The Trinity

An Essential for Faith in Our Time

The Trinity

An Essential for Faith in Our Time

Edited by Andrew Stirling

Evangel
Publishing House

Toll-Free Order Line: (800) 253-9315
Internet Website: www.evangelpublishing.com

Unless otherwise noted, all Scripture quotations are from the New Revised Sandard Version Bible, copyright © 1989, by the Division of Christian Education of the National Council of the Churches of Christ in the United States of America.

Publisher's Cataloging-in-Publication Data
(Provided by Quality Books, Inc.)

The Trinity : an essential for faith in our time / edited by Andrew
   Stirling. – 1st ed.
   p. cm.
   LCCN 2001099477
   ISBN 1-928915-26-4

   1. Trinity. 2. Apologetics. I. Stirling, Andrew.

BT111.2.T75 2002   231'.044
                QBI02-200162

Printed in the United States of America
10 9 8 7 6 5 4 3 2

Table of Contents

Foreword

CHRISTIANS believe in the Trinitarian God. At least, this is the doctrine of the church, which is officially shared and affirmed by most contemporary churches. Many Christians, however, have difficulties with the Trinitarian faith of the church. They feel more familiar with the idea that there is only one personal God, and in this they think themselves in agreement with the way Jesus himself talked about the one God, His heavenly Father. In modern times, even among theologians, powerful tendencies developed to leave the affirmation of three persons in the one God, the Trinitarian dogma of the church, behind as obsolete. But where these tendencies succeed, Jesus is no longer understood to be the incarnation of the eternal Son of God, but is conceived as mere human being among others, though perhaps a most excellent and admirable human being. Thus, the loss of the Trinitarian conception of God entails the loss of central affirmations of the Christian faith. It also deprives Christian monotheism of its distinctive and profound meaning. Therefore, in the theology of the twentieth century, prepared by certain forerunners in the nineteenth century, a resurgence of interest in the Trinitarian concept of God occurred, and in the second half of the twentieth century, new developments in the Trinitarian doctrine became the most fascinating topic in theological discussions, with contributions from many churches and theologians of different countries. The resurgence of Trinitarian theology calls for the attention of every Christian, however, who wants to understand the content of his of her faith and looks forward to a new vitality of Christian teaching and proclamation. Therefore, a common effort like this book must be welcome and will hopefully contribute to new vitality of the Trinitarian faith in the church.

The God of the Trinitarian dogma of the church is, of course, no other than the God whom Jesus proclaimed and whom He addressed as His heavenly Father. He can be no other than the God of the Old Testament and of the Jewish prophets. Since Jesus was a Jew, the God whom He called Father was the one God of Israel, the Creator of heaven and earth. But how can this one God appropriately be described as one God in three persons rather than one person, the heavenly Father? The reason is that Christians believe in God the Father the way Jesus proclaimed Him. Human fancy may invent many images of fatherhood, but for Christians, God is identified as Father by Jesus, the Son, the correlate of God's fatherhood. Therefore, God is not Father without His Son. The Son Jesus Christ belongs to the identification of God the heavenly Father. And if God is Father in eternity, then it must be said with Athanasius, that God the Father was never without His Son, and therefore the Son is eternal like the Father is, and this eternal Son became manifest in human history in Jesus Christ and in His relationship to the God of Israel, His heavenly Father. Furthermore, because the Father and the Son are united by the divine Spirit, who proceeds from the Father, the belief in God the Father entails the affirmation of the Son and the Spirit as eternal correlates of God's fatherhood.

It has often been said that the Trinity is not a biblical doctrine, but emerged centuries later as a doctrine of the church. Now it is true that the biblical writings do not contain an explicit statement on the Trinity, though triadic formulas occur that speak of Father, Son and Spirit—most importantly in Jesus' command to baptize in the name of the Father, the Son and the Holy Spirit (Mt 28:19). As one of the chapters of this volume will show in detail, triadic formulas or phrases occur more often in the New Testament writings than many people assume. They serve as indications of a Trinitarian conception of God. Though they do not specify the exact relationship between the three and their equally eternal and divine nature, they do provide the theological basis for the Trinitarian doctrine. It is the relationship of Jesus to the God whom He called His heavenly Father that forms the basis of the Trinitarian creed of the church. That relationship is implicitly Trinitarian, and the Trinitarian doctrine of the church can be understood as explication of what the relationship between Jesus and His heavenly Father implies.

This is not a deviation from the belief that there is only one God the Father. But His fatherhood entails the Son as its correlate. On the other hand, the monotheistic claim of the Trinitarian faith of the church is safeguarded by the fact that the Son and the Spirit serve the monarchy of the Father, the kingdom of God that Jesus proclaimed and that even presently becomes effective through the Spirit. The monarchy of the Father, the kingdom of God, is not independent of the work of the Son and of the Spirit. God is Father not only in transcendent aloofness, but also in the world of His creation through the Son and the Spirit who further the kingdom of the Father in the world of His creation. Thus the Trinitarian God is not only transcendent, but also dynamically present within the world.

It is possible to look at the Trinitarian doctrine of God as providing the solution to the problem of how God's transcendence and His active presence in the world can be affirmed together. In this sense, the Trinitarian conception of God was prepared in some way in the Old Testament, though we cannot ascribe to any part of the Old Testament a Trinitarian doctrine of God. The God of Israel is transcendent. But He is also present with His people through His "name" that was said to "dwell" in the temple at Jerusalem. The same was said about the "glory" of God that was believed to dwell on the arch between Cherubs. Isaiah experienced this presence of the God of Israel when he received God's call to become a prophet (Isa 6:1-8), and Ezekiel saw in a vision that God's glory left the temple (Eze 8:1ff, 10:1ff), thereby relinquishing the temple and the city to its fate of destruction by the Babylonians. More examples for the presence of the transcendent God with His people and in His creation will be discussed in the first chapter of the present book. With all these examples a question arises: How can God be utterly transcendent and yet at the same time present in the world of His creation? In the Old Testament, the name of God is distinguished from His transcendent majesty, and yet God himself is believed to be present through His name. There is no conception in the Old Testament that reconciles the tension between the idea of God's transcendence and His presence among His chosen people. It is the doctrine of the

Trinity that solves this tension, because it shows how God is transcendent as heavenly Father and yet present in the world through the mission of His Son and through His Spirit.

The Trinitarian faith of the church, then, is concrete monotheism, because it relates to the one God not only in His abstract transcendence, but in the concretion of His presence in the world, without dissolving His transcendence into some form of pantheism. The Trinitarian differentiation in the life of the one God is not opposed to His oneness either. The philosophical discussions on the concept of the absolute One resulted in the insight that the One as opposed to the Many cannot be the absolute One, since the One as opposed to the Many is conditioned by the contrast of the Many. Therefore, the absolute One which is equivalent to the one God has to be conceived as an intrinsically differentiated unity rather than an abstract unity in opposition to the Many. Philosophical reflections like that cannot demonstrate the divine Trinity, but they provide rational plausibility to the Christian affirmation that the one God is Father, Son and Holy Spirit. It is not a logical absurdity to affirm that the one God is concrete in three Persons. Rather, absolute unity has to be an internally differentiated unity like the Christian teaching claims it to be in its Trinitarian concept of God.

Obtaining clarity in these matters is increasingly important in the contemporary situation of intensified interreligious encounter and dialogue. In the face of the challenges of the Christian Trinitarian faith by Jewish and Islamic monotheism, Christians need not develop a feeling of inferiority or a readiness to dismiss this central Christian doctrine celebrated through so many centuries. They should be proud for adhering to a form of concrete, not abstract monotheism and they should learn to argue for it. I hope that this book may contribute to preparing the churches and their members for this task.

Wolfhart Pannenberg
Institut für Fundamentaltheologie und Ökumene
Munich, Germany

Acknowledgments

I owe a debt of gratitude to many people and organizations for their assistance in developing this important project on the Trinity. First of all, my thanks go to the two congregations I served during the writing of the book, Parkdale United Church, Ottawa, Ontario and Timothy Eaton Memorial Church, Toronto, Ontario. Together they afforded me the study-time to ensure that the book reached its fruition. The support of the Trustees of Dominion-Chalmers United Church, Ottawa, Ontario is also greatly appreciated and without their contribution, this book would not be possible. I am also indebted to my wife, Marial, whose constant belief in the project encouraged me to persevere in the work.

I received a great deal of assistance from Peter McEnhill and the library of Westminster College, Cambridge, England as well as the library of the Episcopal Divinity School, Cambridge, Massachusetts and the Andover Library at Harvard Divinity School, Cambridge, Massachusetts. I also gained insights from Peter Wyatt, Phil Ziegler, Dale Skinner, Barry Parker, Graeme Hunter, Brian Stiller, Jim Crighton, and my colleagues Jean Hunnisett, John Harries, and Anne Levy-Ward.

My greatest thanks, however, are reserved for three people who made this work complete. Allen Churchill not only wrote the outstanding work on the New Testament, he was a constant guide throughout the whole process. He not only believed in the merits of the project, he also prayerfully supported every process from the original idea to the final production. He is a man of immense faith. I am also deeply honored that Professor Pannenberg graciously agreed to write the Foreword. His many years of diligence and faithfulness as a scholar of the highest order has challenged and encouraged all of the writers of this book and I hope that the readers will derive benefit from his outstanding scholarship.

Finally, I acknowledge the support of Joseph Allison and the staff of Evangel Publishing House. I hope that their courage in publishing this work will be rewarded by people deepening their faith in God as the Holy Trinity. If that happens, the project will have been worthwhile.

Andrew Stirling
Timothy Eaton Memorial Church
Toronto, Ontario

Contributors

ALLEN CHURCHILL
Former Senior Minister of Dominion-Chalmers United Church, Ottawa, Ontario. He has served as an officer in the Royal Canadian Mounted Police and has a doctorate in New Testament from Oxford University. His area of interest is Biblical Studies.

DAVID CURRY
Rector of Christ Church Anglican Church, Windsor, Nova Scotia. He formerly served the Church of the Advent in Boston, Massachusetts. He is a prolific writer with special emphasis on preserving the historic faith of the church.

DONALD FARIS
Former Minister of North Lonsdale United Church, North Vancouver, British Columbia. He served as the Provincial Minister of Education in the Province of Saskatchewan. He has a doctorate from New College, Edinburgh and has written extensively on Ethics.

KENNETH HAMILTON
Emeritus Professor of Theology and Literature at the University of Winnipeg, Manitoba. He is the author of 17 books, most notably *To Turn from Idols* and *Words and the Word*. His specialty is Systematic Theology.

EDITH HUMPHREY
Professor of Scripture at Augustine College in Ottawa, Ontario. She is active in the Anglican Church of Canada and is part of the Essentials movement. She is the author of *Ladies and the City* as well as articles on various exegetical topics.

DANIEL MEETER
Pastor and Teacher at Old First Reformed Church, Brooklyn, New York. A well-known exponent of the Reformed tradition, he has written extensively on Liturgy and Biblical Interpretation and is keenly interested in ecumenical dialogue. In addition, he is the writer of several hymns. His area of interest is Liturgical Renewal.

JOHN OSWALT
Research Professor of Old Testament at Wesley Biblical Seminary, Jackson, Mississippi. He is author of the commentary on Isaiah 1-39 in the *New International Commentary on the Old Testament* and most recently, *Called To Be Holy*. His area of interest is Old Testament Studies.

GRAHAM SCOTT
A United Church of Canada minister for 34 years and now a member of St. George Antiochian Orthodox Church in Niagara Falls, New York. He was an assistant professor of religious studies at Laurentian University, Sudbury and Brock University, St. Catharines, Ontario and is the past Editor of *Theological Digest*. His area of interest is Church History.

VICTOR SHEPHERD
Professor of Historical Theology and Wesley Studies at Tyndale Seminary in Toronto, Ontario. He is formerly Senior Minister of Streetsville United Church, Mississauga, Ontario. His area of intrerest is Historical Theology.

ANDREW STIRLING (Editor)
Senior Minister of Timothy Eaton Memorial Church, Toronto, Ontario. He is Adjunct Professor of Theology at Tyndale Seminary, Toronto and an Instructor at the University of Toronto School of Continuing Studies. He is a former Visiting Scholar at Harvard Divinity School. His areas of interest are Systematic Theology and Homiletics.

Introduction

A s a preacher of the gospel of Jesus Christ, I often feel torn between two worlds, each of which has its own vocabulary and icons. The first world is the realm of modern North American society in which I exercise my pastoral ministry. In this world, I am daily confronted with the spirit of radical doubt which sees God as the "dream of fools" and His Son as an historical relic. Paradoxically, this is a world where ordinary people ask the church to be relevant and seek from it comfort in an alienating society. I often feel like an alien in this world, as if I am reaching back in time to another era, a distant planet, where the miraculous was accepted and the transcendent was glorified, a world in which faith was considered relevant and did not need to prove itself.

The second world is the world of theology with its protracted use of a dead language (Latin) and its secret codes accessible to an elite few. Who for example gets excited today about a *Filioque* clause or debates about the meaning of *substantia*? In this world I feel like a temporary sojourner, finding it a nice place to visit but a dangerous place to stay.

However, despite the obvious differences between these two worlds, I have come to believe that they are inextricably connected. It is not a choice between Scylla and Charybdis; rather, through my years of ministry, I have become convinced that the world in which I live can only find its relevance when it encounters the world of theology. Likewise, the world of theology realizes its relevance when it is challenged by the doubts and despairs of modern culture. It is precisely this dialectic which motivates the writers of this book.

As Christian pastors and academics, we deal continually with matters of faith and enjoy the pursuit of knowledge. We desire to know more about God in order that our lives and ministries can be enriched. We are cognizant, however, of the needs of our society replete with its moral relativism and materialistic hedonism. We minister to the poor and the marginalized, the disaffected and unfulfilled, and we want to offer them a word of hope and redemption. Above all, we are believers in search of a deeper foundation to our Christian witness. Our starting point is a faith in Jesus Christ and, like St. Augustine of Hippo, we seek understanding in order that we can fulfill our calling as disciples (*Credo ut Intelligam*). This book, therefore, is an attempt to bring together the two worlds in which we live and thereby deal with the world in all its need and God in all His glory. We do so on the basis that God has already made this connection through His Son Jesus Christ who is our Redeemer and Lord. Likewise, we are moved by the power of the Holy Spirit to pay testimony to this fact and believe that the supreme medium which manifests this belief is the doctrine of the Trinity.

The reader will soon realize that there are a diversity of opinions about the Trinity represented in this book. We represent various ecclesiastical traditions, and the unique and distinct nature of our credal beliefs is evident. Nevertheless, we have an unswerving conviction that God is to be called "Father, Son and Holy Spirit," and this is affirmed by our primary authority, the Holy Scriptures.

We begin our understanding of the Trinity with John Oswalt's examination of the Old Testament. He concludes that while the writers of the Old Testament may not necessarily have conceived of God in Trinitarian terms, they say nothing to contradict it. Indeed, on a positive note, Dr. Oswalt's excellent treatment of the pneumatology of the Old Testament causes Christians to deepen their understanding of the Third Person of the Trinity. His conviction that the Old Testament "requires that doctrine [of the Trinity]" is a natural link to Allen Churchill's work on the Trinity in the New Testament. Churchill's highly textual analysis of the New Testament begins with his assertion that the Bible is the supreme source of authority in matters of belief. From this assumption he examines the works of Paul, John, the Synoptic Gospels, and the epistle to the Hebrews. He concludes that this "raw material" affirms that Jesus was God. However, this does not mean that the New Testament writers had a dogmatic formula in mind when they wrote, for Churchill states, "No formal Trinitarian doctrine was formulated in the New Testament." He goes on, however, to say,

> The distinctiveness of the three Persons was kept, often in relation to the specific work of the Father, Son and Holy Spirit. Their unity was maintained in a kind of dynamic tension, as was their hinted equality.

Both Oswalt and Churchill, therefore, support the doctrine of the Trinity on biblical grounds but are rightly not prepared to say that a clear Trinitarian definition is found in Scripture.

When we turn to the history of the church, we see a more clearly developed doctrine emerge. This was mainly due to Christianity's struggle with heretical movements which sought to undermine the essence of the biblical witness. Graham Scott looks at the foundation of the doctrine of the Trinity by placing special emphasis on one of the Cappadocian Fathers, St. Basil. Basil's work is a call for us to see the glory of the triune God and, like many Eastern Christians, he explains why the Trinity is worthy of our praise. Scott concludes with the words of Archimandrite Vasileios, "How beautiful it is for a man to become theology."

In stark contrast to Scott's chapter, Kenneth Hamilton examines the nineteenth century's problems with the doctrine of the Trinity. His study of Schleirmacher, Hegel and Ritschl leads him to see that many of the challenges to the Trinity in today's church find their genesis in the theological liberalism of that era. Those theologians' fatal mistake was replacing the credal basis of the Christian church's belief with self-consciousness. According to Hamilton, this is still a problem in modern theology. He quotes P.T. Forsyth to sound a warning that it is the Trinity who created the church, "and no other God can sustain it."

Hamilton's conclusions are illustrated in the two essays that follow his. In the first, I examine many of the challenges to the Trinity today, believing that most of them stem from societal influences and the church's desire to be relevant. I would argue, however, that the very things which society desires are found in an honest appraisal of the Trinity's relevance; any meaningful enlightenment comes from the Trinity itself. Victor Shepherd moves us on to look at the many faces of unitarianism which exist in the church today. He concludes his treatise by stating, "A recovery of the doctrine of the Trinity would do ever so much to assist mainline denominations with respect to the catholicity of their mission." According to Shepherd, this leads to an ever-deepening devotion to the Triune God, "whose love for a dying world commissions us to love it no less."

It is this devotion to God and concern for the world which are at the heart of the next two essays. Edith Humphrey and Daniel Meeter deal with the importance of Trinitarian worship. The former deals with issues of language and the naming of God, whereas the latter looks at the Trinity as the foundation for liturgical renewal. Humphrey is concerned with liturgical changes and their effect upon Christian unity. Meeter is also a devotee of Trinitarian worship, which he believes enables us to participate in the inter-Trinitarian worship manifested on the Cross.

The penultimate and final chapters address the aforementioned two worlds of ministry. David Curry approaches the need for re-newal within the church. As an Anglican priest who has served urban parishes in the United States and rural ones in Canada, he is con-vinced that the church must enter into the life of the Trinity. This Trinitarian God can be experienced *in se* and is also the Trinity *pro nobis*. He affirms the belief that Jesus Christ desires for us to know the inner life of God and calls us to manifest this love for others.

How the church deals with the complex issues of modern society is the subject of our last essay. Donald Faris is accustomed to deal-ing with practical matters of justice, for he sat as a Member of the Saskatchewan Legislature. He brings this background to his treat-ment of the Trinity and social ethics. Commencing with a series of theological affirmations about the Trinity, he leads us into the realm of practical ethical concerns. He announces that "Christian ethics are based on our communion with God—a God who is Triune."

For the church to be the church in the modern world, it must ground its ethical decisions on the God who reveals himself as Father, Son and Holy Spirit. His concluding Collect states this best, "Enable us to live by the Spirit, that walking with Christ and rejoicing in Your Fatherly love, we may become partakers of the mystery of Your divine being."

It is into this world of the Trinity that the reader is invited to come. Naturally, no single work can cover all facets of the Trinity, but our hope is that this work will cause the church and the world to declare with confidence,

> *Glory be to the Father and to the Son and to the Holy Spirit. As it was in the beginning is now and ever shall be, world without end. Amen.*

Andrew Stirling
Timothy Eaton Memorial Church
Toronto, Ontario

The God of Abraham, Isaac, and Jacob: The Trinity in the Old Testament

John N. Oswalt

Does the Old Testament teach the doctrine of the Trinity? The answer to this question is very simple. It is No. The Old Testament nowhere explicitly teaches that there are three persons in the Godhead. But then it may be argued that the New Testament does not teach that doctrine, either. Nevertheless, the things it does teach require the Trinitarian doctrine if we are to make sense of those teachings. However, the doctrine is not taught as such. Thus, the question for the student of the Old Testament is not whether that collection of books teaches the Trinitarian doctrine, but whether it contains the same kind of data about God which called forth the doctrine of the Trinity from the New Testament. Or, to put the question in a negative way: does the Old Testament contain data which clearly contradict the Trinitarian doctrine?

The answer to the above questions, as the following will seek to show, is Yes and No. Yes, the Old Testament displays some of the same phenomena and descriptions of God that appear in the New Testament and that require the doctrine of the Trinity in order to understand them and No, there is nothing in the Old Testament that contradicts the Trinity. The negative statement is of considerable importance. Clearly the teachings found in the Bible are developmental. The New Testament builds upon the Old. It is not necessary for the Old Testament to contain every teaching of the New in its fully developed form. Neither is it necessary for the New

Testament to affirm everything which the Old Testament teaches. However, if the Old Testament flatly denied the Trinitarian possibility, then there would be serious grounds for questioning the validity of the inferential reasoning from the New Testament which issues in the doctrine of the Trinity. That is not the case. Not only does the Old Testament not deny this possibility, it contains several kinds of data which are distinctly similar to those found in the New Testament. Unquestionably these data at least allow for, if they do not directly point to, the Trinitarian understanding of God.

What are these data? First of all, and undergirding everything else, is the absolute monotheism of the Old Testament. Apart from this teaching, it might be argued that evidence pointing to separate divine entities is simply a reflex of the polytheism which was rampant on all sides of Israel. However, this cannot be maintained because one of the most recalcitrant pieces of data in the entire Old Testament is the insistence upon the unitary nature of God. From Genesis 1 to Malachi 4 God is one. To be sure, we wait until Isaiah (37:19) and Jeremiah (2:11) for the assertion that there are no other gods. But there is never a question from Genesis 1 onward but that God is one without a rival. It is this kind of absolute commitment to monotheism which accounts for those statements like Isaiah 45:7 and Amos 3:6 where God is said to be the author of calamity. The writers of these books were not going to allow for the existence of evil deities who brought about these kinds of events in spite of the good God. Rather, they insisted that God was the ultimate cause of all things, and that if calamity occurred, then it was within his larger purposes. If the reality of the worship of other gods was admitted, the idea that they had any effective power was completely denied.[1] The gods did nothing. All that existed and all that occurred was the sole result of the will and activity of the One God. Yet, as early as Genesis 1:2 we read of the Spirit of God exercising a function in the process of creation. It will be necessary to examine the significance of this information in greater detail later in this study. However, now it is important to point out two things. First, this is not a spirit whom God sent. This is God's Spirit. Second, this Spirit is in some sense God himself. It is not another god. Monotheism effectively rules out this possibility.

Granted then that the Old Testament claims there is only one God, what is the evidence that there are distinct entities operating within the Godhead? The clearest evidence is that which is represented by the reference cited in the preceding paragraph: the activity of the Spirit of God. In this discussion it will be necessary to establish, or at least show the likelihood of, two things: that the references to the Spirit of God are not merely synonyms for God, and that the Spirit carries out distinct activities which are both limited and predictable. The significance of these factors is that if it can be shown that the activity of the Spirit is limited to certain spheres of the total divine activity, then it is unlikely that Spirit is merely a synonym for God. Of course, showing this does not in and of itself rule out some form of modalism whereby God's activity in differing spheres is represented by different terms. However, it is not necessary to disprove modalism here. That can be left to the fuller exposition of the activities of the Trinity in the New Testament. All that is necessary here is to demonstrate that the Old Testament descriptions of God are not at odds with the New Testament ones, which demand the formulation of the doctrine of the Trinity.

The Hebrew word *ruah* may be translated with several different, though related, English words. Among these are "wind," "breath," and "spirit/Spirit."[2] The relationships among these are fairly obvious upon reflection. Since a body without breath is dead, it was easy to equate breath with the enlivening spirit. The wind is analogous to the breath. It is invisible, yet it can be felt; it seems to give life to previously lifeless objects such as tree leaves and the sails of ships. On another level, a person who is passive and inactive may be said to lack "spirit." Finally, there is the issue at hand here: the Spirit, conceived of as a distinct entity within the Godhead, is the One who expresses the life-giving, enabling power of God within the context of creation.

The work of the Holy Spirit in the Old Testament may be categorized in three different areas, but all of these have to do with the manifestation and application of the power of God to creation. First, there is the work of the Spirit in creation; then there is His work in leading and guiding the people of God; and finally there is the supernatural empowerment of humans: in craftsmanship, in military exploits, in leadership, in supernatural insight, and in righteous living. In all of these latter cases it is plain the common denominator is divine empowerment for that which is normally beyond human capability.

Genesis 1:2 is the classic expression of the Spirit as the creative power of God. He is the One who hovers over the void as a mother eagle flutters over her chicks in the nest (Dt 32:11).[3] This creative and life-giving function is further supported by such passages as Job 33:4 where the Spirit of God (also identified as "the Breath [*nisma*] of the Almighty") is said to have made the writer and given him life. Similarly, Psalm 104:30 says that all the creatures of earth are created when God sends forth his Spirit. Finally, Isaiah asks who directed the Spirit of the Lord in his creative activity (Isa 40:13). Are these statements merely another way of saying that God is the Creator? It is difficult to see how this is the case. Unless the Spirit of God is conceived of as a distinct entity within the Godhead, it is difficult to see what value the reference to the Spirit has. Yahweh God is the Creator, as the first two chapters of Genesis make plain. If "Spirit of God" is simply another way of saying "God," what is gained? On the other hand, if the writers are using the concept of the "spirit of God" to differentiate some specific aspect of God and His working, as I think they are, then the ground for the Trinitarian conception is already laid. They may not think in terms of separate persons in the Godhead, and I see no reason to suggest they did. On the other hand, they are saying that it is not enough to say that God is the Creator. It is God in some particular manifestation of His character and nature who is the Creator. And that is to say that it is possible, even necessary, to distinguish functional aspects within the behavior of the one God. This ability to assign certain functions to the Spirit of God is also seen in His role as leader. This is particularly seen in Isaiah 63:10-11, where the Spirit and His leadership are rebelled against so that He is grieved. But it is also implied in the references to the Spirit's "carrying" persons to various places, as in the case of Elijah (1Ki 18:12; 2Ki 2:16)[4] and Ezekiel (8:3; 11:1). The Isaiah references seem to underline the distinct personality of the Spirit, since it is difficult to imagine grieving what is merely a concretion of certain divine functions.

But by far the most common occurrence of the Spirit is in regard to the empowerment of human beings. The first example of this is in Genesis 41:38, where the Pharaoh recognizes in Joseph a supernatural wisdom, and expresses this by asking who else has the Spirit of God in him like this.[5] The manifestation of the divine Spirit is not limited to intellectual matters, as is shown in the case of Bezaleel, the craftsman who was divinely empowered to design and build the Tabernacle (Ex 31:3; 35:31). So also the Spirit empowered the so-called "Judges" to deliver the Israelite people from their oppressors (Othniel, Jdg 3:10; Gideon, Jdg 6:34; Jephthah, Jdg 11:29; Samson, Jdg 13:25; 14:6, 19; 15:14). Eventually, evidence of Spirit-empowerment came to be seen as one of the necessary marks of God choosing the leader of Israel. While this was already the case as early as Numbers 11, where the elders of Israel were given "the Spirit which is upon you [Moses]" (Nu 11:17, 25), it is especially apparent in the cases of Saul and David (1Sa 10:6, 10; 11:6; 16:13, 14). Part of the poignancy of Saul's rejection by God is the removal of the Spirit from him and the filling of the subsequent vacuum by an evil spirit (1Sa 16:15, 16, 23; 19:9).[6]

One of the particular manifestations of Spirit-empowerment was the declaring of a message from God, or prophesying. Again, this appears in Numbers 11:25 with the elders. Apparently this involved some sort of mantic behavior since Joshua was concerned about it (Nu 11:28). The same thing seems to have applied in the case of Saul (1Sa 10:10-13; see also 19:20, 23). Regardless of the association of mantic behavior with prophesying—a more thorough discussion of which is beyond the scope of this treatment[7]—the emphasis in biblical prophecy is upon the deliverance of an intelligible message related to the covenant responsibilities of the person or persons being addressed. This is seen in numerous instances, among which are those involving Balaam (Nu 24:2); David (2Sa 23:2); Azariah, Jehazial, and Zechariah (2Ch 15:1; 20:14; 24:20); Ezekiel (Eze 11:5); and Micah (Mic 3:8). These cases are all similar to Joseph's in that he and they were supernaturally empowered to speak the message of God regarding a particular situation.

It is this that the New Testament particularly picks up on. This is so almost from the beginning, as Peter draws upon the Old Testament promises of the Spirit to make the unusual behavior of the 120 in the upper room explicable to the onlookers (Ac 2:14-21 [Joel 2:28-29]). In the same way, when Paul explains that it is the indwelling Spirit who gives Christians power to conquer sin, he is using a concept which is entirely in keeping with the teachings of the Old Testament (Ro 8:1-16; cf. Isa 32:14-17; Eze 36:27). Nor is this appropriation of the Old Testament teachings an innovation on the part of the apostles. It is Jesus who makes the connections for them when He speaks of the imminent outpouring of the Spirit in such passages as John 15-16. The point of these observations, if that point is not already clear, is to show that the New Testament understanding of the person and work of the Holy Spirit rests upon, and is inseparable from, the Old Testament understanding. The New Testament certainly develops and amplifies the teachings, but there is no contradiction whatsoever between the understandings of the two testaments.

The evidence for the action of the second person of the Trinity in the Old Testament is not as clear as it is for the third person. Nevertheless, there are two kinds of information which are at least suggestive. The first is the interchangeability of "the angel of the Lord" with the Lord himself. This fact emerges already in Genesis 16 where the "angel of the Lord" was the one speaking to Hagar (vs. 7, 9, 11). But Hagar gives the name El-Roi to "the Lord who spoke to her" (16:13) rather than to the angel. Similarly, in Genesis 18 those who appeared to Abraham are variously referred to as "men" (Ge 18:2, 22) and as "angels" (Ge 19:1). Yet, the text has no qualms about saying that the Lord was one of the three men, and that it was the Lord who spoke with Abraham. In Genesis 22 it might be argued that the angel of the

Lord is speaking for the Lord rather than as the Lord, but in view of the previous references, the direct speech from God certainly points in the direction of the identity of the two figures.

The same kind of thing appears with even more definition in Exodus 3:2-4, where it is said that the angel of the Lord appeared to Moses in the burning bush (v. 2) and that the Lord saw that Moses had stopped to look and God spoke to him from within the bush (v. 4). In Exodus 33:2 the Lord makes a distinction between himself and "my angel" when He offers to send an angel in His place to lead the people to the Promised Land. But later (v. 15), God relents and says that His Presence (lit. "face") will go with the people. Yet in Judges 2:1, "the angel of the Lord" says that it was He who brought the people up out of the land of Egypt and brought them into the land "that I swore to give to your forefathers." From this we may infer that while the angel of the Lord is identical to the Lord himself and is a manifestation of the "face" or presence of the Lord, not all angels are such a manifestation. The delightful story of Balaam and his insightful donkey in Numbers 22 makes the same point. What Balaam and the donkey see is "the angel of the Lord" (vs. 22-27, 31-32, 34-35), but it is the Lord who opens both the donkey's mouth and Balaam's eyes (vs. 28, 31).

The book of Judges offers two very clear examples of this phenomenon. The first involves the call of Gideon in chapter 6, and the second appears in connection with the birth announcement of Samson in chapter 13. In both instances the angel of the Lord is clearly a visible manifestation, so much so that the persons have to be convinced He is not just an ordinary human being. But in both cases the narrative makes it plain that when the angel speaks, it is actually the Lord speaking.

There are several other references to the angel of the Lord which emphasize the angel as the visible representation of God, but there are two references in Zechariah which are particularly notable. In Zechariah 1:12-13, the angel of the Lord is depicted as conversing with the Lord in a familiar way and interceding for Jerusalem. And in Zechariah 12:8, the last Old Testament reference, God and the angel of the Lord are treated as synonymous.[8]

The other piece of evidence for the operation of the second person of the Trinity in the Old Testament has just two examples, but both are of considerable significance. In both cases, what is obviously a manifestation of God is explicitly called "a man." In neither of these examples is there any reference to the angel of the Lord. The first is in Genesis 32 where Jacob wrestles with "a man" until daybreak. There is no question that this is a representation of God, as is shown by Jacob's demand that the person give him a blessing (32:26), by the person's refusal to tell Jacob his name (32:29; cf. Jdg 13:17-18), and by Jacob's wondering assertion that he has seen the face of God and yet lives (32:30).

The second example occurs in Joshua 5:13-15, where Joshua meets "a man" dressed as a warrior while he is reconnoitering Jericho. Joshua asks if the man is friend or foe, and He answers that He is neither, but has come as commander of the armies of Israel. His one command to Joshua is that he is to remove his shoes because he stands on holy ground. It is, of course, obvious that this incident is designed to be a conscious parallel to the experience of Moses at the burning bush. As with Jacob, there can be no question that the "man" is God in human form.

If the "Spirit" in the Old Testament is a representation of God's power operative in the world, the "angel of the Lord" and "the man" are physical manifestations of God in visible form. It is significant that in many cases the angel of the Lord appears for the purpose of declaring a message, a word, from God. This is precisely what the second person of the Trinity did in the New Testament after He had become fully incarnate. There is no indication that He was incarnate in His Old Testament appearances; that had to wait until after the Virgin Birth. Nevertheless, the identity with and yet distinction from the Lord while representing Him to His people and declaring His word to them is the very same thing which He was enabled to do in a whole new dimension after the Incarnation. It was not a different ministry which Jesus carried out, rather it was the same sort of ministry which He had carried out before. Only now it was on a deeper level, one whose metaphysical implications were of a profoundly shocking nature.

This essay has shown that in the Old Testament, just as in the New, there is evidence in the description of God, His person, and His activity which points to what was eventually formulated as the doctrine of the Trinity. As was stated at the outset, this evidence hardly constitutes irrefutable proof of the doctrine. Neither can we be certain that any of the faithful in Old Testament times thought in Trinitarian terms. In fact, we may assume they did not. Nonetheless, the descriptions of God which they give are entirely in keeping with those of the New Testament, and when the implications of those descriptions are carried out to their logical conclusions, they are not only consistent with the orthodox doctrine of the Trinity, but it may be fairly said that they require that doctrine.

NOTES

1. For a full, if somewhat overstated, treatment of this theme, see Y. Kaufmann, *The Religion of Israel*, tr. M. Greenberg (Chicago: University of Chicago Press, 1960).

2. For a fuller discussion of this topic see J. Oswalt, "The Holy Spirit in the Old Testament," *The Herald*, 88:5 (1976), 12-13; 88:7 (1976), 16-17, and L. Wood, *The Holy Spirit in the Old Testament* (Grand Rapids: Zondervan, 1976).

3. The word translated "hover" or "flutter" here occurs only three times in the Hebrew Bible: Genesis 1:2; Deuteronomy 32:11; and Jeremiah 23:9. "Move" of NRSV does not seem to be the best translation. NRSV also translates *ruah* as "wind." While this translation is certainly possible, there is no compelling reason to do so. Nowhere else is *ruah elohim* translated "wind of God." Everywhere else it is translated as "s/Spirit of God." In one case (out of a total of 23) the context shows that *ruah yhwh* should be translated as "the wind of the Lord" (Hos 13:15).

4.   The references regarding Elijah are not dissimilar from those regarding Philip in Acts 8:26, 39-40.

5.   A closely similar situation is described in Daniel 4:8, 9, 18 where Nebuchadnezzar describes Daniel as one in whom is the "spirit of the holy God/gods" after Daniel's successful interpretation of the king's dream (see also Dan 5:11, 13).

6.   This discussion raises the question, in all of these cases, is this a description of human emotional or mental states in terms of divine hypostases, and thus not divine reality at all? All that can be said in the limited space available here is that this language is exactly similar to that used in the New Testament. In and of itself, the modern tendency to speak of everything in terms of human states is not necessarily more valid than the biblical descriptions. If the biblical tendency is to explain everything in terms of supernatural causes, the modern tendency is to deny any possible supernatural causes and to explain everything on a rigidly naturalistic basis. Modern thought has no greater claim to be free of bias than does biblical thought.

7.   For a recent discussion of some of these issues, see R. P. Gordon, "Where Have All the Prophets Gone? The 'Disappearing' Israelite Prophet Against the Background of Ancient Near Eastern Prophecy," *Bulletin for Biblical Research*, 5 (1995), 67-86.

8.   For further discussion of this issue, see the following: W. McDonald, "Christology and the Angel of the Lord," *Current Issues in Biblical and Patristic Interpretation*, ed. G. Hawthorne (Grand Rapids; Eerdmans, 1975), 324-325; J. Fossum, "The Name of God and the Angel of the Lord," *Wisenschaftliche Untersuchungen zum Neuen Testament* (Tubingen: Mohr, 1985), 36:307-338; D. Slager, "Who is the Angel of the Lord?" *Bible Translator* (1988), 39:436-438. McDonald takes a position contrary to that presented in this paper. But Fossum shows how this concept was real enough that it played a significant part in Gnostic teachings about the demiurge.

The New Testament and the Trinity

Allen D. Churchill

Where Trinitarian Thought Began and Begins

THE New Testament is the major point of departure or matrix[1] for all Trinitarian thought. This is not to deny an important role to the Old Testament, for this at the earliest stage is the mine for the great ideas which are essential for Trinitarian understanding: a personal God, rich in being, love and power; a God who acts dynamically in creating, sustaining, and redeeming the world; a God who promises the coming of a Messiah and Suffering Servant to bring in His Kingdom; and a God who relates personally to both the hosts of heaven and all the races of the earth. We cannot begin to comprehend a Trinitarian God apart from these theological elements. These are elements that have come naturally into the New Testament, and they have been developed as the divine promises have been fulfilled in the coming of Jesus Christ and the Holy Spirit, and as the earliest church began reflecting upon them.

Nor does the role of the New Testament deny the importance and necessity of theological exploration by systematicians who must exercise freely but judiciously their skills in finding and using ancient and also contemporary language adequate to the formulation of a doctrine of the Trinity that will make this mysterious and difficult reality relevant in each generation as history unfolds.

Nevertheless, the New Testament is where all Trinitarian thought must begin formally. It is also the reference point to which all creative speculation on the Trinity must be brought back for testing and verification, and this for at least four reasons. First, because the New Testament is *chronologically* the premier data bank, supplying actual Trinitarian language and simple but significant formulations, anchored as they are to a unique breakthrough in revelation at a particular point in history. When the New Testament church affirmed that in Jesus the Word had become flesh (Jn 1:14) and could use a personal pronoun to identify the Holy Spirit (Jn 14:26, etc.), it is clear that in the church's mind, a new way of thinking and speaking about God needed to be developed. How could the Father, Son and Holy Spirit, each identifiable individually, be understood and expounded within the framework of an essential monotheism? This was not just one section of the New Testament church that found it necessary to speak in this way. It was a phenomenon common to the church as a whole (e.g., Col 1:15-20; 1Co 2:10ff; Heb 1:1-4; 6:4; 13:8; 1Pe 1:2, 3, 12). It is highly unlikely that the church would ever have conceived, let alone developed, a doctrine of the Trinity had the New Testament not provided the initial impetus, for the idea and doctrine of the Trinity is scarcely credible in either a Hebraic or Greek world.

Second, the New Testament provides the *content* of Trinitarian thought. The Gospels and Epistles identify the persons who make up the Trinity, the particular characteristics of each, whether distinctive or overlapping, the work of each within the framework of the work of one God, and imply an interrelationship between these persons. In addition, the New Testament provides us with the raw material that leads to the development of the idea of the Trinity in the earliest church. That is, the reality of the Trinity existed prior to the creation of time, but the idea and the doctrine of the Trinity developed within time. It was only after the disciples met Jesus of Nazareth and came to reflect on His life and work that they came to realize that He was more than a prophet or teacher. They came to the conclusion, especially after His resurrection, that Jesus was divine (Ro 1:4). Jesus himself bore witness to a special relationship that He shared with the Father (Mt 11:25-27; Lk 10:21-22). The New Testament church was led to ascribe preexistence to Jesus which, in the fourth gospel (Jn 17:24), Jesus himself is said to claim. A similar history of the development of the idea of the Trinity applies also to the Holy Spirit. Whereas at first, and especially in the Old Testament, the Holy Spirit seems to have been considered to be God acting in creation (Ge 1:2; Ps 104:30; Job 33:4) and in people's lives to re-create them (1Sa 10:6; Eze 37:14), to confer upon them leadership abilities (Ge 41:38; Nu 27:18; 1Sa 16:13), and to inspire them as prophets (Nu 11:29; Isa 61:1; Mic 3:8), the Holy Spirit comes to take on a more distinctive role. The Old Testament speaks of a new age of the Spirit (Joel 2:28ff) that will break out sometime in the future. The New Testament speaks of baptism in and by the Spirit (1Co 12:13) into the body of Christ, the church. It speaks of the Spirit penetrating the depths of God and human beings in order to interpret each to the other and reconcile the two (1Co 2:10ff), and to create the sanctified life (Gal 5:22ff). All of this finds its historical focus in a particular event which is as distinctive for the Holy Spirit as the birth at Bethlehem is for Christ, namely Pentecost (Ac 2). Though later theologians have developed and continue to develop the doctrine of the Trinity in the light of theological, philosophical, and practical considerations, the New Testament remains the reservoir containing the basic constitutive elements of this most distinctive component of Christian belief.

Third, the New Testament furnishes the major *practical foci*, the areas of action and application to which the Trinity is related as their source. It is not possible to treat the Trinity merely as a question of being and of the interrelationship of Father, Son, and Holy Spirit. The New Testament insists, in its incomparable and dynamic way, that theological matters be treated equally in terms of being and action. The two are, of necessity, interrelated. Consequently each reference to the Trinity in the New Testament[2] refers to a certain action or actions in whose name or by whose love and power the actions are accomplished. Reference to the Trinity is found in various contexts: missionary (Mt 28:19), pastoral (2Co 13:14), persecution (Rev 1:9),[3] the growth of the church (1Co 12:3-6), the unity of the church (Eph 4:4-6), the Christian hope (1Pe 1:2ff), the plan of salvation (Eph 1:3-23), new relationship with God (Gal 4:4-6), the baptism of Jesus (Mk 1:9-11), life through the Spirit (Ro 8:1ff), standing firm in the faith (2Th 2:13-15), tranformation by the gospel (Tit 3:4-6), resurrection (Ro 8:11), perseverance in the faith (Jude 20f), exorcism (Mt 12:28; Lk 11:20), the sending of the Spirit (Ac 2:33; 5:30ff; 10:38), and the ministry of the Spirit to the church and world (Jn 14:16, 26; 15:26; 16:5-15). The Trinity is not simply a matter of persons and substance (The Council of Nicea), but also of the personal source of a creative, sustaining and trans-forming enterprise and power. The New Testament keeps this essential and practical aspect clearly before us.[4] In fact, there are numerous New Testament texts which are action-oriented, that demonstrate how the earliest church came to appreciate the persons of Christ and the Holy Spirit as being somehow divine and as such to be accounted for in close relationship to the Father. As the early church was faced with the growing realization that Jesus was more than just an itinerant Jewish preacher and healer, that human terms alone were inadequate to describe Him and His work, so it was necessary to revise upward her estimate of Jesus' identity. We will examine some of these texts as our investigation unfolds. The main point here is that the "economical" evidence of God's action in time and space in and through Jesus Christ and the Holy Spirit as provided in the New Testament furnishes a basis for developing a way of speaking about the "immanent" Trinity, the triune God himself.

Fourth, the New Testament supplies us with more than an historical and practical foundation for discussing the Trinity. It provides us with an *authoritative* source. New Testament scholars today, grounded in historical and literary criticism, are often loathe to speak of the Bible as the Word of God. There is a tendency to develop a "canon within a canon,"[5] or to give away some or even much of the original text in favour of reason[6] or experience.[7] St. Augustine, in his study on the Trinity,[8] treated the Bible as authoritative, using mainly a face-value or plain or literal reading of the relevant texts. "The Holy Scripture," he said, "suits itself to babes." It uses language and analogies that can be understood by the ordinary person.[9]

Under the influence of the Enlightenment, the study of Scripture became increasingly dominated by the methods of secular criticism. The Bible was to be interpreted as any other book would be. The presuppositions of the interpreters often got in the way, and the results were frequently chaotic. Recent post-modern methods have been attractive, focusing as they do on a literary and pre-suppositional approach, finding expression in either the language of the text independent of the author's intent or in the reader's response. Unfortunately, few of the modern methods of interpretation have commanded unanimity among scholars either on the meaning of the text or on the question of its authority. Yet these are matters that cannot be ignored. The Bible claims an authority for itself as the locus of a special Word that demands our attention, "Thus says the Lord." It is only in Scripture that we hear the Word of God that went forth first to Israel and then to the church.[10] It is only in Scripture that we learn about the special relevation given in and through Jesus Christ. It is this that the church recognized at the Third Council of Carthage (AD 397) when the traditional twenty-seven books of the New Testament containing this message were recognized as authoritative. How these authoritative books were to be interpretated was a question that remained open. The question of the appropriate method(s) of interpretation have, from the beginning, been debated. Allegorical, typological, spiritual, and moral approaches have been attempted and assessed. Dominant since the Reformation, the literal or plain-sense of Scripture continues to prove the most useful. It corresponds to what the text itself requires, and in this way remains the most scientific of approaches. The data determines the method of interpretation.[11]

This means that historical material in the New Testament requires an historical method of interpretation.[12] A considerable amount of material in the New Testament is historical, especially that of the Gospels and the Acts of the Apostles, but also parts of the Epistles, which provide some of the earliest written material in the New Testament. In addition to this descriptive material, there is also a considerable amount of didactic material. This didactic material needs to be interpreted by a method complementary to its nature. Because it is theological in nature, it requires a theological method for purposes of exegesis and exposition. The newer post-modern methods of interpretation, being more philosophically and politically oriented, consequently correspond less to the New Testament material than historical and theological methods; they are therefore less useful and in many cases create confusion and even error. At the very least, whenever an extraneous method of interpretation interferes with the historical and theological purpose of the New Testament and diminishes the importance of such meanings of the text, we should be skeptical.

Where one commences the process of exegesis and exposition is crucial. The attempt to identify the biblical text as the witness to and interpretation of the unique revelation of God, but as separate from and not a part of that unique revelation,[13] is an unnecessary reaction to certain forms of fundamentalism, is a denial of the role that Scripture plays as an inextricable element of the revelation God offers the world for its salvation. This practice has lead to a radically diminished effectiveness in the old-line churches' witness to the world. Scripture is not only a witness to divine revelation but is an integral component of that revelation. The Bible is part of and participates in revelation at the very least in the sense that the revelation that God has given of himself as Father, Son, and Holy Spirit, is not other than or different from the message that Scripture alone provides. There is no other source of such revelation, and we cannot in all honesty contemplate another source which could speak this revelation so well.

Scripture is therefore not merely a witness to the Word of God, it is the Word of God in its written form.[14] This is not to deny the reality of the Word of God in its incarnate form in Jesus Christ, or the value of the Word of God in the form of proclamation.[15] In a way, this three-fold understanding of the Word of God bears some considerable resemblance to the Trinity and suffers some similar problems in the process of explanation. The important thing is to try to maintain and clarify the distinctives without denying the basic unity involved. For example, there is a distinction between revelation as an act in history in, say, the Exodus or in the life, death, and resurrection of Jesus, and the interpretation of the meaning of such historical events and the impact of the saving influence of these events. Yet the act and the interpretation and the influence belong together. None is complete or intelligible without the other. Indeed, some have argued that an historical event is composed of both an act and its meaning. We need not pursue this particular point. What we can say is that revelation is made up of both a saving act and the identification and communication of the significance of that act in a way that brings about personal transformation. Scripture reports the saving act and declares the meaning of that act. Broken down into its constituent parts, the report contains historical information about the act and the declaration conveys the theological meaning of that act. Yet the process of this revelation remains incomplete until and unless the same Holy Spirit, who was working in the act and guiding the interpreter in the defining of the meaning of that act, brings the event before our consciousness and conscience in a provocative and persuasive way.[16]

This brings us back to the question of the authority of the Bible as the theological impetus for undertaking a study of the Trinity and for insisting that such a study should begin, after considering Old Testament antecedents, with the New Testament. When we consider the various historical and literary strands of Christology, pneumatology, and Trinity in what may be called their pre-canonical stage in the history of the development of the Bible, is it merely as descriptive material that we peruse this data,[17] or is it also as prescriptive? In other words, do the various strands of biblical material gain their theological authority only when the canon of Scripture is complete and recognized, or are they authoritative as individual pericopae in the developing process prior to that? Presumably those scholars who see the final form of the text as the only normative basis for a biblical theology[18] would take a different view from those who support the view of a "canon within a canon,"[19] whose authority is an aggregate of texts chosen on the basis of their own perceived intrinsic merit. In fact, representatives of the latter group impose a kind of canonical status on their selected texts largely on the basis of their own presuppositions which they bring to the text. These presuppositions form a screen through which the biblical data is made to pass and undesirable texts are excluded from those which are by the same test accepted. On the other hand, the full canonical view of Scripture accommodates a broader amalgam of the various texts. The coercive power of those various texts makes itself felt and leads to the formation of the full canon of Scripture. The process that leads to the formation of a "canon within a canon" is controlled by a narrower view of what is permissible as authoritative. The full canonical approach recognizes the apostolic and ecumenical diversity of the multitude of texts on a given theme, and under the power of all of those texts the complete biblical canon has been formed. The full canonical view, related to a given theme, considers each text as possessing authority from the outset of its literary history. The other view, being more subjective in its evaluation of each text and consequently producing a partial or more limited canon, is more inclined to wait to pronounce a text authoritative until it has seen how each text fits into an acceptable theological view. In the former view, the authority of the text is granted in advance. In the latter view, authority is given or withheld by the reader as each text is evaluated. Since the text of Scripture belongs formally to the revelatory process of God, it is consistent and profitable to view each text as authoritative from the earliest stage of its existence.

But how does this scriptural authority work? What is its nature? A recent proposal in the currently popular genre of narrative theology[20] argues that the task of reading the New Testament is never a purely literary or a purely historical study, but also theological; that theology is done within a worldview; that a worldview is identified by its stories, questions, symbols, and action; that theology focuses on certain particular dimensions of a worldview, highlighting its god-dimension; that in this context theology tells its story, answers basic personal questions about the human condition, provides appropriate symbols, and promotes a particular lifestyle; that this gives rise to a system of basic mandatory beliefs and more or less mandatory consequent beliefs; that theology becomes a necessary tool in studying Scripture, involving awareness of contemporary culture just as theology needs biblical insights to inform itself; and that this biblical and theological story is in some way authoritative. Since proof-texting has been abandoned, and since there has been a general agreement to disagree on whether a descriptive or prescriptive reading of Scripture is followed, largely on the assumption that both readings are imposed by presuppositions that arise from outside the historical task itself, it may be that stories or narrative may have the capability of conveying authority. The example cited is that of a Shakepearean play, part of whose fifth act has been lost. The first four acts are rich in plot and characterization. In order to stage the play, it is recommended that the fifth act be completed, not by a playwright whose work would freeze the play into one particular form, but by highly skilled actors who would immerse themselves in the first four acts and then work out a fifth act for themselves. The first four acts would be the authority against which the various versions of the fifth act would be tested for authenticity. The fifth act could be innovative each time it was worked out, but would always have to be consistent with the first four acts. Applying this to Scripture, the biblical story would consist of four acts of creation, fall, Israel, Jesus, and the first scene of the fifth act would be formed by the New Testament which would supply hints as to how the play is supposed to end. Thus the church would live under the authority of the extant story. In each generation, then, those who were so led would work out the last scenes of the fifth act in the light and under the authority of the biblical story.

This is an intriguing proposal, which is not altogether strange because many of us do live our Christian lives under the powerful influence and authority of the biblical story. But the biblical authority is more than narrative. Narrative, by definition, is descriptive. Biblical authority is based primarily on the prescriptive "Thus says the Lord." It is based on the movement of the Spirit of God who interferes with and penetrates human lives, so that Christians live not only voluntarily by copying the greatest example who ever lived but compulsively, under the constraint of the divine imperative and in the presence and with the direct encouragement and aid of the risen Christ. This authority is more than an authority attached to a great story, however moving and mobilizing in practical terms. It is an authority based on saving events in history, interpreted by eyewitnesses under the guidance of the Holy Spirit. It also includes an invitation to believe and be saved, and an imperative to live in the light and power of that saving event.[21]

There is, however, a marked difference between story and history. Whatever value 'story' has in the context of Christian revelation, it will only be as a servant of the history of God's saving activity in the experience of Israel and the earliest church. This was a history preeminently about the life, death, and resurrection of Jesus Christ and His ministry that transformed people's lives. That saving event could only occur and make a difference in human lives by virtue of the presence and agency of the Holy Spirit. The church proclaims this good news of the presence and work of the Holy Trinity in the light and under the impetus and authority of the first and only written revelation, the Bible, and more particularly the New Testament. The danger of narrative theology is that in viewing it as operating within a particular worldview it may inadvertantly or even consciously allow the authority of the biblical text to be defined or controlled by the worldview within which it works. That is, the text may be controlled by the context of the reader and not by the story itself. The testimony of the canonical text however is to listen to the voice of God rather than to the opinions of men (Ac 4:19; 5:29). The full canonical approach permits the ecumenical and apostolic texts to be heard, whatever the theme and, by the power of the Holy Spirit, to transform lives by a saving and sanctifying experience of God in three persons.

Identifying and Evaluating the New Testament Texts Regarding the Distinctiveness of Jesus

THE EARLIEST CHURCH'S ACCOUNT OF THE MESSIAH.

Chronologically, the earliest church came to think of the Trinity only when it became apparent to her that Jesus of Nazareth was more than a prophet or teacher and that the Holy Spirit was more than merely a description of God in action. Whatever it consisted of, the evidence had to be more than a little persuasive in order to be convincing to Jewish disciples raised in a completely monotheistic atmosphere. Many, of course, have argued that the Trinity as such arose not in the earlier Jewish ecclesiastical environment, but in a later Gentile environment as the church branched out around the Mediterranean Sea. Such a view requires a deliberate fragmentation of the New Testament data and the unnecessarily late dating of its Trinitarian texts, not to mention the limiting of the number of texts that may be construed as Trinitarian. We need to be clear at the outset, however, that there are many more texts that can be identified as 'Trinitarian' than is often assumed.[22]

It is unnecessary, even perverse, to require a Trinitarian formula, such as appears in Matthew 28:19 and 2 Corinthians 13:14, for a text to be identified as "Trinitarian." I want to argue that in a very real sense many, if not all, of the earliest texts about Jesus are incipiently "Trinitarian." We can argue with some justification that very early in the life and ministry of Jesus, the texts that reflect astonishment at His wisdom and mighty works (Mk 1:22; Mt 13:54) indicate an awareness of distinctive qualities that set Jesus apart from other teachers and healers. From the outset, Jesus' teaching was unique. He declared that the kingdom of God was not a future dream, but had actually broken onto the horizon (Mk 1:15). "The time is fulfilled," Jesus said. That is, the promises of God were now coming to pass. This was not to be confused with religious sentiment or speculation. This was God acting. His reign had now broken in, in Jesus himself (Lk 17:21). This authority of Jesus was evidenced and confirmed by His dominance over the powers of darkness (Mk 1:27). The unclean spirits themselves knew they were being confronted by an extraordinary personality (Mk 1:24; 5:7). It takes a spirit to know a Spirit! They knew, when the scribes did not perceive who Jesus was (Mk 2:6f). It was to prevent a misunderstanding of His identity and purpose that Jesus delayed the public proclamation of His identity by means of what is called "the Messianic secret." This He engaged in at the very outset of His ministry (Mk 1:25, 44).[23] It was as Jesus' kingdom-ministry unfolded and addressed the diverse conditions of many people that it became increasingly obvious that here was someone who did not fall into the common category of what we might call a great man. Here was someone who dared to act in God's stead in forgiving sin (Mk 2:1-12),[24] exercised special authority in telling parables about God's kingdom (Mk 4; Mt 13; Lk 8),[25] and asserted a sovereign attitude towards the Torah (Mt 5:17ff)[26] and over the Sabbath (Mk 2:28). Add to these Jesus' choosing of the twelve apostles (Mk 1:16ff,19ff; 2:14; 3:13ff; Mt 10:1ff; Lk 6:12ff), which indicates an attitude of authority equal to God's choosing the twelve tribes of Israel,[27] and the triumphant entry as a king, with spiritual and political overtones, into Jerusalem (Mk 11:1-10).[28]

We need to remember, however, that it took time for the earliest church to appreciate who it was that was in their midst. Jesus' identity did not change from the earliest days of His ministry; yet the church's perception of that identity did. When Jesus addressed Simon and Andrew by the Sea of Galilee, "Come after me, and I will make you become fishers of men" (Mk 1:17), the disciples had no way of knowing who Jesus really was. As His ministry unfolded, there were obvious and provocative hints. But Jesus' deliberate reticence to identify himself boldly as the Son of God and Messiah stood in the way. Moreover, there is a certain ambiguity attached to the titles Jesus used, or that were used about Him.[29] What we are faced with, then, as we pursue an historical study of the development of the church's awareness of Jesus' identity, commencing with the earliest perception that here was a great prophet, teacher, and miracle worker, to a deeper appreciation that this was the promised Messiah, and finally to the awareness that this was none other than God incarnate is a development in perception. A modern reader of the New Testament might come to faith believing simultaneously that Jesus is both human and divine, but the disciples of the earliest church, given their historical situation and without immediate direct revelation that Jesus was also divine, had to develop their Christology "from below"[30] as it became increasingly clear that Jesus' identity, person, and work could not be fully accounted for in purely human terms. In retrospect, John's Gospel was able to depict Jesus from both human and divine perspectives. It is only later, with all the evidence in, that the earliest church could recognize Jesus in his fullness and think in terms of a Christology "from above." We will recognize, of course, that in our spiritual journeys both approaches are valid, and that both can find mutual accommodation. They are two sides of the same coin.

Some of the earliest descriptions of the person and work of Christ are found in the *kerygma* or preaching of the apostles.[31] In comparing the sermons of Peter (Ac 2:14-39; 10:34-43) and Paul (Ac 13:16-41; 1Co 15:1-11; cf. also Ro 1:1-4; 8:11-34; 10:8-9) it becomes apparent that there is a considerable amount of agreement on the substance of the church's proclamation: (i) The day of fulfillment of the Old Testament prophecies has dawned. (ii) This has occurred in the ministry, death and resurrection of Jesus. (iii) Through His resurrection from death and the grave, Jesus has been exalted to God's right hand as Messianic head of the new Israel, as Son of God with power, and as Lord of the living and the dead. (iv) The Holy Spirit has fallen upon the church. (v) Christ will return as Judge and Savior.

It has been mentioned that there are three points in the Pauline *kerygma* which do not explicitly occur in the Jerusalem *kerygma*. The latter omits any reference to Jesus dying for our sins, or to the exalted Christ interceding for us. Most significant for our purposes, however, is that in the Jerusalem *kerygma* Jesus is not explicitly called "Son of God." What He is called here is "Lord and Christ" (Ac 2:36). The Old Testament, which refers to God as "Lord," is used in the preaching of the earliest church in Jerusalem to refer to Jesus (Ac 2:21). Jesus is predestined to be Savior. He offers peace and healing. Being exalted to God's right hand, He receives and pours out the Holy Spirit. He offers forgiveness and judges the world (Ac 2:23, 32ff, 38; Ac 10:36, 38, 42ff; compare Ac 13:23, 29f, 39). We are told in the narrative of Acts 9:20 that Paul preached Christ as the "Son of God" in the synagogues of Damascus. Is this an attempt on Luke's part to show what Paul's preaching later developed into? That is possible, but not likely. For Luke identifies Paul's early *kerygma* as already containing reference to the Son (Ac 13:33), by way of a quotation of Psalm 2:7, interpreting this in relation to Jesus.[32] It would seem then, that the omission of the title "Son of God" from the Jerusalem *kerygma* is not overly significant for our purposes. It was already a significant, if not amazing step for the Jerusalem church to have designated Jesus "Lord," the Old Testament title for God!

There are two important questions to be considered here. How early is the Jerusalem *kerygma* and what exactly does "Lord" as applied to Jesus signify? With respect to the dating of the earliest *kerygma*, we need not be compelled to assume that the speeches are free compositions of the author, even if we agree that Acts was written as late as between AD 70 and 90. There is evidence that the author was restrained by the existence of sources to which he kept reasonably close, that he was apparently not influenced by the existence of Pauline theology, and that both the speeches and their narrative context contain "Aramaisms" that reflect the common language of the earliest church.[33] Whether or not the author has preserved the actual words of Peter and Paul is widely debated. Some would argue that neither the outline nor the content of the speeches are original. Some would argue that the outline is probably original, but not the content. Still others would hold that both the outline and the content are reasonably accurate. It does appear that each speech is unique and remarkably suited to its own peculiar occasion, while generally maintaining a common or shared focus. It is highly unlikely that the author could have created such speeches, with their individual distinctives and yet common similarities. Without claiming complete identification, it has not yet been proven that the words and their frameworks bear little or no relationship to what was actually spoken on their respective occasions. It appears very likely then, that the Jerusalem *kergyma* dates from much earlier than the date of the writing of Acts.

Does the *kergyma* date from the mid-thirties (AD)? The author's use of the Septuagint (the Old Testament in Greek) has been said to point to a later dating. But the Septuagint translation had been completed approximately two hundred years prior to Pentecost (Acts 2); was regarded by Philo, the influential Jewish thinker and exegete (ca. 20 BC to AD 50), as divinely inspired (Vita Mosis, II, 34-40); would have been used at least in Hellenistic synagogues of Palestine, such as the Jerusalem synagogue of the Freedmen (Ac 6:9); and is likely to have been quoted by Peter to the assembled Jewish throng on the day of Pentecost since many, if not the majority, of them were from the Diaspora where the Septuagint was commonly used. It was because the Septuagint was the popular version of the Old Testament among early Christians that the Jewish community later came to use only the Hebrew text.

The second reason for ascribing a fairly early date to the Jerusalem *kerygma* is the nature of its theology, which shows little development, especially when compared to the Pauline epistles or to Paul's *kerygma* (Ac 13:39; 1Co 15:1-8). The death of Jesus is described as a fact, without any particular positive purpose or effect. Apart from the ascription of "Lord" and "Christ" to Jesus, there is no development of thought regarding the incarnation. Moreover, none of the standard language later associated with salvation (e.g., justification, regeneration, reconcilation, redemption) is used. Rather, salvation is offered in terms of repentance, baptism in the name of Jesus Christ for the forgiveness of sins, and the receiving of the Holy Spirit (Ac 2:38).

The third reason for admitting an early date for the Jerusalem *kerygma* is the acceptance, also at an early date, of a more highly developed *kerygma*, which included but went further than the earlier Jerusalem *kerygma*, by St. Paul. Paul expressly states around AD 55 (1Co 15:3) that this *kerygma* which he preached was not of his own construction, but one which he received from an earlier source. Despite his disclaimer (Gal 1:11-18) that he derived it from a human source, nevertheless Paul states clearly that he submitted his gospel to Peter, James, and John at Jerusalem for their approval, which they gave (Gal 2:2). When did Paul receive this tradition? His conversion occurred around AD 33-34. It was no more than three years later that Paul first visited Jerusalem, during which time he stayed with Peter for fifteen days (Gal 1:18). What did they discuss during this time? What would a new convert like Paul be likely to discuss with Peter, the chief apostle? It is unthinkable that they focused on anything other than the facts and meaning of the gospel. In the fourteen years following this initial contact with Peter, when Paul had no direct contact with the primitive church (Gal 2:1), there is no evidence that he had any opportunity to learn more about early apostolic experiences and traditions. The burden of proof lies on those who would claim otherwise. In other words, Paul was made aware of the basic elements of the early Christian message no later than seven years after the death of Jesus! Indeed it could be earlier, since we can legitimately assume that Paul knew what the early church was preaching for some time before his conversion while he was busy persecuting the church.

We must now ask what "Lord" as applied to Jesus in the Jerusalem *kerygma* meant. This term is here used in conjunction with "Messiah" (Ac 2:36). The term "Messiah," we must recognize, is not by itself indicative of divine nature. Jewish messianic expectation varied, as we can see, from its four main sources. In the Old Testament the prophets spoke of a coming messianic age which would bring physical and spiritual hope to God's people. Sometimes there is no reference to an actual Messiah (Isa 26-29; Eze 40-48; Da 12; Joel 2-3). On other occasions reference is made to a Messiah, often considered to be of the line of David (e.g., Isa 9:7; 11:1ff; Mic 5:1ff; Eze 44:23ff; Jer 23:5f).[34] This means that the coming king and leader is royal in the human sense, but is he royal in the divine sense? The major text suggesting the latter is Isaiah 9:6-7. It has been suggested that this is a dynastic oracle celebrating the succession of a great and good king who would come and deliver his people. The titles stated are considered to be ceremonial names bestowed on this royal deliverer who will bring in an era of justice and righteousness. But this is less than adequate. In fact, all four titles imply divinity. The one who is "wonderful in counsel" is none other than Yahweh himself (Isa 28:29). Yahweh is "the mighty God" (Isa 10:21; compare Dt 10:17; Neh 9:32), and also "the everlasting Father" (Isa 63:16; compare 1Ch 29:10; Ps 68:4ff). Moreover, it is the Lord who is "Prince of peace" (Isa 26:3,12; compare Isa 57:19). It must be noted that the person designated in Isaiah 9:6-7 is never explicitly described as "anointed," which is what *Messiah* (*Christ*) means. In fact, "anointed" is never in the Old Testament used in connection with a future Davidic king, with the exception perhaps of Daniel 9:25 and Zechariah 4:14, which are uncertain as to meaning. But although anointing is not always referred to explicitly, we do know that kings were appointed to their office by anointing (1Sa 2:10; 2Sa 2:4; 1Kgs 1:39; Ps 18:50), even a heathen king (Isa 45:1). It is likely therefore that the special Davidic deliverer would be assumed to be appointed in this way. During the intertestamental period, we know from the Apocryphal and Pseudepigraphical literature, the messianic hope took different forms. The predominant expectation was that a Davidic king would come and establish an earthly kingdom for Israel, banishing her enemies. The messiah was a political agent with spiritual concerns (PS 17:36; 18:6,8), and was seen sometimes in an apocalyptic setting (4Ezr 7:27ff; 12:31ff). In the Qumran literature there are divergent views. Two anointed figures are identified, a high priest descended from Levi and a king from Judah (1QS 9:11; 4Q Test). A messiah from Aaron is said to take precedence over the messiah from Israel (CD 12:23).[35] Finally, rabbinic material on the messianic hope before AD 70 is scarce. Josephus' only reference to the Messiah (Christ) concerns Jesus (Antiquities 18.3.3), and this has been judged by many to be a later Christian interpolation in part or in total. Philo says nothing about a messiah. Jewish prayers, elements of which may be dated in New Testament times, look forward to the coming of an anointed one descended from David.[36] It is obvious from this brief survey that the idea of a coming messiah was widespread among the Jews, but that this figure's nature and purpose was variously defined. The closer to New Testament times, the more likely the authors of various Jewish literature on the subject thought of the coming deliverer primarily in political terms as a savior from foreign domination.

It is clear, however, that the author of Acts, and prior to that the author of the Jerusalem *kerygma* (whether Peter himself or someone else) thought of the Messiah in terms of spiritual deliverance.

This at any rate is what we find in Acts 2:36 and its context. The Messiah here is identified with Jesus, who brings forgiveness of sins for those who are repentant and upon whom the Holy Spirit is poured out as a gift (Ac 2:33,38). Who is it in Old Testament terms that offers forgiveness and pours out the Holy Spirit? It is God himself. What does this mean then for our understanding of the nature of Jesus Christ in this passage? True, there is no reference here to the preexistence of Christ as was later to be introduced by Paul, John, and the writer of Hebrews, but there are other factors in this passage that imply a remarkably high Christology dating from a very early stage.

It has been suggested[37] that we probably have here a primitive kind of Adoptianism: the idea that there was once a time when the crucified Jesus was not Lord and Messiah and that the man Jesus was elevated to these high positions by virtue of His vindication through resurrection. But three things speak against Adoptianism here. First, Adoptianism assumes advancement by moral merit. There is no reference here at all to Jesus meriting anything by virtue of living a holy life.[38] Rather we are told, second, that Jesus was raised from the dead because it was not possible that He should be held by it (Ac 2:24b). In support of this, Psalm 16:8-11 is then quoted. This Psalm cannot refer to King David but to the one he pre-figured, "Great David's greater Son," the messianic king. That is, Jesus was raised from the dead because of who He was by nature, not by the merit of a holy life. This is why it was impossible for Him to be held by death. Third, Jesus is identified not just as "Messiah," but simultaneously as "Lord." Two Old Testament passages are quoted in connection with Pentecost (Ac 2:17-21, 34-35) to show that the events involving Jesus were in fulfillment of the Scriptures. In Joel 2:29-32, God the Lord is the One who in the last days will pour out His Spirit and thereby bring about the proclamation of the Word (prophesy), signs and wonders (miracles), and the experience of salvation. In the Jerusalem *kerygma* it is Jesus who, in fulfillment of this promise, has poured out the Holy Spirit. Psalm 110:1 cannot refer to David, who did not ascend into the heavens, but to the Messiah. In Acts, this passage is cited as referring to Jesus. The "Lord" referred to in both Old Testament passages is in this *kerygma* ascribed to Jesus.[39] Jesus is here treated as in some way standing in the place of God. God and the Messiah are brought together in the same name, "Lord," and by the same saving functions. At the same time, they are clearly distinguished. Without the use of specific Trinitarian language, the primitive *kergyma* obviously contained significant elements of Trinitarian thought.

Peter's subsequent speech to Cornelius (Ac 10:34-43) is evidence of how the primitive *kerygma* was used in addressing a Gentile who had accepted Jewish monotheism and worshiped in the synagogue. Like the speech in Acts 2, this one also affirms Jesus as "Lord" (Ac 10:36) and "Judge" (Ac 10:42), who was raised from the dead (Ac 10:40), and who provides forgiveness of sins to those who believe in Him (Ac 10:43). All of this is covered in brief compass. What is developed more here is the historical data concerning Jesus (10:35-38), His life and ministry. The Greek of this section is strangely rough and ungrammatical: strange because the Greek of the author of Acts is usually first rate. It is almost certain that these verses are a translation of an earlier Aramaic version. When the Greek of this section is translated word for word into Aramaic, it becomes lucid and grammatical.[40] In other words, the section which uses the title "Lord" of Jesus and declares Him "anointed" by God issues from the earliest Aramaic-speaking church. There is no further development of Trinitarian thought, but the raw material for such thought is again affirmed and that as belonging to a very early date. True, God the Father is at every stage behind the life and ministry of Jesus. God sent, anointed, accompanied, raised, chose, ordained (Ac 10:36, 38, 40-42). But to be "Lord of all" and "Judge of the living and the dead" is to stand in the place of God. It is, in some way, to be God!

St. Paul's Contribution Regarding the Distinctiveness of Jesus.

Paul's *kerygma*, as demonstrated primarily in his sermon at Pisidian Antioch (Ac 13:16-41), contains both similarities and developments in comparison with the Jerusalem and Caesarean speeches of Peter (Ac 2:14-40; 10:34-43). The history of Israel is traced, albeit briefly, to show how God has worked out His purposes under the leadership of the judges and kings, David being "the man after my own heart, who will do all my will." God, according to His promise, has from David's seed raised up for Israel a Savior whose name is Jesus. John the Baptist prepared the way for His coming by preaching repentance and by pointing to Jesus as one of greater importance and authority than he. The message of this salvation has been sent to both Jew and God-fearing Gentile. The rulers and citizens of Jerusalem did not recognize Jesus for who He was, nor realized that in condemning Him they were fulfilling the very Scriptures they heard read each Sabbath. They had no reason to want Him dead, but demanded it of Pilate. They buried Jesus (the burial is strangely attributed to the Jews rather than to Joseph of Arimathea), but God reversed their action by raising Him from the dead. Jesus appeared on numerous occasions to the apostles, who then witnessed to the people confirming that Jesus was again alive. This is what we declare to you as gospel, says Paul—the very promise that was made to the fathers of Israel (Ac 13:32). The resurrection of Jesus is the means whereby the promise of salvation to Israel's fathers is made available now to the children of the fathers. All of this is in fulfillment of the Scriptures (Ps 2:7; Isa 55:3; Ps 16:10) which bear witness to the coming Savior. Through this Jesus ("Savior"—Ac 13:33) is offered forgiveness of sins. The person who believesis justified by Him in respect tp everything from which one could not be justified by the law of Moses. To scoff at such an offer brings the warning of the Scriptures (Hab 1:5ff) of which they are aware.

It is unlikely that Paul's original speech was so brief. What we have here is presumably an outline by Luke of what Paul said. Luke may himself have been following an outline he received, since there is some evidence of Aramaic showing through the Greek.[41] This means that Paul's speech was not the later product of the Hellenistic church. It also means that the idea of justification (Ac 13:39), though not developed here, was relatively early. Moreover, we seem to have confirmation here that the title "Son of God," which is attributed by Luke to Paul's preaching shortly after his conversion (Ac 9:20), is not as late as some scholars have suggested.[42]

But how is the reference to "my Son" (Ac 13:33), as conceived by the author of Psalm 2:7, which is being quoted here, to be understood? If Psalm 2 were simply a royal psalm referring to the enthronement of the king of Israel, then the idea of sonship here would likely also be limited. But the promise to this monarch is that God would upon request give him the nations and the ends of the earth to possess (Ps 2:8). Such universal authority can hardly be offered to an ordinary king. The psalm must therefore be messianic in focus and scope, and the king referred to must be messiah in an unlimited way. That is, "Messiah" (anointed one) was understood in a variety of ways. The conception in Psalm 2 seems to be of a messiah that is a world ruler, not one whose authority is limited to the borders of Israel. This theme is connected naturally to Paul's offer of the message of salvation to both the children of Abraham and Gentile God-fearers (Ac 13:26). The title "Son of God" is not out of place with such an extraordinary messianic expectation.[43] It appears that the earliest church recognized the appropriateness of Psalm 2 as containing the promise of the coming of God's Son, so that it could with legitimacy be quoted as referring to the person and work of Jesus of Nazareth, who died for our sins and rose again. Psalm 2 is quoted explicitly in Hebrews 1:5 and is often accepted as being implicitly behind Romans 1:4, both passages referring to a Son of God who is more than merely a political liberator or learned exponent of the Law.

There is the possibility however that the quotation of Psalm 2:7 in Acts 13:33 suggests that the early church considered Jesus to be Son of God not from His conception or because of His preexistence, but from the occasion of His baptism when He was addressed as "You are my beloved Son..." (Lk 3:22), or from the point of His resurrection and enthronement. This would be the Adoptionist view. Jesus, the man, would be granted the position of Son of God with such authority and power as goes with the title. But as we have argued on a previous occasion, adoption assumes merit. What we have in Jesus is not primarily a matter of merit, however righteous He was (Ac 13:28), but of identity and status. Jesus was not made Son of God by virtue of being raised from the dead. He was raised from the dead because He was the Son of God.[44] "Today I have begotten you" probably refers to the day of Jesus' resurrection. This is true in respect to the use of all three Old Testament references in Acts 13:33-37 (Ps 2:7; Isa 55:3; Ps 16:10). With respect to the use of the second Old Testament passage (Isa 55:3), the point is that the resurrection of Jesus makes the mercies offered in the Davidic Messiah "sure." God's grace can be counted on because God himself is faithful. The word translated "sure" also means "faithful." The means of assurance is the resurrection of Jesus which allows the risen Christ to make forgiveness universally and constantly available. God has acted faithfully. With respect to the use of the third passage (Ps 16:10), the point is that God will not "allow" His Son to disintegrate in His grave. The means of achieving this is by God raising up Jesus from the dead. Working backwards from the obvious meaning of these texts, we can see that "begotten" (Ac 13:33b) refers to resurrection. If that is not the meaning of Psalm 2:7 in its original context, it seems clear that this is what Luke meant by it here. But if "begotten" refers to Jesus' resurrection, it is not a corollary that the meaning is that Jesus began His Messiahship from that day. The reason is that this whole speech is set within the context of the purposes of God. It was God who elected Israel and sent the kings (vv. 16ff), raised up a Savior (vv. 23ff),[45] sent the message of salvation (vv. 26ff), issued the promise (vv. 23, 32), and fulfilled the promise by raising up Jesus (vv. 30, 33ff). The whole history of salvation has been in God's hands from start to finish, including the offer of good news (v. 32), forgiveness (v. 38), and a new status before God (v. 39). It is in such a context—that is, one of election—that "begotten" must be interpreted. The reference is almost certainly to resurrection. But what is the full significance of this event? To pick up the original meaning of Psalm 2, the significance of Jesus' resurrection is enthronement. That is, Jesus' coming out in full glory in a public act! It is an act of revelation. Nothing is added to Him; rather, He is proclaimed publicly to be the King

He always was and ever shall be. The promised Messiah is the Son of God, the Savior of all.

When we turn to Paul's *epistles* we find that he affirms what we have discovered to be his focus in at least one sermon in Acts.[46] He was accustomed to preaching Jesus Christ as the Son of God (2Co 1:19). The literary context confirms that this was the focus of his preaching, and that of other evangelists', to the unconverted at Corinth. It was not something reserved for those already initiated into the Christian faith.[47] Moreover, "the Son of God" was preached as the affirmation that all the promises of God in the Old Testament were fulfilled in Jesus. In other words, it was preached to Jews who would be able to identify those promises in their Scriptures. God-fearing Gentiles, who worshipped in the Jewish synagogues, would also be somewhat familiar with those promises (cf. Ac 18:4). The content of this preaching is that everything that God promised by way of a new beginning for the people of God has now been made available in Jesus the Son of God. The theological context is God and His purposes. The Son of God must here be seen in relation in the Father of mercies and the God of all comfort (2Co 1:3). It is this God and Father who made the promises (2Co 1:20), who makes the Christian secure in Christ, commissions (anoints) the Christian for service (2Co 1:21), and grants the guarantee of the Spirit to the believer (1Co 1:22).[48] The literary and theological context is also a missionary context.

Let us now consider 2 Corinthians 8:9 (ca. AD 55-56). The context of this famous Pauline text is the need for Christians with plenty to support poor Christians in their specific time of physical need. Sacrificial giving is the essential practical expression of the Christian's experience of divine grace. The historical expression of that divine grace is the incarnation of Christ. The principle of benevolence is built on the prior foundation already laid (compare 1Co 3:11), which is the person and work of the Son of God in flesh. Just how powerful the argument for earthly love among Christians is is what Paul is attempting to communicate here. "For you know the grace of our Lord Jesus Christ, that though he was rich, yet for your sakes He became poor, so that by His poverty you might become rich." The argument for love in the community of faith is found in the depths of God's love and the distance and degree to which He would go to save mankind as a whole.

The Christians in Jerusalem were being ostracized by the Jewish community, from which they came, because of their new Christian faith. They were consequently being impoverished. They found it difficult to make money and to live. Paul had appealed to the Christian churches around the Mediterranean Sea to dig into their pockets and give practical assistance. A collection was being taken up to be sent to the saints at Jerusalem. To justify and increase the donation of money, Paul appealed to the theological center of the Christian faith. No one was richer than the preexistent Christ; He was with God in heaven. Yet for our salvation, He gave up His status and benefits in heaven and came to earth. "None was richer than he; none became poorer than he."[49] Christ became a man in order to bring mankind back to God. He not only came to earth, He suffered and died for the world. Through this impoverishment of His status and through His sacrificial suffering for others, wealth in the form of a new life is granted free of charge to believers. This is the basis of all Christian ethics; this is the reason, Paul says, why Christians abroad should give sacrificially to Christians in need in Jerusalem.

The preexistence of Christ is essential for Paul's argument here. It is not merely his working hypothesis; it is assumed as given in the theology of the early church. The similarity between this passage, Philippians 2:5-8, and Colossians 1:15ff is obvious.

The third relevant passage of Paul's relating to the Son of God is Romans 1:3ff (ca. AD 57). The whole epistle, and every aspect of its theology and ethics, is drawn from the apostle's view of Jesus Christ. He is the good news promised by the prophets in the Holy Scriptures. This Jesus is God's Son, who in the flesh descended from David and who, by the Holy Spirit, was raised from the dead and by this resurrection designated Son of God in power. The text cannot legitimately be made to support an Adoptianist view of Christ. Nor can it be persuasively used to argue that Jesus was foreordained to become Son of God at His return.[50] First, the grammar of the passage clearly states that it was God's Son who was born of the seed of David. The language, if anything, suggests the preexistence of the Son.[51] Second, the point of resurrection is that Jesus' Sonship is thereby marked out and confirmed.[52] The verb and the prepositional phrase, "in power," go together. It is as the risen Son of God that Jesus begins to assert His authority over the lives of those to whom the good news is proclaimed. It is good news because He is now mighty to save and to sanctify, and to bring people into His service. It is generally admitted that Paul is quoting or at least borrowing from an earlier confession that already existed in the church.[53] The role of the Holy Spirit is explained later by Paul in Romans 8:11. The Holy Spirit is the agent of resurrection. Some have suggested that Psalm 2 may lie behind the language here.[54] If this is true, it is added evidence that Jesus as Son of God is at least universal in authority, if not also divine in being. If we are correct in seeing here more than a hint of Paul's belief in the preexistence of Jesus, then we can be assured also that Paul is here thinking of a divine Son of God.[55] At any rate, the point Paul is making is that Jesus, who in the period of His earthly existence is Son of God in apparent weakness and poverty, now by means of His resurrection, has been appointed Son of God with power.[56]

The fourth relevant passage is Philippians 2:5-11 (ca. AD 63). The context here is ecclesiastical and ethical. Paul wants harmony in the church, and advocates humility among the members so that it may be achieved (Php 2:1-4). A community cannot be united and harmonious when each member is wrapped up in his or her own interests. The apostle points to Christ as the supreme example of Christian humility. Look to Christ, Paul says, who might well have insisted on the honor rightly ascribed to one who, being in the form of God, was equal with God, but who chose to forego such honor for the sake of mankind. Instead, He stripped himself by taking the form of a servant, being born in the likeness of men. Moreover, being found in the form of a man, Christ humbled himself not just to the point of dying like everyone, but by suffering the ignominy of criminal execution for sinful mankind. Therefore, since Christ has so acted for the salvation of sinners, God has reversed everything. He has exalted Christ and given Him the highest name, before which all mankind shall kneel in acknowledgment of His true identity, and all the tribes shall confess Him as Lord, so as to bring glory to God for His great saving act.

A number of significant points about the nature and work of Christ are made here by Paul. First, Christ was preexistent. Prior to His incarnation, Christ existed in relationship with God. In this relationship He was equal with God. Second, Christ is capable of exercising personal choice in becoming incarnate. Third, in His incarnation He is both human and divine. Fourth, He is instrumental in overcoming sin and death for mankind. Fifth, Christ will be confessed as Lord by every tribe and nation. That is, all humanity will finally learn humility, whether willingly or by the compelling persuasiveness of divine truth.[57]

It has often been argued that Paul has here borrowed from an earlier tradition. It has been attributed to Gnostic origins,[58] but most of the evidence adduced is later than the New Testament. Redemption occurred by the revelation of special saving knowledge, not by a "redeemer" as such, and the heavenly primal man was linked to mankind's creation and embodied the saving truth about its origin and therefore was not likely an individual person at all, but rather a symbol of some specific truth.[59] Others have suggested not Gentile, but Jewish origins.[60] The case for this is based on the passage's hymn-like form and style: vocabulary and theology that is un-Pauline, the passage disrupting the ethical context, the Greek being stilted, and familiarity with Old Testament language. There is a considerable amount to be said on the other side of the debate, however. Almost half of the 104 verses in this letter have been recognized to fall naturally into poetic form. How can this passage then be put into a special category? Even if it were a hymn, Paul might have written it himself. The language is not strictly un-Pauline; several of the words used here appear in cognate form in his other letters. The proportion of unusual words is numerically similar in this passage as it is for the letter as a whole.

The theology of the passage is in fact quite Pauline. We should note the Adam-Christ typology here, which is found only in Paul. The reference to "death on a cross" is strictly Pauline, and has to be treated as a Pauline addition by those who see the hymn as pre-Pauline. The passage attributes incarnation as an act of choice by Christ and is therefore highly consistent with the context which is promoting an ethic of humility.

The point of the passage is that Christ, who was in the form of God, stooped to accept equality with the human race which, like Adam, was created in human form but grasped after equality with God.[61] The divinity of Jesus is here assumed and stated from the beginning and then stated again in terms of self-emptying. This is a self-emptying of power, status, and authority brought about by a change of form and function. Nowhere in this passage is an ontological self-emptying suggested. The language of the passage is itself suggestive. The author deliberately chose such words as "form" (*morphe*), "fashion" (*schema*), "likeness" (*homoioma*) to make the point that what was at issue here was Christ's self-denial through a change of condition rather than a relinquishment of His divine nature or attributes. In assuming human nature, Christ did not give up His original divine nature. What He demonstrated in His incarnation was an attitude and manner devoid of all self-aggrandizement.[62] This is the author's purpose in pointing to Christ as the great example for us all in emptying ourselves of selfish ambition and conceit. The eternal uniqueness of the Son in relation to the Father is clearly expressed in this passage, as in no other, in terms of the preexistent Christ who desires nothing for himself but gives himself in complete servanthood to the task of establishing the kingdom of God so that the Father whom He loves might be brought near to the world in love, and in doing so might bring full glory to the Father.[63] If we wonder how Christ's divinity, with its superlative attributes of omniscience, omnipotence, and omnipresence, remains intact in the process of incarnation, perhaps we need to think of these not so much in terms of compression or condensation but of concentration and interspersion. At any rate, in this passage the ontological issues are not pursued, only the ethical. The theological elements are clear: the preexistent Jesus became incarnate to save the world; He was then exalted and would eventually be acknowledged by all as Lord!

The fifth passage to be considered is Colossians 1:15-20. This letter is probably Pauline,[64] and was written from Rome between AD 61 and 63. What is relevant for our purposes in this passage is the reference to Christ as the image of the invisible God (v. 15), who created the world (v. 16), in whom all things hold together (v. 17), and in whom all the fullness of God was pleased to dwell (v. 19). The context is one of prayer in which the apostle expresses his gladness for the faith, love, and hope which Christians at Colossae have received through the gospel, and for the fruit and growth they are manifesting as they continue to mature in the faith. Paul prays that they may be filled with spiritual wisdom and understanding so as to be enabled to lead a life worthy of the Lord—fully empowered with God's might so as to endure with patience in all circumstances, demonstrating joy and gratitude to God. It is God the Father who qualified them to share with all believers in the inheritance of light, and who delivered them from the realm of darkness, transferring them into the kingdom of His beloved Son.

But are these verses really Pauline? Many scholars view this section as a hymn derived from one of three possible sources: Jewish,[65] Hellenistic,[66] or Gnostic.[67] There are problems with this somewhat popular theory. It requires the excision of words that are out of place in this passage and their identification as glosses by the final editor. There is a common assumption often made by scholars that biblical authors are limited in their choice and use of vocabulary where it is more likely that they had access to a larger common stock of ideas and vocabulary. Certainly the exalted claims made here for Christ are not specifically parallel in the other letters of Paul, but each of the Pauline letters contains distinctive theological ideas peculiar to it as might be expected. None of his epistles is intended to contain a complete systematic theology. Each is written for a particular purpose, and often in response to special needs or questions. Even if the "hymn" theory were to be accepted, we must recognize that the meaning of the passage is what Paul intended it to mean.

The study of Christian origins is important but must not be allowed to control the final exegesis of a passage. What we need to recognize in the exegesis of this particular passage is the direction of Paul's thinking as evidenced in the context in which these verses appear. Paul is focusing on the authority ("the Kingdom of His beloved Son") and the work ("redemption, the forgiveness of sins") of Jesus Christ (Col 1:13-14). The gospel to which these Colossians have responded so magnificently in faith, love, and hope (Col 1:4-5) consists of the saving work of Christ. He has redeemed, reconciled, and released them from the guilt and power of sin (Col 1:14, 22), through His death and resurrection (Col 1:18, 22). This redemption has been and is so effective that it can only reflect the authority of the One who has accomplished it. The redemption effected through Christ reflects the fact and importance of the reign of Christ. Therefore, the Colossian Christians should "live a life worthy of the Lord," "bearing fruit in every good work," "being strengthened with all power according to His glorious might" (Col 1:10ff). Paul, in other words, arrives at his understanding of Christ's place in creation through His role in bringing about the new creation (cf. Col 3:10; 2Co 5:17; Gal 6:15; Eph 2:15). We begin to see the greatness of Christ, in relation to God the Father and the world, through the impact of His saving power and love.

On the question of textual origins, a more persuasive theory than that of a pre-Pauline "hymn" was suggested over seventy years ago.[68] It is that Paul himself is responsible for this passage (Col 1:15-20), and that he was adapting a rabbinic midrash on two Old Testament passages for Christian purposes. The rabbinic hypothesis is that the reference to Wisdom in Proverbs 8:22 as the "beginning" (*reshith*) of God's way is to be seen as suggested in the "beginning" (*bereshith*) of God's creation in Genesis 1:1. That is, Wisdom (or Torah) was the instrument of creation. Paul is here claiming that in reality the reference is to Christ (compare 1Co 10:1ff).

Nowhere else in the Pauline corpus is there a higher or richer exposition of the person and work of Christ. Within the literature of the New Testament, only John 1:1ff and Hebrews 1:1ff are comparable. The scope of Christ's work and authority encompasses the creation and preservation of the physical world, the salvation of mankind, the headship of the church, and His special ontological relationship with God. It helps to break the passage into three sections. The first (Col 1:15-16) focuses on the simultaneous relation of the Son to the Father and to the universe. Paul uses two significant words to this end. Christ is the "image" (*eikon*) of the invisible God and the "firstborn" (*prototokos*) of all creation. God as Father is invisible, but the incarnate Son, who is not merely one creature among many creatures but the preeminent ("firstborn") historical being of all time, is most definitely visible. As such He is more than merely the Wisdom of God (Proverbs 8:22). He is the perfect revelation ("image") of God (compare 2Co 4:4; also Jn 14:6). What Paul means by "firstborn" he elucidates in Colossians 1:16. The Son is the agent ("in Him", "through Him") and goal or focus ("for Him") of creation. Paul's thought here moves freely and fluidly back and forth between the Son's creative activity in His preexistence and His saving activity in His incarnation.

This is extended in the second section of this passage (Col 1:17-18) to include a third mode of action. The incarnate Christ who came to save mankind from sin and who was once the preexistent agent of creation and its coherence is now the exalted Lord who continues as the agent of coherence. He holds the creation, which He made and saved, together. The tense of the verbs changes from past to present.[69] The present tense of the verb "to be" is repeated three times, presumably for emphasis. The Son precedes all things in importance. He holds all things together. He is the head of His body, the church. He is the beginning and source (*arche*) of the new creation, the first to rise from the dead. Christ is thus in all things preeminent, and He is this in the present.

So we come to the third and final section (Col 1:19-20). Here is the climax and indeed apex of Paul's assertions about Christ in this and all his epistles. "In him (Christ) the whole fullness (of God) was pleased to dwell." The clue to the meaning of "fullness" is given in Colossians 2:9: "For in Him the whole fullness of deity dwells bodily." In other words, the total essence of God resides in Christ.[70] There is complete wisdom and knowledge (Col 2:3) in Christ. He is more than a prophet or teacher. He is more than a secondary divine being, more than the sum total of intermediary aeons (Col 1:16; 2:8, 15) of which Gnosticism spoke. Paul is saying, you can account for Christ in His preexistence, historical existence and exalted existence, and all the work He undertook and undertakes in each form of existence, only by recognizing His real identity. He created, preserves, and redeems the world because of who He is. Christ's preeminence is to be explained by His "fullness" (*pleroma*). What makes Christ uniquely preeminent over all things is that He actually represents everything that God is, and this in incarnate form (Col 2:9). All that God is is to be found living dynamically in Christ.[71] It is because of this ontological reality that Christ is able to be the revelatory "image" of God (Col 1:15), as well as the agent of creation and coherence with respect to the universe (Col 1:16-17). The reference to "fullness" is deliberately used by Paul in response to the Colossian heresy, which is one of the main reasons for writing this letter. The same term was used by the Gnostics to refer to the sum total of intermediary aeons, "all the supernatural denizens of the interspace between the invisible, uncreated God and the visible, created world."[72] Paul's point is that real "fullness" is to be found in the incarnate and glorified Christ, and that this "fullness" does not consist of anything that is intermediary, but of God himself.[73] Central to Paul's theme, of course, is an element which does not appear in Gnostic theology: reconciliation (Col 1:20). Moreoever, Paul's theology of reconciliation is based on the shedding of the blood of the Savior. This is the special wisdom which goes far beyond the wisdom of Gnosticism.[74]

The sixth passage we must consider briefly is 1 Timothy 3:16. The thought contained here in hymnic form contains the following elements: preexistence, incarnation, resurrection, and exaltation. The main focus is on the revelation of the divine mystery through the coming of Christ. The incarnation is described in revelatory terms. "He was revealed in the flesh." Preexistence is thus implied. Resurrection is described as justification by the Holy Spirit (cf. Ro 8:11). This implies His atoning death, which would otherwise be construed as a defeat. Being seen by angels and being preached among the nations covers the two-directional proclamation of Christ's saving activity, in heaven (cf. Eph 3:10; 1Pe 1:12) and on earth. The hymn concludes with the note of vindication and triumph. He was "believed in throughout the world," and was "taken up to glory." The mystery is thus a Person, but which person: Christ or perhaps God himself? To whom does the masculine relative pronoun refer? The subject in the immediately preceding verses is God (v. 15). This probably accounts for the alternative reading in some manuscripts. The more likely reference however is to Christ. "The mystery of our religion" refers everywhere in Paul's writings to the saving activity of Christ (1Co 2:1,7ff; 4:1; Eph 1:9; 3:3ff, 9; 6:19; Col 1:26ff; 2:2; 4:3; 1Ti 3:9).[75]

We look finally at three verses in the Pauline material that may or may not reflect a high Christology.

Romans 9:5. This verse is set in the context of Paul's list of all the privileges and blessings that belong to the chosen nation of Israel. "To them belong the sonship, glory, covenants, law, worship, promises, patriarchs." From them, according to the flesh, comes either the Christ, "who is God over all, blessed forever, amen," or "God, who is over all, be blessed forever, amen." The translation depends on the punctuation. The original Greek text, of course, did not carry any punctuation marks from which Paul's meaning could be discerned.[76] There is one substantial argument against the view that Paul is here referring to Christ as God, and it is that Paul nowhere in the rest of his corpus makes this claim.[77] Yet Paul could say: "God was in Christ reconciling the world to himself" (2Co 5:18ff); "Christ is the likeness of God" (2Co 4:4; Php 2:6); "Christ is the Son of God" (Ro 1:4); and that "in him all the fullness of God was pleased to dwell" (Col 1:19; cf. Col

2:9). Christ was "in the form of God" (Php 2:8), and "equal" with God (Php 2:6). Moreover, Paul could pray to Christ (1Co 16:22; 2Co 12:8). Passages reflecting the subordination of Christ to the Father (e.g., 1Co 15:28) are probably to be read as referring to His incarnate humanity, not to His divinity. In favor of the view that Paul is here designating Christ as God are the following three considerations: (a) If the concluding words are a doxology to God the Father, the participle (on) would be unnecessary. (b) Paul's normal practice in a doxology is to connect the subject to the person immediately prior (e.g., Ro 1:25). (c) The word "blessed" (*eulogetos*) would normally be placed at the beginning of a doxology rather than toward the end. Paul's grammar and theology therefore strongly support the ascription of divinity to Christ here.[78]

There remains the psychological argument that because of his strong Jewish monotheism Paul could not have made such an assertion.[79] But this assumes that Trinitarian thought cannot be made compatible with monotheism. It is unwise to limit the human mind, regardless of its cultural conditioning, to what it can or cannot come to believe or write.[80] New ideas can spring up in strange places. This, for example, is the whole purpose of education. Besides, Paul was no longer limited to a single "typical" Jewish way of thinking. His experience of the risen Christ (Ac 9) and his subsequent reflection on that experience (Gal 1:17) would undoubtably have been the cause of new ways of thinking. He saw God at work, and revealing himself in a remarkable new way, in Jesus. That Paul should eventually take the step, especially in moments of ascending spiritual thought, and give the name God to Christ should not be at all surprising.

Titus 2:13. This text provides us with another occasion where Christ is probably called God. The theological reasons are strongly in favor of doing so. First, the initial setting is the return of Christ in which the focus is naturally Christological. There are not two appearings, one of God and another of Christ. Second, the context turns immediately to the theme of redemption and Christ's act of purifying for himself a people for His own. Third, the phrase "God and Savior" is a formula which is probably not to be torn apart. Grammatically, had there been any intention of differentiating between God and Jesus, a second article would normally have been used.[81] The question of authorship does not have to be firmly settled in favor of Paul for this text to be influential. It is sufficient to recognize Pauline influence behind it.

2 Thessalonians 1:12. It is possible, but according to much scholarly opinion less likely, to support the interpretation that here Christ is referred to as God.[82] The argument in favor is built on the fact that only one definite article is used. This would not be a weighty argument if the expression "Lord Jesus Christ" were a technical term which could exist without an article. Further, the context focuses on judgement by God and the return of Jesus. Both are active in these eschatological events. It would not be out of place, then, for grace to be seen to flow from both the Father and the Son. On the other hand, in the immediate context, the focus is specifically on "the name of our Lord Jesus...glorified in you, and you in Him." If it is this glorification that Paul is referring to here as deriving from grace, then it may very well have led him to see that grace as coming preeminently from Jesus. In such a case it would be natural for Paul to ascribe this grace to Jesus as God, since God is the traditional and likely source of grace. The translation would then read: "According to the grace of our God and Lord, Jesus Christ." The final question would be an historical one. In the development of doctrine in Paul's mind, especially as relating to Christology, is it likely that Jesus would be identified with God so early in Paul's ministry? Second Thessalonians was probably composed in AD 49-50. Colossians, with its high Christology, was written more than 10 years later. This would provide time for Paul's thought to develop. A sign of such development during that period would be Romans 9:5 (ca. AD 57). Titus 2:13 would date from some time after AD 62.[83]

We conclude that Paul's preaching focused on a magnificent work of salvation carried out by Jesus the Messiah, who is the Son of God, enthroned as Savior of the world. There is no question that Paul saw God and Jesus in a special relationship, working together to provide deliverance and hope for all mankind and for all of creation, animate and inanimate (Ro 8:18ff). This is a concept that has similarities with the teaching of Jesus concerning "the renewal of all things" (Mt 19:28), which will take place at the enthronement of the Son of Man when He undertakes the judgment of the world. The apocalyptic literature refers to this event in terms of the coming of a new heaven and earth (Rev 21:1). Paul saw Jesus, the Son of God, as the preexistent Christ who, at the appropriate time in God's purposes, became incarnate in time and space. This preexistent Christ was not only to be Savior in His incarnate work, but is also the agent of creation and the One who held and holds the world together. There is also evidence that Paul could describe Jesus as God, marking a distinct breakthrough in the development of Trinitarian thought. It is little wonder that Paul could pray to Jesus to return (1Co 16:22), a prayer that no Jew would dream of praying to a mere prophet or teacher of God but only to God himself.[84] What may be surprising is that Paul could pray such a prayer so early in his Christian pilgrimage. Yet his thinking in 2 Corinthians 8:9 indicates that the intermingled ideas of incarnation, preexistence, and deity came earlier than many have thought possible.

EVIDENCE FROM THE EPISTLE TO THE HEBREWS.

The introductory verses of this letter, which is to be dated prior to AD 70 and the fall of Jerusalem, refer to God's Son who, "in these last days," is the spokesman for God bringing revelation to the world and is the "heir of all things." This is the preexistent Son who, as in the Pauline passages, is the agent of both creation and providence. Moreover, when the Son came into the world, He provided purification for sin, returning to sit at the right hand of God from whence He came. This Son of God is none other than Jesus (2:9; 3:1; 4:14; 5:7, etc.). His status is defined in three particular ways.

First, Christ has become superior to the angels (Heb 1:4). This superiority is the result of enthronement as the Son takes His place at God's right hand when He has completed His work of atonement (Heb 1:3). In the background is the human development of the incarnate Jesus, who later in the letter, is described as being made a little lower than the angels (Heb 2:9). He shared our humanity (Heb

2:14), was tempted as we are (Heb 2:18) though without sinning (Heb 4:15), and was made perfect through suffering (Heb 2:10; 5:8). That is, Christ's life on earth was completely human. He experienced life in a sinful world, undergoing everything sin could do to Him, yet remained faithful, making atonement for mankind (9:15), and receiving vindication, He became for mankind its Apostle bearing good news of salvation and High Priest conveying salvation (3:1). Christ, being exalted, entered heaven, into the very presence of God, and there as High Priest of a higher order, that of Melchizedek (7:11ff), acts as an advocate on our behalf (9:24). Having accomplished the work of salvation once for all, Christ will return a second time to bring a final salvation for those who await Him (9:26-28; 10:10). This Christ undertakes His priestly ministry on the authority of an indestructible life (7:16), and He lives in His resurrection power to intercede for those who come to God through Him so that they might be completely saved (7:25). Having therefore been a little lower than the angels, because He has experienced real incarnate life and fought His way through to victory over sin and death, Christ has been elevated above the angels. This was where He was before His incarnation, in His preexistence with the Father (1:5). Superiority over the angels is the clear mark of the high status of the Son of God. It belongs to Christ from the beginning, and also because He earned His place above the angels by virtue of His unique and victorious work of salvation. It is for these two reasons that Jesus Christ is described in this letter as "the same yesterday and today and forever" (Heb 13:8).

Second, "he [the Son] is the reflection of God's glory and the exact imprint of God's very being" (Heb 1:3). The letter to the Hebrews focuses certainly on the great work of salvation Christ has undertaken and accomplished, but it also underlines the work of revelation which He in addition undertakes. The salvation needs to be made known, if it is to have any effect on people's lives. Christ undertakes and achieves both of these tasks. He paid the ransom for our sins (Heb 9:15). He is also "the pioneer and perfecter of our faith" (Heb 12:2). That is, Christ is the One upon whom we should "fix our eyes," because He conveys the message of this great salvation to us. Faith is our response to a prior revelation. Jesus Christ reveals in whom and in what we should believe. Consequently, He is "the apostle," the one sent with the message (Heb 3:1). The point is that this Jesus is an extraordinary, indeed unique "apostle," for He not only conveys the message, He is the message. This is the point of the two Greek words *apaugasma* and *charakter* (Heb 1:3) as they are applied to the Son. They refer not so much to His work as to His being. Better, the work of revelation springs from Christ's being. There is no idea here of Jesus' being the adopted Son of the Father. The issue here is the special interrelationship between the Father and the Son, one that is unique and permanent.[85] The imagery used by the author is one of light, which is common enough in descriptions of the divine but which here is distinctive. It is distinctive not only in being used of the Son as well as of the Father, but also in that the meaning must surely be an active radiating and not merely a passive reflecting of God's light by the Son.[86] References by scholars to the influence on this passage by WS 7:26 and Philo (*De Opificio Mundi*, 146) are questionable. In the former, *apaugasma* is used of the Wisdom of God, which though personified is not thought of there as a personal being. In the latter, *apaugasma* is applied to the *logos*, but here also the *logos* was never understood as personal. It was merely the personification of a divine attribute. Closer parallels can be found in the idea of the image (Col 1:15) and of the visible glory of God in the Son (Jn 1:14). In Hebrews, the Son is the effulgence or brilliant light of God as He makes His purposes and work known. The tense is present, the point being that this is who Christ is, unchangingly. The second word, *charakter*, means that the Son is the impress of God's being. To see the Son is to see the Father (cf. Jn 14:9). These two Greek words were specially chosen by the author to explain the nature of the Son in relation to the Father and His work as revealer.

Third, "But of the Son he says, 'Your throne, O God, is forever'" (1:8). To translate this quotation from Psalm 45:6 as "God is Thy throne forever and ever" is not at all persuasive.[87] The usual translation involves treating the nominative as vocative, but this can be paralleled elsewhere (e.g., Jn 20:28). The significance of this verse can hardly be overestimated. It means that for this author, the Son can be addressed as God. To the Son is being applied here a text which in the Old Testament refers entirely to God in His sovereignty. In Hebrews, the meaning is that the Son's kingdom knows no end. Moreover, it is a kingdom that is characterized by true righteousness. Not even the angels can boast of such a kingdom. This is why the angels must worship the Son (Heb 1:6) and obey Him (Heb 1:13). It is this Son that as incarnate Messiah has been anointed by the Father (Heb 1:9). This high Christology compares favorably with that of Paul and with that of John, to which we now turn.

EVIDENCE FROM THE GOSPEL OF JOHN.

How early is the Christological evidence of this Gospel? The dating of the Fourth Gospel depends largely on four factors. First, it depends on whether its background is primarily Jewish and therefore associated with the earliest church, or primarily Gentile and associated with the later church. Increasingly, its Hebraic character is being recognized. Old Testament allusions, ideas and references are ubiquitous. Second, the dating depends on whether or not the author was an eyewitness. The author in fact displays considerable knowledge of Jewish customs and history, Palestinian geography, and gives several hints of having been there, hints that are totally insignificant to the narrative, therefore all the more believable (e.g., Jn 2:6; 6:19; 21:8, 11). That John the apostle is author is the traditional view (Irenaeus) and has considerable support in the Gospel (Jn 1:14; 19:35; 21:24). Alternative theories present numerous problems. If John the apostle were the author, or at least the main source, then the apparent eyewitness testimony would be explained. Third, the dating depends on whether or not the author was combating Gnosticism,[88] which in its maturer forms would make the appearance of this Gospel much later. This theory however is offset by others which hold that one does not have to go so far afield; that John was undertaking a polemic against unbelieving Jews, or refuting certain docetic views that draw distinctions between the divine and the human in Christ, or presenting the true relationship between Jesus and John the Baptist. Even if there are Hellenistic ideas addressed in Greek terms, this need not require a late date. Hellenistic thought was brought into Palestine and its environment with Alexander the Great, some three hundred years before Christ. Evidence of this influence has been found in the Qumran community. Fourth, the dating is related to whether or not the Fourth Gospel is dependent upon the Synoptic Gospels. This of course depends upon the dating of the latter. If the date for Mark is set around AD 64-70, then John could follow between AD 80-90.[89] If, however, as some hold, there is little evidence of literary dependency and John's Gospel represents an independent tradition,[90] then the dating could legitimately be altered. Depending on one's determination of the preceding issues, it is conceivable that John could be dated much earlier, even earlier than AD 70.[91]

We will consider five texts from this Gospel which will provide a clear indication as to the Christological view of the author.[92]

The Prologue (1:1-18). John's description of the ministry of Jesus is given not, as in Matthew and Luke, in an historical framework but rather a theological one. The incarnate Son of God (v. 14) has His origins outside of time and space in the preexistent Word.[93] This Word represents clearly both the being and action of God.[94] The author takes us back to the beginning of all things (Gen 1), to the agency of creation-salvation-revelation that is found in the eternal divine Word (Jn 1:1-5). Prior to the world and time, the Person who came to be known as Jesus already existed. He was the Word who existed with God; that is, in the presence of God.[95] This being with God includes the idea of relationship.[96] God was not alone.[97] The two ideas probably present are those of accompaniment and of relationship.[98] That there were no limitations to the being and actions of Jesus, the author makes clear in the third phrase of his opening declaration. "The Word was God." This phrase cannot with justification be re-interpreted to mean "The Word was like God." If the author had wished to say the Word was merely divine, the adjective was readily available (cf. Ac 17:29; 2Pe 1:3). In fact, there is here no sense of subordination of the Word to God at all. The Word is equal with God. Nor does the omission of the definite article before "God" mean that the Word is not actually God, but only "a god" or divine in nature, a kind of divine emanation.[99] The definite article is omitted by the article for a simple grammatical reason, because "God" is the predicate.[100] The author is making a literal claim when he calls the Word "God."[101] The question as to why we are reminded that the Word "was with God in the beginning" (v. 2) is answered in at least two different ways: to avoid the erroneous assumption that there is no distinction at all between God and the Word[102]; or to emphasize that the Word does not come to be with God, but is with God from the beginning.[103] The former emphasizes the distinction between the Word and God in their relationship. The latter emphasizes the glory shared between the Word and God (Jn 17:5), and therefore their oneness in fellowship. A third way of taking this verse is to see it as a bridge between the being and action of the Word and God, as the author now turns to the agency of the Word as Creator (v. 3), Savior (v. 4), and Revealer (v. 5). Each of these three activities the Word undertakes in His relationship to the Father. The former is undertaken as the preexistent Word, the latter two are undertaken as the incarnate Word. The point may well be that the Word is in relation with the Father in carrying out the Father's purposes. The agency of the Word is grounded in His ontological relationship with the Father. The language of "the Word" and "God" (v. 1) becomes that of "the Son" and "the Father" (v. 14). That we are still meant to remember the dual ideas of being and action throughout the Prologue is evident from the author's introduction of the words "only-begotten," "glory," and "fullness" (1:14,16). The incarnate Word is one of a kind (only-begotten), full of grace and truth which in substance and completeness can come only from the Father. He has come to convey that grace for salvation and the revelation concerning it to the world. There is a glory that the incarnate Word has in all of this, and it is a glory not only to be found in the action of bringing it to the world but also in the relationship He has with the Father (cf. Jn 17:5).

The next four texts we must look at in the fourth gospel are found in the narrative and may be taken as the basis on which the author expounded his high Christology in the prologue. Where else would he have found the ideas of which he writes in the prologue, if not in the life and ministry of Jesus? This is surely what he means when he says, "We have seen His glory...full of grace and truth" (v. 14), if we consider this in relation to various references of glory throughout the Gospel narration (Jn 2:11; 11:4; 12:41; 14:13; 15:8; 16:14; 17:4, 10, 24), and the author's stated purpose in writing this book (20:30f). These four texts are not exhaustive, but typical of the elevated Christology throughout this Gospel.

Honoring the Father and Son (Jn 5:23). In the teaching of Jesus, we are instructed to honor the Son to the same degree that we honor the Father. The honor of the Father and the Son is identical.[104] The context of this passage focuses on the themes of resurrection and of judgment. The Son is endowed with what must otherwise be considered as divine prerogatives. In Jewish theology, only the Father can give life by raising the dead and only the Father can condemn the guilty to death. Here, this authority is in both instances recognized as having been conveyed to the Son. All of this comes out of a debate between Jesus and the Jewish authorities over the question of the use of the Sabbath for purposes of healing the sick (Jn 5:16ff). Jesus claims the authority to do so on the grounds that He and the Father share a work that is always underway. The point is that the Father doesn't always rest on the Sabbath day! This would seem to the Jewish authorities to be a breach of Scripture (Ge 2:2), and therefore untenable teaching. That Jesus also was guilty of making himself equal with God by speaking of Him as His own Father (John 5:18) compounded the offense. What follows is Jesus' explanation of His relationship with the Father. He begins by saying that He depends on the Father to show Him what to do. But once the Father shows Him this, then the Son must act for there is a special bond between them. To illustrate the degree of interaction and inter-relationship, Jesus points to two acts that are of the highest order: raising the dead and judging the world. It follows, Jesus is arguing, that to act in these areas is to act in the place of God himself, and therefore, makes Him worthy of equal respect, honor, and presumably worship.

In fact, says Jesus, not to so honor the Son is to deny honor to the Father, because it was the Father who sent the Son. There is here more than a hint of the preexistence of the Son. In this passage two things are unmistakable: the distinctiveness, but also the unity of the Father and the Son. As such they share a common dignity. This shared function and authority between the Father and the Son carries over in the following verses (Jn 5:24-30) to the mission of Jesus' preaching of the Word that brings eternal life which obviates any necessity of judgment for the believer and the apocalyptic events of resurrection and judgment. Jesus ends by returning to the note of His human dependency on the Father. By himself he can do nothing. He lives to serve the Father (Jn 5:30). In this passage we have the oneness and yet the distinction of the Father and the incarnate Son.

Preexistent to Abraham (Jn 8:58). "Before Abraham was, I am." Of all the classical "I am" sayings of Jesus in this Gospel (Jn 6:35; 8:12; 10:7,11; 11:25; 15:1), this is the most striking in strictly ontological terms. The other sayings in this group tend to focus on the nature and scope of Jesus' ministry. This one focuses on His identity and His relationship with God. Two points are being made in these cryptic words: "I who exist now existed before Abraham and I continue to exist." That is, Jesus is pointing to His preexistence and to His eternal being.[105] But is He here also making a claim to a special and equal status and relationship with the Father? Some scholars[106] deny that Jesus is here identifying himself with God, building on one of the mysterious Jewish formulas used to avoid direct mention of the divine name or Old Testament text (such as Dt 32:29; Isa 41:4; 43:10; 46:4; 48:12; or Ex 3:14), on the grounds that the simple phrase "I am" would have to serve as both subject and predicate for the more complex "I am who I am" or "I am the 'I Am.'" But even if we cannot identify the particular Old Testament texts that Jesus is thinking of, what else can these words mean but eternal equality with God? The context would seem to make this plain. Jesus has been arguing He is from above and not from this world (Jn 8:23). He has the truth that sets people free (Jn 8:31-32, 36). Who can do such things but God? And following Jesus' claim, the Jewish authorities (who are quite aware of the enormity of His claim) pick up stones to execute Him for the sin of blasphemy (Jn 8:59). The least this passage can mean is surely: "Before Abraham came into being I eternally was, as now I am, and ever continue to be."[107]

Is there any likelihood that Jesus actually made such a public claim or is this the creation of the early church? Certainly the Jewish authorities saw something blasphemous in Jesus' claims. Another "I am" (Mk 14:62) provoked the high priest to make such a charge and call for Jesus' death. There is no convincing evidence that Jesus was crucified simply and only because He was a social, ethical, or political reformer. There was certainly something deeper that provoked such a violent reaction by the Jewish authorities.[108] Moreover, is it likely that Jewish Christians would have even speculated about the possibility of ascribing deity to Jesus? The chances are nil. Nor would Gentile Christians have been likely to embrace the necessary concomitant doctrine of incarnation had they rendered Jesus divine. In fact the idea of incarnation would not have been popular with either Jew or Greek. It was a doctrine that had to force its way through to acceptance. We can, therefore, come to the reasoned conclusion that John 8:58 was not the creation of the early church. The alternative view that this text may have sprung from the fertile mind of Jesus is far more believable. Whether we believe such a claim to be true is, of course, up to the individual reader.

The Glory of the Father and Son (Jn 17:5). The context of this verse is the "high priestly prayer"[109] of Jesus to the Father for glory (Jn 17:1-5). *Glory* and *glorification* in this prayer are used to refer to different kinds and occasions of glory. First, Jesus asked to be glorified so that He might glorify the Father (Jn 17:1). The occasion is Jesus' approaching death. He asked to be vindicated in His dying so that He, by His death for the world, might bring eternal life to people and glory to God. Second, Jesus states that He has already brought the Father glory through His earthly ministry (Jn 17:3). This is borne out in various places in this Gospel (Jn 1:14; 2:11; 11:4,40; 12:28). Third, Jesus requests the return of the glory that He had with the Father before the world existed (v. 5). This is a prayer for exaltation and ascension[110] to the heavenly glory that Jesus shared with God in His preexistence.[111] That glorification will take place in the Father's presence (*para seauto*). The relationship between the Father and the Son is one of unity (Jn 17:21) and of love (Jn 17:24), before the incarnation in His earthly ministry and afterwards. It is an expression of the clearest kind that so far as the author is concerned, Jesus knew He had come from the Father and would return to the Father (cf. also Jn 16:28). There is here a unity and yet a distinctiveness between the Father and the Son.[112] Does this prayer originate with Jesus or with the early church? This prayer has many characteristics of Jesus' prayers as we know them from the Synoptic Gospels: His looking up to heaven; His use of "Father"; parallels to the Lord's Prayer (glorification, doing God's will and work, deliverance from the evil one). It is also highly unlikely that such a prayer could or would be attempted so successfully by the church.

Thomas' Confession (Jn 20:28). This is the final Christological pronouncement in the fourth gospel. Thomas, seeing the risen Christ for himself, confesses Him as "My Lord and my God." If chapter 21 is a supplement, then this confession would appear to be the climax and culmination of this Gospel, and this despite the caveat that those who have not had the privilege of actually seeing the risen Christ are also blessed (Jn 20:29). The latter is presumably addressed to those who will respond to the apostolic preaching as the church continues her ministries through the centuries. Thomas' confession goes far beyond earlier confessions, such as "My Master" (Jn 20:16 KJV).[113] The message of the fourth gospel has now been borne out. It began with the declaration that "the Word was God" (Jn 1:1). It has now been demonstrated how that conviction came about in the early church through the life and ministry of Jesus.

We have seen from the text of the fourth gospel how the Father and the Son are distinct, yet equal. "I and the Father are one" (Jn 10:30). "He who has seen me has seen the Father" (Jn 14:9). This oneness and equality of God and the Word are not abrogated by the obvious subordination of the incarnate Son to the Father. The Son can do nothing by himself (Jn 5:19). "The Father is greater than I" (Jn 14:28). "You have sent me" (Jn 17:25). These are the admissions of the incarnate Christ from the point of view of His humanity. The same kinds of expressions of Jesus' humanity are found also in the Synoptic Gospels (Mk 13:32; Mt 24:36) and in Paul's writings (1Co 15:24, 28). The Son is subordinate to the Father in His humanity and equal in His divinity. But is there a similar emphasis on Jesus' divinity in the Synoptic Gospels?

EVIDENCE FROM THE SYNOPTIC GOSPELS.

It is important to consider the words and works of Jesus in the Synoptic Gospels as they bear upon the issue we are considering, if we are to discover to what degree Trinitarian thought can be traced back to Jesus himself. We have seen how the roots of such thought are to be found in Paul, in the writer of Hebrews, and in John, as well as earlier in the proclamation of the early church as testified to especially in the book of Acts. Scholarship, however, has never been satisfied until the synoptics have had their say, since they continue to be held, probably by the vast majority of scholars,[114] to be the chief avenue into the life and ministry of the historical Jesus. The epistles of the New Testament take for granted the historical reality of Jesus. The theology of the New Testament is grounded in the historical revelation of God in Jesus. Peter was bold in his assertion "We cannot keep from speaking about the things we have seen and heard" (Ac 4:20). Paul is directed to preach the things that he has "seen and heard" about Christ (Ac 22:14). Luke researches the data carefully before he writes his Gospel (1:1-4). The author of 1 John writes about the Word of life and the basis of what he has heard and seen and touched (1:1-4). The resurrection of Jesus is believed and proclaimed by the apostolic church on the basis of "eyewitness testimony" (e.g., 1Co 15:4-8). It is clear that the life and ministry of Jesus is foundational (1Co 3:11). Paul could not have preached "the bare cross" (1Co 2:2). The cross has a broader context. There is no theology in the New Testament that does not have its assumptions rooted and grounded in the historical Jesus. The great doctrines of the faith—the preexistence and incarnation of the Word, the atonement through Christ, and the verifying and vindicating act of the resurrection of Jesus—are not doctrines that would naturally have come from rabbinic Judaism or incipient Gnosticism. Yet these are the revolutionary ideas the early church was preaching within a few years, if not a few days following the crucifixion of Jesus. From an historian's point of view, where did these ideas originate? How did they develop? They forced their way through the screen of various, largely antagonistic, presuppositions held by both Jew and Gentile. It is highly improbable that these revolutionary ideas came from one or more theological "think tanks," scattered throughout the ancient Near East. The question needs to be asked: how did such think-tanks themselves ever emerge, if there were such? It is infinitely more likely that the source was Jesus himself! It is not just a case of arguing that great thoughts and actions usually originate from individual geniuses as they reflect on life and certain select traditions by means of the power of their own peculiar intellects, which would, from a purely historical point of view, point to such a person as Jesus being a more credible source of His own message. We must also look at the influence the church has when she turns her full attention and allegiance to her Lord, in comparison to the influence she has when she tries to substitute an alternative as her message. In the former case, the impact has been incredible in the transformation of life and lives. In the latter case, the impact proves to be ineffectual at best and disastrous at worst.

When we turn to the synoptic gospels, we find Jesus takes over God's authority to forgive sins (Mk 2:1-12); exercises authority over nature (Mk 4:35-47, 6:30-44; 6:45-56); sits supremely in the council with Moses and Elijah, the representatives respectively of the Law and the Prophets (Mk 9:2-13); assumes authority to interpret the Law (Mt 5:17-48); claims to be greater than Jonah and Solomon, the representatives of the prophets and wisdom tradition (Mt 12:41-42); chooses twelve disciples, the same number as the tribes of Israel over whom God alone reigns, to conduct his mission to the world

(Mt 10:1-42); claims to be the unique Revealer of the Father (Mt 11:25-30; Lk 10:21-22);[115] claims to be God's Son in the parable of the tenants (Mark 12:1-12); prophesies with accuracy His death and resurrection (Mk 8:31; 9:31; 10:32f); claims to be the Son of Man, not merely to describe His humanity but borrowing the title from Daniel 7, He applies it to himself as the Mediator between God and His people, ransoming their lives by the sacrifice of His own life (Mk 10:45); and claiming to be the Messiah, He earns the charge of blasphemy by the high priest (Mk 14:61ff). Admittedly, many or all of these passages have been challenged by scholars skeptical of their authenticity. Yet it needs to be asked in all fairness what Jew or Gentile would be likely to make such outlandish claims in order to create a religion that on the basis of human expectations would hope to succeed? Yet these claims and actions found in the synoptics (and John) would be of such a kind as to pose a clear threat to organized religion and result in a charge of blasphemy. It is obvious that the religious authorities could not allow Jesus to live. Had he been a madman making such claims, He would simply have been ignored. But the authorities realized that Jesus was not out of His head. They realized He was sane and serious. He could not be permitted to live. The charge was blasphemy, and from their theological point of view the Jewish authorities were right. But for the Roman political and military authorities to act, the charge had to be couched in political messianic terms. What neither Jew nor Gentile saw was the vindication of Jesus' radical claims by means of a resurrection, and the experience of the Holy Spirit at the Pentecost. When all is said and done and despite the different language, the synoptic picture of Jesus is not greatly different from the Johannine account. Certainly both accounts affirm a view of Jesus of Nazareth that includes both His humanity and a special filial relationship with God the Father that is characterized by oneness, distinctiveness, and equality.[116]

The Holy Spirit

The Holy Spirit is the third Person of the Trinity. What basis is there in the New Testament for concluding that the Holy Spirit is a divine Person, in union with, but also distinct from and equal to, the Father and the Son?

EVIDENCE FROM THE OLD TESTAMENT.

By way of background, in the Old Testament, the Holy Spirit brings order out of chaos (Ge 1:2); continues as the source of human life (Ge 6:3; Job 27:3; 32:8; 33:4); cares providentially for people (Ps 104:29f; 139:7ff); endows humans with artistic and intellectual powers (Ex 35:30f); confers leadership qualities upon judges (Jdg 3:10; 6:34: 14:6), kings (1Sa 11:6; 16:13), and prophets (Eze 2:2; Hos 9:7; Mic 3:8; Zec 7:12); confers ability upon the promised Messiah (Isa 11:1-2), the coming Servant of the Lord (Isa 42:1-4) and the coming Anointed One (Isa 61:1); and is the agent of Israel's revivification (Eze 37) and the promised new Pentecost (Joel 2:28). The intertestamental period does not stress the doctrine or work of the Spirit, with the exception of a few references in the Qumran Scrolls (1 QS 3:7-9; 4:21; 1 QH 16:12; 17:26; frag. 2:9ff; CD 2:12). In the Qumran literature, some reference is made to the Spirit of Holiness granted to the Messiah and to the Spirit of truth, but there seems to be little understanding there of a personal Holy Spirit, or, a Spirit who works in a person's heart to bring about faith and righteousness, or an accompanying Paraclete, such as appears in the gospel of John.

EVIDENCE FROM THE SYNOPTIC GOSPELS.

When we turn to the New Testament, and in particular to the synoptic gospels, we find the Holy Spirit referred to in relation to the birth, mission, and teaching of Jesus. With respect to birth and mission, the Spirit conceives Jesus within Mary (Mt 1:18; Lk 1:35), guides the words which Simeon pronounces over Jesus (Lk 2:25ff), is present at and comes upon Jesus at His baptism (Mt 3:16; Mk 1:10; Lk 3:22), is stated to be the element in which Jesus will baptize His disciples (Mt 3:11-12; Mk 1:7-8; Lk 3:15ff), leads Jesus out into the wilderness to be tempted by Satan (Mt 4:1; Mk 1:12; Lk 4:1), initiates Jesus' ministry (Lk 4:14ff), is the power by whom demons are exorcised (Mt 12:28; cf. Lk11:20), and brings joy to Jesus when the disciples' ministry in His name is effective (Lk 10:21). With respect to the teaching of Jesus, there are only a limited number of statements of Jesus' about the Holy Spirit, but these few are more than a little significant. Jesus teaches that blasphemy against the Spirit is unforgivable (Mt 12:22-32; Mk 3:22-30; Lk 12:10); the Spirit will give the disciples their defense in times of persecution (Mt 10:19-20; Mk 13:11; Lk 12:12); the Spirit was instrumental in inspiring David in writing Psalm 110 (Mt 22:43; Mk 12:36); the Father will give the Holy Spirit to those who ask (Lk 11:13); the church should baptize new disciples in the name of the Holy Spirit as well as in the name of the Father and the Son (Mt 28:19);[117] and finally, the disciples should stay in Jerusalem until they have been clothed with power from on high (Lk 24:49), obviously a reference to the descent of the Spirit at Pentecost (Ac 2). We may observe, on the basis of this data, that Jesus continued in the Old Testament prophetic tradition in His ministry through and teaching of the Spirit. The main events of Jesus' life are deliberately portrayed as stemming from the activity of the Spirit. Yet the synoptic gospels say very little directly about the person and work of the Holy Spirit. Reasons given by scholars for this vary. It may have been because the church was living each moment in the Spirit. No one disputed the presence of the Spirit. Therefore, there was no need to prove it by the words of Jesus.[118] It may have been because the ancient world had more than enough "spiritual men" and the church did not want to depict Jesus as one of them, putting potential believers off. Perhaps Jesus downplayed His own inspiration, refusing to detract from the significance of God's ongoing action in history in His own life. Perhaps Jesus wanted to keep His messiahship a secret early in His ministry, and to have claimed possession of a significant measure of the Spirit would have been equivalent to making an open confession of messiahship. Perhaps also Jesus saw that the kingdom, though inaugurated, was not present in the fullness of its power. Therefore, mention of the Spirit, which would naturally be linked to the kingdom, had to be restrained.[119] The time for the coming of the Holy Spirit would be between the time of Jesus' resurrection and His return. The disciples would have to experience the Spirit for themselves. Perhaps Jesus said so little about the Spirit because any such teaching in the New Testament would be more intelligible with the actual experience of the Pentecost.[120] And yet the New Testament texts more than hint that the Spirit is divine, bringing about transformation, healing, and communication. There may also be hints of personality in the texts dealing with blasphemy against the Spirit and the Spirit's counsel in times of persecution.

EVIDENCE FROM THE GOSPEL OF JOHN.

In John's gospel the personal distinctness of the Spirit becomes clearer.[121] Most of the material is contained in Jesus' teaching to the Twelve on the eve of the Passion; and yet there are references prior to this. In the earlier part of the gospel there is one narrative passage and five teaching passages to consider.

John the Baptist is recorded as describing the descent of the Spirit like a dove upon Jesus (Jn 1:22-34). The baptism is not actually mentioned, but is assumed. The experience here is not just visionary but something more realistic. That is, something seems to have been visible to John's eyes, but it was not a dove, only something like a dove. Luke 3:22 catches the same nuance. The Spirit was in bodily form, like a dove. What clinches this argument is that the Spirit "abode" upon Jesus (i.e., stayed with Him and affected the whole of His ministry). Artists who insist on painting this scene, with a literal dove included, miss the point of the text. The experience, so far as John the Baptist was concerned, was a revelatory one. It enabled the Baptist to identify the "coming one" logically as Jesus, christologically as the Son of God, and soteriologically as the baptizer in the Holy Spirit. From this passage we can legitimately take hints that the Spirit who came upon Jesus and revealed Him to John the Baptist as the Son of God, and who we may assume was sent by the Father just as John the Baptist was sent by the Father (1:6, 32), is both divine and personal, and perhaps even equal, at least in the sense of being up to the task. It would seem that scholars may have to lengthen their list of Trinitarian New Testament passages to include this one.

We turn now to John 3:1-5 and to Jesus' teaching on the role of the Spirit in regeneration. There are at least four points being made here. First, spiritual rebirth is essential for a person to see (i.e., "experience" or "enter"; cf. Jn 3:5, 36) the Kingdom of God (v. 3). Religion or tradition or the moral life are unable to provide a basis for such an experience. A person must be invaded by the power of God. Judaism avoided such language, probably because such experience was uncontrollable by the community.[122] The legal tradition was more predictable. But a moment of discontinuity in which the whole human nature is dramatically reviewed was and is what is needed. Second, rituals cannot bring about such renewal, only God himself can. Even John the Baptist's baptism in water led only to moral reformation. It did not change a person's spiritual nature. Who could bring about such a recreation but the One who was the agent of creation, the Spirit (v. 5)? Third, against the possible rabbinic argument that a man can bring about remarkable changes in himself if he puts his mind to it, Jesus replies that humans can achieve only a human solution, only the Spirit can achieve a divine solution (Jn 3:6; see Jn 1:13). Fourth, the results of new birth have to be left in divine hands (Jn 3:8).

In this latter verse, Jesus uses a simile or parable. The mystery and movement of the Spirit of God is like that of the wind.[123] The symbolism of the wind fits the Spirit closely: the visible effects of an invisible power; the controlled power that is sometimes gentle and sometimes boisterous; the force that has a will of its own. What is underscored here is the spontaneity and surreptitiousness of the Spirit at work bringing about the new birth. How it happens, under what circumstances, with such-and-such a timetable, sometimes with one and not with another—all of this comes not from some wild and uncontrollable power but from a mysterious and sovereign will. What we have here is not an allegory of the Spirit controlled by the vagaries of natural forces, but an analogy to which a natural phenomenon (wind) is pressed into service insofar as it can serve the purpose. It provides a play on words since the same Greek word (*pneuma*) can mean both wind and Spirit. And it can provide reflection on the ways of the Spirit. But the subject of this passage is the Spirit and the supernatural work of the Spirit. Therefore, we are justified in seeing a mysterious sovereign will at work here. This is not a Spirit who is out of control, violent one minute and peaceful another. This is the Spirit bringing a son or daughter into the Father's kingdom. The language in this passage is not far from that in later chapters in John. The Spirit here is not only portrayed as powerful, but sovereign and very close to personal.

In John 3:34, we have Father, Son, and Holy Spirit brought together within the context of the preaching of the Word. The point made is that the Father gives the Spirit to the Son without measure, and thereby the Son is able to speak the true and complete Word so that at least some may hear and accept it as the true Word of God (see Jn 3:31-32). God makes every effort to provide the full teaching and interpretative assistance of the Spirit to enable people to believe. It is without measure. Here we have the full cooperative work of Father, Son, and Holy Spirit, engaged in a ministry of revelation and hence salvation, while maintaining the distinctiveness of each member of the Trinity.

In John 4:24 the issue is true worship. The way to such worship is to recognize that God is pure spirit and therefore not restricted to tribal locations such as Mount Zion or Mount Gerizim. Moreover, He is to be worshiped in the Spirit and according to the truth. Only those who are born of the Spirit (Jn 3:3-8) and who accept the truth of God as revealed in Jesus can so worship.[124]

In John 6:63 the issue is spiritual life. The context is the consumption of the Bread of Life and the results. Lest anyone misunderstand His words, Jesus focuses not on the material but on the spiritual. He has just said: "He who eats my flesh and drinks my blood has eternal life" (Jn 6:54). This could be construed as cannibalism and Jesus will have none of that. Nor will He have His words construed in extreme sacramentalistic or woodenly pietistic terms. His words are, in fact, about faith in the incarnate One who died on the cross and rose again for the sins of the world. Those who feed (believe) on Him will live (Jn 6:57b). Only the Spirit can produce this life. They do this through the words of Jesus (cf. Jer 15:16; Eze 2:8–3:3; Rev 10:9ff), and the words of Jesus in turn convey the Spirit and life (cf. Dt 8:3). The Spirit and the Word of God work hand in hand. The church's theology and life must be one of both Word and Spirit. In Trinitarian terms, God works dynamically and in perfect cooperation with the Spirit and the Son.

In John 7:37-38, we are given the first hint that the Holy Spirit is yet to be conferred in a dramatic way. The passage is complicated both by the grammar and the difficulty in identifying accurately the Old Testament reference. The passage can be read in such a way that the living waters flow either out of believers or out of Christ. There are no scriptures that refer to the former (see Eze 47:1-12; Joel 3:18; Zec 14:8), unless the reference is to John 4:14. It seems better, though it is not without its own difficulties, to take the reference as one to Christ. This could make Christ the dispenser of the Spirit which coincides with John 15:26 and 16:7. We are told here that the Spirit is yet to be given. If the Old Testament reference is to Zechariah 14:8, we may be able to see the connection to Jesus for He is the source of the New Jerusalem. The point is, for our purpose, the identification of a new age of the Spirit, who would be sent by Jesus after His glorification (i.e., crucifixion, resurrection, and ascension).

We come now to the Holy Spirit in John's Passion narrative (Jn 14:16-17, 26-27; 15:26-27; 16:5-15). While there are different segments of this teaching, the various passages reflect similar thoughts and occur within a single setting. Therefore we will consider them as a unit.

The source of the Spirit is God, who will respond affirmatively to the prayer of Jesus (Jn 14:16). There are two other ways of saying the same thing: "The Father will send [Him] in my name" (Jn 14:26) and, "I will send [Him] to you from the Father" (Jn 15:26; cf. 16:7). That is, the initiative is not with man but with Jesus. The Spirit goes out from the Father at the Son's request. But first, the Son must depart (Jn 16:7; cf. Jn 7:39). The coming of the Spirit is therefore to be a major event in the future. Only believers can understand the

Spirit, because they will gladly receive Him into their lives (Jn 14:17). The world will not be able to understand or accept the Spirit.[125] But the world does not have final control over the work and influence of the Spirit.

The function or purpose of the Spirit is to glorify the Son (Jn 16:14) by making all the Son's words known (Jn 14:26; 16:14). He will witness to Christ (Jn 15:26). The Spirit is self-effacing, seeking not His own glory but that of the Son (Jn 16:14). The Spirit brings no new truth beyond that which the Son offers. He will speak only what He hears. If Jesus is the servant Messiah, the Spirit is also a servant! The Word comes from the Father through the Son by means of the Spirit (Jn 16:15). In this sense, He is the Spirit of truth (Jn 14:17; 15:26; 16:13), and will serve to guide people into the whole truth (Jn 16:13). This will include the truth about the future. "He will disclose to you what is to come" (Jn 16:13). In other words, the Spirit has inside information on the eschaton which He will make known. And yet this is not information peculiar to himself, for He will speak only what He hears from the Father and from the Son (Jn 16:13-15). Central to the Spirit's task will be two things: first, to teach Christians the whole council of God (14:26), and second, to bring the world to faith (Jn 15:26-27; 16:8ff).

The nature and character of the Spirit can be determined from five pieces of evidence. First, the Spirit is holy (Jn 14:26), deserving respect and response. The adjective is used only here and at the baptism of Jesus (Jn 1:33), and before Jesus' departure (Jn 20:22). Second, He is the Spirit of truth (Jn 14:17; 15:26; 16:13). That is, the Spirit is with the Father, the source of truth (Jn 8:28, 40) and with the Son, through whom grace and truth come (Jn 1:17). Consequently what the Spirit bears witness to is true. Third, the Spirit is called "Paraclete" (Jn 14:16, 26; 15:26; 16:7), which may be rendered by the English words Helper, Advocate, Counselor, or Comforter. The root meaning of the Greek word is "one called alongside." Whether the source of this title is the law courts or the prophetic work of preaching (cf. Ac 4:8ff; 1Co 14:3), or the pastoral work of consoling (Isa 40:1), the work is such as only a person could carry out. Fourth, this is confirmed here by the reference to "another" Paraclete (Jn 14:16). The context suggests a continuity between the work of Jesus and that of the Spirit. The work of the Son and the Spirit is interconnected yet distinct and personal. Fifth, there is the striking use of the masculine pronoun (*ekeinos*) to designate the Spirit on three occasions (Jn14:26; 15:26; 16:8,13, 14). This undermines radically any suggestion that the Spirit is an impersonal force. Here we have clear evidence that the Spirit is a Person. The Spirit, who will be with the church forever (Jn 14:16), shares the same intimacy with the believer that the Father and Son do. All three will live with and in the believer (Jn 14:17, 23). In this they are personally and equally present.

EVIDENCE FROM THE EPISTLES OF PAUL.

In the epistles of Paul, the work of the Holy Spirit is widely referred to, affecting every aspect of the Christian experience and life. The Spirit is behind the proclamation of the gospel (1Co 2:4; Eph3:5; 1Th 1:5) and initiation into faith (1Co 12:13; 2Co 1:22; 5:5; Eph 1:13-14; 1Th 4:8). He is active in the believer's life to illuminate (1Co 2:10-16), to liberate (Ro 8:2, 13; 2Co 3:8; 17-18,; Gal 3:2; 5:1), to give access to God (Eph 2:18), to adopt (Ro 8:14ff; Gal 4:6), to sanctify (Ro 15:16; 1Co 6:11; 2Th 2:13), to intercede (Ro 8:26f; Eph 6:18; Php 1:19), and to mature and give hope (Ro 5:3; 14:17; Gal 5:22f; 6:8, Col 1:8). So far as the community is concerned, the church and her members enter the kingdom by baptism in the Spirit (1Co 12:13) and experience many infillings (1Co 12:13; Eph 5:18), and the Spirit equips the church for ministry (1Co 12:4-11; cf. Ro 12:3-8; Eph 4:11).

But does Paul speak of the Holy Spirit as God? Not directly, but certainly indirectly. First, "the Spirit searches everything, even the deep things of God" (1Co 2:10). The Spirit penetrates to the deepest understanding of God. Who can do this but God himself? And yet the Spirit who performs this is distinguished from God, upon and in whom the Spirit acts! Paul's argument is that just as man's own inner-spirit best understands himself, the same thing can be said of God's Spirit when it comes to understanding God (vs. 11-12). It is this Spirit who is the agent of revelation to man (v. 14). Second, we are God's people and

God's Spirit lives in us (1Co 3:16-17; 2Co 6:16). Paul can say in another place "Your body is a temple of the Holy Spirit" (1 Co 6:19).[126]

Is the Spirit a person? Putting aside those specific Trinitarian passages for the moment, consider for example the language of Romans 8. Paul's focus here is new life through the Spirit. A new law (order) is in effect, one that surpasses and in a way replaces the old law. It is the law of "the Spirit of life" that sets us free from the law of sin and death (v. 2). "The Spirit of life" means the Spirit that initiates life. The verbs of which the Spirit is the subject in this passage are significant. The Spirit liberates (v. 2), controls (v. 9), raises (v. 11), leads (v. 14), testifies (v. 16), helps (v. 26), intercedes (8:26f), and possibly works together for good in every situation (v. 28). A Spirit as a force or power could suitably be the subject of some of these verbs but such a subject would hardly suit "dwells," "testifies" or "intercedes." These are more easily understood as the actions of a person. And a person could very easily fit as the subject of the other verbs that are used of the Spirit in Romans 8.

But is the Spirit distinct from Christ? On one occasion Paul refers to the Spirit as the Spirit of Christ (Ro 8:9b; cf. 2Co 3:17). But in the same verse he speaks also of the Spirit being the Spirit of God (Ro 8:9a, 14; cf. 1Co 3:16). We should not here confuse the Spirit with either God or Christ. The Spirit is probably to be understood here as sent by God at the request of Christ (see Jn 14:16).[127] It is, of course, possible that the Greek word (*pneuma*) is being used by Paul in at least two different ways in Romans 8 to refer to the Holy Spirit (e.g., 8:2, 5, 9, etc.) and to refer to the spirit or attitude or authority of Christ (cf. 8:9b). This latter would be a usage similar to the "spirit of adoption" (8:15), preferred by some scholars although "the Spirit which confers adoption" is preferred by others.[128] At any rate, it seems that Paul is here identifying three distinct persons: God the Father who initiates the work of salvation by sending His own Son in the flesh to provide the means of salvation in order that we might live according to and by the dynamic of the Spirit (Ro 8:3-4). The emphasis in Romans 8, however, is on the work of the Spirit. The Greek word for "Spirit" appears at least eighteen times here.

EVIDENCE IN OTHER NEW TESTAMENT PASSAGES.

In other New Testament texts, we discover that Peter who rebukes Ananias for lying to the Holy Spirit, states that he has not lied to men but to God (Acts 5:3-4). Paul is quoted in Acts 28:25f as attributing to the Holy Spirit a passage that in the Old Testament is attributed to the Lord of Hosts (Isa 6:9). Peter declares that the Word of God is inspired by and therefore must be interpreted by the Holy Spirit (2Pe 1:20f). Hebrews is able to distinguish between God, who provides signs and wonders and various miracles, and the Holy Spirit by whom gifts are given (Heb 2:4). Also, Hebrews 10:17 ascribes to the Holy Spirit a text that in the Old Testament is ascribed to Yahweh (Jer 31:34). Christians are partakers of the Holy Spirit (Heb 6:4) or of Christ (Heb 3:14). The author of the Apocalypse of John is able to distinguish between God the Father, Jesus Christ (the firstborn from the dead and the Alpha and Omega), and the Spirit in whom he finds himself on the Lord's Day (Rev 1:1, 5, 6, 8, 10; cf. Rev 21:2, 6; 22:6, 12, 17).

GENERAL OBSERVATIONS.

Does the New Testament ever ascribe prayer or worship to the Holy Spirit? The closest any text comes to declaring that worship is to be given to the Spirit is in the fourth gospel (Jn 4:24). That is, "God is Spirit" would not be anything the Jews or even the Samaritans would not know. What was new was what was deduced from this, that worship was to be through the Holy Spirit and the truth of the Gospel or Word of God (cf. Jn 14:26; 16:13). Worship is to be given to God only as He is revealed by the Holy Spirit. In doing so, we may be found worshiping the Holy Spirit (cf. Jn 4:10, 14; 6:63; 7:37ff). By a similar kind of argument, we may come legitimately to pray to the Holy Spirit if He is known to make intercession for us (Ro 8:26). We may ask Him to continue to do so.

What is the basis for the Holy Spirit's being separated at least in function from God? The answer is probably twofold. First, in the Old Testament, the Word of God is sometimes seen as having a distinctive and identifiably separate life from God (Isa 55:11). Second, the same can be said of the Wisdom of God (Prov 8). A third point may justifiably be made: the Old Testament may have already begun a tradition of separating the Spirit from the Father (cf. Ge 1:2; Isa 63:10; Zec 4:6).

The Trinitarian Texts

Here we must consider four different kinds of passages: those (a) where deliberate Trinitarian formulae are used; (b) where a deliberate triadic form is used; (c) where the three persons of the Trinity are mentioned together without any clear triadic structure; (d) where actions normally attributed to God are ascribed to Christ (e.g., creation) or to the Spirit (e.g., signs and wonders).

DELIBERATE TRINITARIAN FORMULAE.

Deliberate Trinitarian formulae appear in 2 Corinthians 13:14 and in Matthew 28:19.

The Pauline text is a benediction which dates from about AD 55-56, a little over twenty years from the crucifixion. Some have argued that this is not a part of a self-consciously formulated doctrine of the Trinity.[129] Others have suggested that this may have already become a liturgical formula.[130] Paul normally concludes his letters with a simple reference to the grace of Christ (e.g., Ro 16:20b; 1Co 16:23; Gal 6:18; Php 4:23; 1Th 5:28; 2Th 3:18; Phm 25). But in 2 Corinthians the benediction is obviously more complex. It commences with a reference to the saving grace offered through the work of the Lord Jesus Christ, continues with the reference to the love which is behind the saving purposes of God, and concludes by referring to the church's experience of the Holy Spirit. The latter has been defined in two major ways, referring either to the fellowship of believers created by the Holy Spirit (subjective genitive)[131] or to a participation in the Holy Spirit (objective genitive).[132] These two views are not all that far apart, for it is in fact by participation in the Spirit that the fellowship of believers results.[133] It can only have been through the early church's experience that she came to speak in such a language as appears in this Trinitarian formula. This would certainly be true of Paul himself. What we have here, then, can be summed up as the language of the church's initial appreciation of and exploration into the "economic Trinity." This was to be the raw material on which the church fathers were subsequently to reflect as they worked towards a satisfactory understanding of the immanent Trinity. So far as Paul is concerned in this Trinitarian benediction, he is specific in the role assigned to each person of the Trinity but makes no distinction of status between the persons. At the same time, there seems to be more than a hint of the unity of the three persons here, otherwise why does Paul mention the three together so succinctly?[134] The benediction may legitimately be taken as a summation of Paul's teaching about Father, Son, and Holy Spirit in this letter.

The Matthean Trinitarian formula (28:19) is, from the manuscript evidence, an intrinsic part of the original text, and is associated with the church's mission to preach and teach the gospel and to baptize. The date of this gospel can be reasonably estimated to be before AD 115 (Ignatius) and, since it seems dependent on Mark, after AD 65, in other words around AD 80-85. The argument that the formula cannot have been used early is based on the simpler and earlier formula used for baptism in the earliest church, that is baptism in the name of the Lord Jesus (Ac 2:38; 8:16). There are, however, points to be made in favor of the text as it stands. First, the Trinitarian formula was known and used as early as AD 55-56 (cf. 2Co 13:14). If this formula was used as a benediction, could it not also have been used for baptism, especially since baptism in the Spirit was apparently standard practice for the church at that time (cf. 1Co 12:13)? Second, what does a "baptismal formula" mean? It need not be a liturgical set piece to be said at each baptism, but rather a theological description of the meaning of baptism or of what is accomplished.[135] Third, the matter of baptism "in the name of Jesus" is not so clear as some suppose. In Acts 8:14-17, there seems to have been something wrong with baptism as practiced by the Samaritans. They had been baptized "only" into the name of the Lord Jesus; they had not receive the Holy Spirit. Because all believers have the Spirit in order to be believers (Ro 5:5; 8:9; 1Co 12:13), this would suggest that there was a deficiency in the initial baptism of the Samaritans. Peter and John corrected this deficiency. In Acts 2:38f, baptism in the name of the Lord Jesus seems to provide three things: forgiveness and the gift of the Holy Spirit, as well as the reception of the promise of God's call. The same thing can be said in the baptism in Ephesus (Acts 19:5). They had received only John's baptism, which was for repentance. Paul provided baptism "in the name of Jesus" and this included baptism in the Spirit. It is highly unlikely that in the baptism no reference at all was made to God the Father. In other words the evidence from Acts is not so different from the evidence from Matthew. Fourth, it is unlikely that the Matthean baptismal formula was so certain a part of the original manuscript evidence without having enjoyed a considerable authority behind it. The most creditable authority for this purpose is Jesus himself, especially since we know He had this mission very much on His mind (Mk 6:6b-13; Mt 9:35-38; 10:1ff; 13:1ff; Lk 9:1ff; 10:1ff), and that the Twelve were actively and progressively engaged in baptizing disciples which, though Jesus is reported as not himself baptizing, must at least have had His approval (Jn 4:1-3). Having made what may be considered to be a *prima facie* case for the authenticity of Matthew 28:19, we need to point out the distinctiveness of the three persons, the role of each of whom has been indicated in the teaching of Jesus which the church is commanded to pass on (Mt 2:19-20). At the same time, baptism is into "the name of" (singular), not "into the names of" (plural), Father-Son-Holy Spirit. The unity of the Trinity is thus maintained. Moreover, to baptize in or into "the name of" means "to pledge allegiance to, to come under the authority of, and to enter the fellowship of the Holy Trinity." It appears, therefore, that here each person of the Trinity possesses equal authority.

It is probable that Revelation 1:4 contains a similar formula, relating not to baptism (Mt 28:19) nor to a benediction (2Co 13:14) but to an address or greeting. This can only be true if the seven spirits refer to the Holy Spirit, symbolized as sevenfold and therefore perfect.[136] This would place the Spirit between God the Father, "who was and is and is to come," and Jesus Christ, "the faithful witness, the firstborn from the dead, and the ruler of all earthly sovereigns." It would be very strange indeed if a reference to the angels of the seven churches were inserted between the Father and the Son. Hence we take it as referring to the Holy Spirit. Again, the three persons are distinct, but united in a common purpose. The theological significance of each is developed throughout the book.[137]

TEXTS ON THE TRINITY IN TRIADIC FORM.

First Corinthians 12:4-6 needs to be understood within the context of a divided church. Part of the cause is division over leadership (1Co 1:10ff). There is also division over who has the better gifts for service (1Co 12:27ff; 14:1ff). Here Paul seeks to remedy the problem by focusing on different categories of gifts, services, and workings, each of which comes from the same Spirit, the same Lord, and the same God. Christians have different roles to play. Uniformity is not to be expected. The differences are shared for the common good (1Co 12:7). They also have a deeper source of unity. Unity lies ultimately in the Spirit who gives, in the Lord who serves and is served, and in the God who is at work! Commentators describe this formula as "embryonic"[138] and "the more impressive because it seems to be artless and unconscious."[139] This is fair comment, provided we recognize that embryos contain *in nuce* all that will eventually emerge in maturity. On the other hand, while Paul seems to use Trinitarian language naturally, he seems to do so in a conscious and orderly way. He deliberately makes his point and makes it persuasively, that the church's unity lies in the one unifying author, God, who as Father, Son, and Holy Spirit is cooperatively active in the church's life and ministry. That Paul is consciously answering the problem of divisions is evidenced in his use of the adjective "same" with each of the three persons of the Trinity. His use of the reverse order of the three persons is dictated by his point of departure, which is the Spirit.

In Ephesians 4:4-6, Paul speaks of "one Spirit...one Lord...one God and Father." The reverse order of the three persons is determined by the context in which Paul is stressing life (unity) in the Spirit and the source of gifts, using Psalm 68:18 as his Old Testament focal point. The singular Spirit, Lord, and Father is the basis for the church's singular life, hope, faith, and identity. The persons of the Trinity are simply given, without any attempt to correlate their inter-relationship. They are distinct as persons, and yet are each involved in the life and work of the church. The emphasis is on "one" Spirit, and "one" Lord, and "one" Father, a parallel to the use of "same" in 1 Corinthians 12:4-6. In Ephesians 1:3-14, the three persons of the Trinity are introduced in more expansive form.

In 1 Peter 1:2, the triadic form is linked more closely with the specific work associated with the three persons of the Trinity. God's elect are chosen "according to the foreknowledge of God the Father, by the sancifying work of the Spirit, to the obedience to Jesus Christ and sprinkling by His blood" (NASB). The date of 1 Peter can be estimated at around AD 63-64. The three persons are kept distinct and yet are seen as working cooperatively in creating and developing Christian faith and life. Peter continues this focus on the Father, Son, and Holy Spirit throughout his epistle (1Pe 1:3ff, 10ff, 13ff; 2:4ff; 3:15ff; 4:1ff, 12ff). The opening statement (1Pe 1:2) is highly compressed and denotes the initiating work of the Father, the authoritative agency of the Son, and the dynamic sphere of the Spirit in and by whom Christian life is lived.[140]

TEXTS WITH NO CLEAR TRIADIC STRUCTURE.

The third group of texts refer to the three Persons of the Trinity but without the text manifesting triadic structure. Among these we may list the passages we have already considered in John (14:16f, 25f; 15:26f; 16:5ff). The Father sends the Spirit in the Son's name and at His request. The Son is also said to send the Spirit who proceeds from the Father. All three Persons are involved in the work of revelation and salvation. These passages are unique and central to the development of Trinitarian thought.

In addition we may cite Mark 1:9-11, the record of the baptism of Jesus in which the Father and the Spirit appear. Other passages in this category are Galatians 4:4-6 (God sent His Son for our redemption and the Spirit to grant us adoption as sons); Romans 8:1ff; 2 Thessalonians 2:13f; Titus 3:4-6; Jude 20f. In all of these passages the three persons of the Trinity are closely linked. The use of language cannot have been accidental.

Conclusion

In the New Testament, Trinitarian language is used consciously and creatively, though naturally, to indicate the action and function of the Father, Son, and Holy Spirit as it relates to the purposes of God for salvation and sanctification, for the building and maturing of the church, and for the effective undertaking of the church's ministry and mission.

The origin of Trinitarian thought within the church arose from the growing awareness that Jesus of Nazareth could not be accounted for strictly on human terms. There was obviously something more here than met the eye. Jesus himself claimed a special relationship with the Father (e.g., Mt 11:27ff; Lk 10:22; Mt 12:28f; Lk 11:20; Mk 12:1ff; cf. Jn 10:30) and special authority to forgive sins (Mk 2:1-12, etc.). Moreover, the church was forced, against several antagonistic presuppositions, to accept the evidence for His physical resurrection from the dead. On top of this, the church's experience at Pentecost (Ac 2) convinced them that a new age of the Spirit had broken in.

The problem for the church was how to account for the special status she felt had to be accorded to Jesus and the Spirit without compromising her monotheism. The church simply could not postulate the existence of three Gods. What allowed the church to move forward was her awareness that God was always active in the Son and in the Holy Spirit, as well as being active as Father. What had been kept a secret, a mystery, was now in these last days being revealed. A new sense of the richness of God, a richness that had always been there but hidden, was developing. A new dynamic revelation was breaking through. The promises of God were being fulfilled in a radically new and unexpected way.

No formal Trinitarian doctrine was formulated in the New Testament, not at least in any expansive way. The distinctness of the three persons was kept, often in relation to the specific work of the Father, Son, and Holy Spirit. Their unity was maintained in a kind of dynamic tension, as was their hinted equality. The precise relationship among the three persons was not worked out in the New Testament. The closest that any New Testament author comes to identifying some of these issues is John. That the three persons possess some kind of individual personality was apparent from the beginning for at least the Father and the Son.[141] The Father had always been considered a person who spoke and was approachable. The Son could be seen to have personality for historic or incarnational reasons. The personhood of the Spirit was presumably more difficult. Yet if the Spirit is of God, then ultimately it is necessary to ascribe personality to the Spirit, especially as the Father is transcendent and the Holy Spirit is immanent, as in the Baptism of Jesus, the experience at Pentecost, and the ministry of the church (Ac 16:6).

NOTES

1. See R.S. Franks, *The Doctrine of the Trinity* (London: Duckworth, 1953), c. 1.

2. The word *Trinity* actually never occurs in the Bible, only the persons who exist and work in the trinitarian relationship.

3. The "seven spirits before the throne" likely refer to the seven-fold Holy Spirit, and not to angelic beings such as perhaps the seven archangels of Jewish angelology, as R.H. Charles suggests. See *The International Critical Commentary: The Revelation of St. John* (London: T. & T. Clark, 1920), ad loc. It would be incredible for an author to replace the Holy Spirit with angels in a passage that refers also to the Father and the Son. The reference to "seven" conveys the idea of unity rather

than diversity and the ubiquitous presence of the Holy Spirit through the "seven" (i.e., the whole church).

4. The New Testament provides us with more data on the Trinity than is often thought. For example, the British Council of Churches Study Commission on Trinitarian Doctrine Today, entitled "The Forgotten Trinity" (Delta Press, 1989), states: "There are few biblical texts which can be claimed to have an explicitly trinitarian significance" (p. 7). This is true if we accept as significant trinitarian texts only those that are written in a deliberate formulaic style (e.g., Mt 28:19; 1Co 13:14). But, as we shall point out, there are others that are just as important. Some are in triadic form, others without triadic structure, not to mention the material in John 14-16. In addition, there are christological and pneumatological texts that need to be considered. Otherwise, the British study is laudable.

5. That is, some books or verses are selected as more authoritative than others.

6. For example, some liberals.

7. For example, some charismatics.

8. See Augustine, *de Trinitate*, written approximately between AD 400 and 428.

9. Of course, Augustine's exegetical methods varied. See Augustine, *de Trinitate*, I.1.2. See also M. Simonetti, *Biblical Interpretation in the Early Church* (Edinburgh: T. & T. Clark, 1994), pp. 103ff.

10. And, of course, to the world.

11. See T.F. Torrance, *Theological Science* (Oxford: Oxford University Press, 1978); *The Ground and Grammar of Theology* (Belfast: Christian Journals Ltd., 1980).

12. See M. Hengel, "Historical Methods and the Theological Interpretation of the New Testament," Section III in *Earliest Christianity* (London: SCM, 1979), pp. 127-136.

13. In The United Church of Canada, this view was maintained by J.M. Shaw, *Christian Doctrine* (Lutterworth: 1953), p. 18; and by D.M. Mathers, *The Word and the Way* (Toronto: United Church Publishing House, 1962), c. 8. "The Bible is like a telescope: it is for looking through, not looking at. It is not itself revealed, it is the witness to revelation, the record of revelation...Why didn't Jesus write a book? To save us from a false view of faith and from a false view of inspiration" (Mathers, p. 95).

14. See Karl Barth, *Church Dogmatics* (Edinburgh: T. & T. Clark, 1956), I.2, pp. 473ff.

15. As R. Bultmann emphasized.

16. See D.G. Bloesch, "Historical-Pneumatic Hermeneutic," in *Holy Scripture: Revelation, Inspiration, and Interpretation*, in Christian Foundations, vol. 2 (Downers Gover, IL: InterVarsity Press, 1994), pp. 200ff.

17. See R.S. Franks, op. cit., p. 3.

18. See Brevard Childs, *Introduction to the Old Testament as Scripture* (Minneapolis: Fortress Press, 1979); *The New Testament as Canon* (Fortress, 1985); *Biblical Theology of the Old and New Testaments* (Fortress, 1993).

19. See E. Kasemann, "The Canon of the New Testament and the Unity of the Church," *Essays on New Testament Themes* (London: SCM, 1964), pp. 95-107.

20. See N.T. Wright, "Theology, Authority, and the New Tetstament," c. 5 in *The New Testament and the People of God* (Minneapolis: Fortress Press, 1992), pp. 121-144.

21. See the helpful evaluation of the various kinds of narrative theology by D. G. Bloesch, op. cit., pp. 208-218.

22. See David S. Yeago, "The New Testament and the Nicene Dogma, a Contribution to the Recovery of Theological Exegesis," in *Pro Ecclesia*, vol. 3, no. 2, Spring, pp. 152-164.

23. See William Manson, *Jesus the Messiah* (London: Hodder and Stoughton, 1943), who, over fifty years ago, answered most effectively the contention of William Wrede (*Das Messiasgeheimnis in Den Evangelien*, 1901) that the early church read her post-Easter knowledge of the majesty of Jesus back into the non-messianic traditions of His earthly appearance. Wrede held that Mark's portrayal of Jesus' ministry is therefore historically suspect. But once Wrede's hypothesis on the messianic secret is answered satisfactorily, it goes without saying that his negative evaluation of Mark's gospel as history is also laid to rest. We need to remember that age-old hypotheses founded often on speculation engendered by an Enlightenment approach to Scripture, have been unnecessarily sanctified by time and reputation, and need to be scrutinized from a balanced point of view. Many of them, including Wrede's, need to be put to rest once and for all. Then, we can address the text of Scripture with greater confidence.

24. See E. Fuchs, *Studies of the Historical Jesus* (London: SCM, 1964), p. 20f; J. Jeremias, *The Parables of Jesus* (SCM, 1963), p. 132.

25. See E. Schweizer, *Jesus: The Parable of God* (Allison Park, PA: Pickwick Publications, 1994), pp. 24, 32.

26. See M. Hengel, *The Charismatic Leader and His Followers* (London: T. & T. Clark, 1981), p. 70.

27. See J.H. Charlesworth, *Jesus Within Judaism: New Light from Exciting Archaeological Discoveries*, Anchor Bible Reference (New York: Doubleday, 1988), p. 136.

28.   Ibid, p. 138.

29.   See G.B. Caird, *New Testament Theology* (Oxford: Oxford University Press, 1994), pp. 317, 416.

30.   See Wolfhart Pannenberg, *Systematic Theology*, vol. II (Grand Rapids: Eerdmans, 1994), pp. 278ff; *Jesus, God and Man* (Philadelphia: Westminster, 1968), pp. 33ff.

31.   See C.H. Dodd, *The Apostolic Preaching and Its Developments*, 3rd ed. (London: Hodder and Stoughton, 1963).

32.   On these two passages in Acts, see C.K. Barrett, *The International Critical Commentary: Acts*, vol. 1, (London: T. & T. Clark, 1994), pp. 463f, 645f, who points out that the term 'Son of God' is not developed in a metaphysical sense. Barrett thinks the title was not of special significance to Luke, that he was not claiming that Paul was the first Christian to use so important a title, and that there is no indication in Acts of a belief in the essential identity of the Father and the Son.

33.   See C.H. Dodd, op. cit. pp. 17ff; Matthew Black, *An Aramaic Approach to the Gospels and Acts*, 3rd ed. (Oxford: Clarendon Press, 1967), ad loc; M. Wilcox, *The Semitisms of Acts* (New York: Oxford University Press, 1965), ad loc; D. Guthrie, *New Testament Introduction*, 3rd ed. (Downers Grove, IL: InterVarsity, 1970), pp. 359ff; M. Hengel: *Earliest Christianity* (London: SCM, 1979), pp. 1-68.

34.   Whether or not Psalm 2:1-9 is messianic depends on whether it refers cultically to an historic king or prophetically to a special kingship. The reference to universal dominion suggests the latter.

35.   See F.F. Bruce, *Second Thoughts on the Dead Sea Scrolls* (London: Paternoster, 1956), pp. 70-84, for a discussion of the Qumran messianic hope.

36.   See I.H. Marshall, *The Origins of New Testament Christology*, 2nd ed. (Downers Grove, IL: InterVarsity, 1990), p. 84; A.S. van Der Woude: TDNT, IX, pp. 521ff.

37.   For example, most recently by C.K. Barrett, *Acts*, vol. 1, p. 152.

38.   See R.S. Franks, op. cit., p. 12.

39.   The title "Lord" has sometimes been suggested to derive from Hellenistic rather than Hebraic sources and to be therefore much later. See William Bousset, *Kyrios Christos* (New York: Abingdon, 1970; German original 1913). This is clearly erroneous. In addition to the Hebrew Scriptures, which provide the title "Lord" quoted in Acts 2, the occurrence of *Maranatha* ("our Lord, come") in 1 Corinthians 16:22 is clear evidence of its use in the Aramaic-speaking Palestinian church. That is, "Lord" is used of Jesus at a very early date.

40.   The original work was carried out by C.C. Torrey, *The Composition and Date of Acts* (Cambridge, MA: Harvard, 1916). See C.H. Dodd, *The Apostolic Preaching*, p. 27.

41.   See M. Black, Op. Cit., on vss. 25, 28 and 32.

42.   cf. R. Bultmann, *Theology of the New Testament*, vol. 1 (SCM: 1952), pp. 128-133.

43.   Granted that "Son" is also used in 2 Samuel 7:14 in relation to the house of David.

44.   See I.H. Marshall: Op. Cit., p. 119f; M. Hengel, *The Cross of the Son of God* (SCM: 1986), p. 62; D. Guthrie, *New Testament Theology* (InterVarsity: 1981), p. 316f.

45.   The aorist passive is a circumlocution for God's action.

46.   Though see Acts 9:26.

47.   D. Guthrie, Op. Cit., p. 318.

48.   See M. Hengel, Op. Cit., p. 9: "The Son Belongs Together with the Father."

49.   P.E. Hughes, *The Second Epistle to the Corinthians* (Eerdmans: 1962), p. 299.

50.   See J. Weiss, *History of Primitive Christianity*, vol. I (1937), pp. 118ff, for the former argument, and R.H. Fuller, *The Foundation of New Testament Christology* (London: 1965), pp. 166ff, for the latter.

51.   R.S. Franks, Op. Cit., p. 28; T.W. Manson, "Romans," *Peakes' Commentary on the Bible* (London: 1962), ad loc; M. Hengel, Op. Cit., p. 58.

52.   This is the primary meaning of the Greek verb, *horizo*.

53.   Cf. M. Hengel, Op. Cit., p. 57; C.K. Barrett, *The Epistle to the Romans* (London: 1967), pp. 18ff, who maintains that the phrase "in power" was added by Paul to avoid any suggestion of a naive adoptionism. This may or may not be so. More likely, "in power" describes the impact of the risen Christ on people's lives.

54.   Cf. L.C. Allen, "The Old Testament Background of *(pro)horizein* in the New Testament," *New Testament Studies*, 1970, pp. 104ff, who traces both the verb and the use of the title here to Psalm 2.

55.   Cf. D. Guthrie, NTT, p. 317, who states, "nowhere does he (Paul) suggest that the pre-existent status of Jesus was a man."

56.   C.E.B. Cranfield, "Commentary on Romans," ICC (T. & T. Clark: 1975), vol. 1, p. 62.

57.   This is not to argue in favor of universalism. It is clear from Paul says elsewhere that we must willingly accept Jesus as Saviour and Lord to be saved.

58.   Cf. R. Bultmann, NTT, vol. I, p. 175. It should be noted that R. Reitzenstein, *Die hellenistischen Mysterienreligionen nach*

ihren Grundgedanken und Wirkungen, 3rd ed. (Leipzig: 1927), who prompted the view of a widespread Graeco-oriental myth of primal man who came down from heaven to redeem mankind from its fallen condition, did not apply his theory to this text!

59.   G.B. Caird, *Paul's Letters from Prison* (Oxford: 1976), p. 103f.

60.   E. Lohmeyer, *Kyrios Christos: Eine Untersuchung zu Phil. 2:5-11* (Heidelberg: 1928); O. Cullmann, *The Christology of the New Testament* (Philadelphia: 1959), p. 174f; R.H. Fuller, Op. Cit., pp. 204ff; I.H. Marshall, Op. Cit., p. 106.

61.   G.B. Caird, *Paul's Letters from Prison*, p. 97.

62.   On the issue of *Kenosis*, see P.T. Forsyth, *The Person and Place of Jesus Christ* (1909, repr. Eerdmans,:1964); W. Pannenberg, *Jesus, God and Man* (Westminster: 1968), pp. 307ff.

63.   See W. Pannenberg, *Systematic Theology*, vol. II (Eerdmans: 1964) pp. 377ff.

64.   See G.B. Caird, *Paul's Letters from Prison*, pp. 156ff, for a very incisive argumentation in this regard.

65.   C. Masson, *L'Epitre de Saint Paul aux Colossiens* (Neuchatel: 1950), pp. 97-107.

66.   M. Dibelius, *An die Kolosser, Epheser, an Philemon*, 3rd ed. (Tubingen: 1953), pp. 14ff.

67.   E. Kasemann, *A Primitive Christian Baptismal Liturgy: Essays on New Testament Themes* (SCM: 1960), pp. 149-168.

68.   C.F. Burney, "Christ as the ΑΡΧΗ of Creation," *Journal of Theological Studies*, xxvii. 1925-6, pp. 160ff.

69.   The verb *sunesteken* ("to hold together") is a present intransitive, which accommodates both past and present. The Son, who before he came in history created and kept the world

together, continues as its exalted Lord to give creation coherence.

70. Cf. D. Guthrie, NTT, 1986, p. 357f; C.F.D. Moule, *The Epistles to the Colossians and Philemon* (Cambridge: 1962), pp. 70f, 164ff; G.B. Caird, *Paul's Letters from Prison*, p. 180f.

71. The verb *katoikeo* is used here in the present tense much as a Greek perfect tense is used, to denote the continuance in the present of a state begun in the past. So Moule, Op. Cit.,. 93.

72. See Moule, Op. Cit., p. 165.

73. Ibid, p. 169.

74. Paul's thought moves back and forth throughout this passage between the Son's activity in His pre-existence and His activity in His incarnation. Paul's language is highly flexible. The supposed tension between J.B. Lightfoot's emphasis on Christ's pre-existence and G.B. Caird's emphasis on Christ's incarnation in this passage is unnecessary.

75. See M. Hengel, *Studies in Early Christology* (T. & T. Clark: 1995), pp. 285ff.

76. See B.M. Metzger, "The Punctuation of Rom. 9:5," *Christ and the Spirit in the New Testament*, ed. by B. Lindars and S.S. Smalley (Cambridge: 1973), pp. 95-112.

77. See C.H. Dodd, *The Epistle of Paul to the Romans* (Hodder: 1932), ad loc; V. Taylor: *The Person of Christ*, pp. 55-57; R. Bultmann, TNT, vol. 1, p. 129.

78. O. Cullmann, *The Christology of the New Testament*, rev. ed. (Westminster: 1963), pp. 312ff; D. Guthrie, NTT, p. 339f. See also the excellent discussion by C.E.B. Cranfield, *Romans II* (1989), pp. 464-470.

79. C.F.D. Moule, *The Origin of Christology* (Cambridge: 1977), p. 137.

80. A.W. Wainwright, *The Trinity in the New Testament* (London: 1962), p. 57.

81. See Cullmann, Op. Cit., p. 313f; and Guthrie, NTT, p. 340.

82. Cullmann, Op. Cit., p. 313; Guthrie: NTT, p. 340; Wainwright, Op. Cit., p. 70.

83. See B.M. Metzger: "A Reconsideration of Certain Arguments Against the Pauline Authorship of the Pastoral Epistles," *Expository Times* 70, 1958-9, pp. 1991ff, against P.N. Harrison, *The Problem of the Pastoral Epistles*, 1921.

84. See Rev. 22:20.

85. B.F. Westcott, *The Epistle to the Hebrews* (London: 1892), p. 9.

86. F.F. Bruce, *The Epistle to the Hebrews* (Eerdmans: 1946), p. 5; against H.W. Montefiore, *A Commentary on the Epistle to the Hebrews* (London: Black, 1964), p. 34f.

87. N. Turner, *Grammatical Insights into the New Testament* (T. & T. Clark: 1965), p. 15, describes it as grotesque.

88. R. Bultmann, *The Gospel of St. John* (Blackwell: 1971), pp. 7-9.

89. C.K. Barrett, *The Gospel According to St. John* (London: 1978), p. 127.

90. E.g., P. Gardiner-Smith, *St. John and the Synoptic Gospels* (1938); C.H. Dodd, *Historic Tradition in the Fourth Gospel* (Cambridge: 1963).

91. For example, J.A.T. Robinson, *The Priority of John* (SCM: 1985).

92. It is not necessary for our purposes to enter into a full discussion of the author's identity.

93. The Greek word is *Logos*.

94. Not just the action of God, as emphasized by O. Cullmann, op. cit., p. 265.

95. See Mark 6:3 for this issue of "pros" with the accusative in New Testament Greek. It is unclear as to the meaning of translations such as "in relation to God" or "a word addressed to God."

96. Raymond Brown, *The Gospel According to John*, vol. 1 (Doubleday: 1966), p. 4f.

97. R. Bultmann, *John*, p. 32.

98. Leon Morris, *The Gospel According to John* (Eerdmans: 1971), p. 76.

99. As per Origen, *de Principius*, Bk. I, frg. 5.

100. E.C. Colwell, *Journal of Biblical Literature*, LII, 1933, pp. 12-21. R. Bultmann, *John*, p. 33, recognizes these points in agreement, yet he can go on to say that "in the Revealer God is really encountered and yet that God is not directly encountered, but only in the Revealer" (p. 34).

101. So Cullmann, *Christology*, p. 266.

102. Cullmann, Op. Cit., p. 266; Bultmann, *John*, p. 34; Morris, *John*, p. 79.

103. Barrett, *John*, p. 156.

104. Bultmann, *John*, p. 256.

105. Pre-existence could have been asserted by the imperfect.

106. Bultmann, *John*, p. 27.

107. Barrett, *John*, p. 352, suggests that the Old Testament text in mind is Psalm 90:2, not Exodus 3:14. No reason is given.

108. Brown, *John*, vol. I, p. 367f.

109. Despite Barrett, *John*, p. 500.

110. Barrett, Op. Cit., p. 504.

111. This can hardly be compared with the thought form of the Gnostic myth as Bultmann, *John*, p. 496, suggests. The idea of incarnation that is found in John's theology is far too materialistic to reflect Gnosticism.

112. It is unclear what Cullmann, *Christology*, p. 305, means when he declares that according to Paul, Hebrews and John (citing 17:5) that the Son will be "absorbed" in God when his redemptive work is complete. This kind of incipient Gnosticism is hardly borne out by the evidence.

113. So Bultmann, *John*, p. 694f; Morris, *John*, p. 853f; Cullmann, *Christology*, p. 265f, 308.

114. Contrary to the outlandish claims of the so-called "Jesus Seminar."

115. A "Q" passage, therefore early.

116. Among those scholars who think it possible to construct a credible historical account of Jesus are the following: M. Bockmuehl, *This Jesus: Martyr, Lord, Messiah* (T. & T. Clarke: 1994); G. Bornkamm, *Jesus of Nazareth* (Harper & Row: 1960); F.F. Bruce, *The New Testament Documents: Are They Reliable?* (InterVarsity: 1984); H. Conzelmann, *Jesus* (Fortress: 1973); C.H. Dodd, *The Founder of Christianity* (Macmillan: 1970); A. Hanson, ed., *Vindications: Essays on the Historical Basis of Christianity* (SCM: 1966); C. Blomberg, *The Historical Reliability of the Gospels* (InterVarsity: 1987); M. Hengel, *Earliest Christianity* (SCM: 1979); M. Hengel, *The Charismatic Leader and His Followers* (T. & T. Clark: 1981); J.D.G. Dunn, *The Evidence for Jesus* (Westminster: 1985); M. de Jonge, *Jesus, the Servant-Messiah* (Yale: 1991); William Manson, *Jesus the Messiah* (Hodder: 1956); J.H. Charlesworth, *Jesus Within Judaism* (Doubleday: 1988); E.P. Saunders, *The Historical Figure of Jesus* (Penguin: 1993); G.N. Stanton, *The Gospels and Jesus* (Oxford); E. Schweizer, *Jesus: The Parable of God* (Pickwick:

1994); N.T. Wright, *Who Was Jesus?* (Eerdmans: 1992); J.P. Meier, *A Marginal Jew: Rethinking the Historical Jesus*, vols. 1-2 (Doubleday: 1991, 1994).

117. This baptismal formula need not necessarily be a stereotyped addition by the later church, designed to safeguard trinitarian thought and practice by reading it back into the authoritative text, as per C.K. Barrett, *The Holy Spirit and the Gospel Tradition* (SPCK: 1966), p. 102f; E. Schweizer, *Good News According to Matthew* (SPCK: 1976), p. 531f. The fact that the early church at first baptized explicitly in the name of Jesus (Acts 2:38; 8:16; see also 9:17-19; 10:44ff) may simply reflect natural but unauthorized practice, as the church recognized the dynamic presence of the risen Christ. Second, at least some parts of the early church later came to recognize that the Holy Spirit also was involved in baptism (Acts 8:16; cf. 2:38; 10:44). Third, the role or presence of God the Father in baptism may well have been taken for granted in the early baptismal services. Fourth, the dominical teaching in Matthew 28:19 may reflect the theologically ideal liturgy which was intended from the beginning but which took some time to be implemented in the church in such a clear formula. Fifth, this may in fact not be a liturgical formula for the rite of baptism at all, but rather a theological description of the meaning of either the sacrament or the underlying faith of the Christian discipline.

118. V. Taylor, "The Spirit in the New Testament," *The Doctrine of the Holy Spirit*, ed. by N. Snaith (Epworth: 1937), pp. 53ff.

119. See C.K. Barrett, *The Holy Spirit and Gospel Tradition*, pp. 140-162, for the above suggestions.

120. D. Guthrie, *New Testament Theology*, p. 525f.

121. G.B. Caird, *New Testament Theology* (Oxford: 1944), p. 212.

122. C.K. Barrett, *John*, p. 207, thinks Judaism avoided this because it annihilated the distinction between this age and the age to come.

123. C.K. Barrett, *John*, p. 211. "The Spirit, like the wind, is entirely beyond both the control and compulsion of man: It breathes into this world from another." This is very close to the meaning, except that the impersonal "It" does not capture the personal aspect of the authority, power and mystery of the Spirit in action here.

124. R. Bultmann, *John*, 190f. He goes further to assert that this is worship of the eschatological age in which there is no temple (Revelation 21:22). This age has already arrived.

125. This does not mean that the Spirit cannot influence non-believers at all. We are told that the Spirit can convict the world of sin (John 16:8), will testify effectively about Jesus (John 15:26), and bring the saving righteous works of Jesus before them for their decision, therefore obviously persuasively (John 16:10). Even Cyrus, the unbeliever, became God's anointed servant (Isaiah 45:1). Paul argued that unfaithful ministers can preach the Word effectively, presumably because the Holy Spirit is using them despite their lack of personal qualifications. D. Guthrie's discussion of this is brief and inadequate (cf. *New Testament Theology*, p. 533).

126. See John Calvin, *The Institutes*, I. xiii. 15.

127. In 2 Corinthians 3:17f, Paul shifts the word "Lord" from God to Christ to Spirit, then back again to Christ, and finally again to the Spirit. See G.B. Caird, *New Testament Theology*, p. 206f.

128. See W. Pannenberg, *Systematic Theology*, vol. I, p. 266.

129. E.g., P.E. Hughes, "The Second Epistle to the Corinthians," NICNT (Eerdmans: 1962), p. 488.

130. E.g., H. Lietzmann, *Die Briefe des Apostels Paulus an die Korinther* (Mohr: 1949), ad loc.

131. F.F. Bruce, "1 and 2 Corinthians," *The Century Bible* (Oliphants: 1978), p. 255.

132. Cf. J.Y. Campbell, "KOINONIA and Its Cognates in the New Testament," J.B.L. 51 (1932), p. 352ff. Also, C.S.C. Williams, "II Corinthians," *Peake's Bible Commentary* (1962), p. 972.

133. Cf. D. Guthrie, *New Testament Theology*, p. 562.

134. "The salutation undoubtedly gives expression to their relationship but in no way posits deity of all three." —W. Pannenberg, *Systematic Theology*, vol. I, p. 302. It is, however, a reasonable assumption from the way they are listed that Paul regards the three Persons as co-equal.

135. W. Albright and C. Mann, *Matthew* (Doubleday: 1972), p. 362f; R.H. Gundry, *Matthew*, 2nd ed. (Eerdmans: 1994), p. 596.

136. G.B. Caird, *New Testament Theology* (1994), p. 212.

137. See G.B. Caird, *The Revelation of St. John the Divine* (London: 1966).

138. C.S.C. Williams, "I Corinthians," *Peake's Bible Commentary* (1962), p. 961.

139. C.K. Barrett, *I Corinthians* (London: 1971), p. 284.

140. J.N.D. Kelly, *The Epistles of Peter and of Jude* (London: 1969), pp. 42ff.

141. D.M. Baillie, *God Was In Christ*, 2nd ed. (Faber: 1955), p. 143, points out that "personality in God must be very different than personality in us." This is not to say, however, that there aren't similarities as well.

The Foundation of
The Doctrine of the Trinity:
The Early Church

Graham Scott

THIS essay attempts to show that the doctrine of the Trinity developed by the Fathers of the church is more biblical than
philosophical, more Hebraic than Hellenistic, more Christ-cen-
tered than academic. The patristic church used the Greek
translation of the Old Testament called the Septuagint; did this
Hellenistic work compromise their theology right from the start?
The patristic church, as well as the medieval, assumed that God
was unchangeable; did this assumption import an alien concept
into their doctrine of God? The Fathers were largely indebted to a
classical education and to a Neoplatonic point of view; did this
background distance them from the Jesus Christ of the New Testament? To answer this last question, one turns to Basil the Great's
most important work, *On the Spirit* (AD 379), for it was influential
and it is accessible.

For a history of the development of the doctrine of the Trinity,
what better is there than Jaroslav Pelikan's project on the Christian
tradition, especially the first volume, *The Emergence of the Catholic
Tradition: 100-600* (University of Chicago Press: 1971)? For contemporary studies by Reformed and Orthodox theologians resulting
in an agreed statement on the Holy Trinity, which attempts to bridge
the gulf between eastern and western theological developments, see
the two volumes, *Theological Dialogue between Orthodox and Reformed Churches*, both edited by Thomas F. Torrance (Scottish
Academic Press: 1993).

109

This essay is limited to the three questions above and to the existential question of how the patristic doctrine of the Trinity bears on one's faith and life.

Bible or Philosophy: Hebrew or Greek?

The Catholic doctrine of the Trinity strikes many people today as unhelpfully abstract, intellectual, and philosophical. The so-called Athanasian Creed gives them little encouragement, coming as it does in the *Canadian Book of Common Prayer* after the "Form of Consecration of a Cemetery." Its sonorous cadences, "Such as the Father is, such is the Son, and such is the Holy Ghost; The Father uncreated, the Son uncreated, the Holy Ghost uncreated," etc., easily lead our contemporaries to say, as Dorothy Sayers noticed, that the doctrine of the Trinity is this: "The Father incomprehensible, the Son incomprehensible, and the whole thing incomprehensible."[1]

THE QUESTION OF THE SEPTUAGINT.

Even Christian students of the Old Testament have suspected that the early church formed the doctrine of the Trinity out of Greek dialectical categories rather than the witness of the Hebrew Bible. It is a fact that the Bible of the New Testament church was the Greek translation of the Hebrew known as the Septuagint (LXX). Professor G.A.F. Knight writes that the concepts which the church used "in the discussion on the nature of God which are the basis of the doctrine of the Trinity, or on the relationships of the persons of the Trinity, were as often as not concepts taken from the LXX version of the OT."[2]

The Septuagint was written by Alexandrian Jews for their community about a century before Christ's birth. Legend has it that it is the result of 70 scholars translating independently yet arriving at exactly the same wording. The number of scholars gave it both its current Latin name and its abbreviation, LXX. Modern scholars consider it to be less a true translation of the Hebrew and more a paraphrase. They are in good company. In his lecture on Genesis 4:7 Luther said, "The translators of the Septuagint appear not to have had adequate knowledge to cope with the vastness of the task they had undertaken."[3]

Professor Knight claims that "the LXX translators of the Pentateuch, under the influence of the Greeks, cut out if they possibly could all references to change in God,"[4] presumably because they accepted the Hellenist view of God as immovable, static, impassive, pure Being. Indeed God's name is revealed from the burning bush in Exodus 3:13-14 as "I AM THAT I AM" (AV) or "I WILL BE WHAT I WILL BE" (NRSV alternative reading). This statement is rendered by the LXX as, "I am Being" (*ego eimi ho on*). Knight says, "The LXX thus gives a totally wrong impression of the Hebraic approach to God's self-revelation."[5] But Being (*ho on*) is full of dynamic possibilities; it is a verbal form; translating God as Being no more requires that God be static than it excludes His being dynamic. We will return to this point in the next section on "God: Static or Dynamic" (p. 126ff).

It is true that the LXX does not always deliver the impact of the Hebrew. Knight cites Genesis 6:6 as a case in point.[6] The NIV translates the Hebrew thus: "The LORD was grieved that he had made man on the earth, and his heart was filled with pain." I translate the LXX thus: "And God was concerned that He had made man on the earth and He bethought himself." The difference is clear, but in verse 7 the NIV says, "For I am grieved that I have made them," and the LXX says, "Because He was very angry that He had made them." There is no abstract, impassible description of God in the LXX's verse 7. The LXX does not give a "totally wrong" impression of the Hebrew, however inadequate it might be at certain points.

Perhaps the translators of the LXX had something of Luther's attitude about New Testament discrepancies like the genealogies of Matthew and Luke. "These are questions that I am not going to try to settle. Some people are so hairsplitting and meticulous that they want to have everything absolutely precise. But if we have the right understanding of Scripture and hold to the true article of our faith that Jesus Christ, God's Son, died and suffered for us, it won't matter much if we cannot answer all the questions put to us."[7]

In any case, the early church believed the LXX to be inspired. After all, the LXX was the NT church's Bible. By the fifth century, St. Augustine could say that "the same Spirit who was in the prophets when they spoke these things was also in the seventy men when they translated them, so that assuredly they could also say something else, just as if the prophet himself had said both, because it would be the same Spirit who said both."[8] Augustine was prepared to accept both the Hebrew text and the LXX text because, he said, the apostles themselves quoted from both.[9]

The LXX was indeed written within a Greek philosophical milieu, but any translation would bear the imprint of its language and worldview. Such imprint need not frustrate God's self-revelation, which is not limited to the Hebrew text. This is obvious not only because portions of the OT are written in Aramaic, but also because the NT is written in Greek. If one can argue that God's election of Israel meant God's choice of the Hebrew language,[10] it would follow that God's sending of Jesus in the "fullness of the time" (Gal 4:4)—that is, *inter alia* a largely Greek-speaking world—meant God's choice of the Greek language also.

The preference of the Reformers for the Hebrew text and canon is admitted. The work of Hebrew scholarship over the last hundred years in expanding our understanding of the Old Testament is valued. We bless God for the Reformers' and the modern scholars' findings and insights. But it is surely an overstatement to suggest that "our modern study of the Nature of God as revealed in the Hebrew Scriptures has opened up to us a much clearer understanding of God as a Trinity of Being than has been possible for those theologians who had only the LXX version of the Scriptures as the source from which to draw both their concepts and their actual language when they sought to erect a systematic Christian theology."[11]

The early church was not impoverished because it used only the LXX. It was influenced not only by the apostles, at least two of whom could be recognized as having been with Jesus (Acts 4:13), but also by the worship of the Jerusalem Temple and of the synagogue.[12]

LANUGAGE AND FAITH.

It takes more than a knowledge of Hebrew to enter into a discussion of the Trinity. St. Gregory Nazianzen (AD 329-389) said, "It is a great thing to speak of God, but still better to purify oneself for God."[13] St. Gregory of Nyssa (ca. AD 330–395) said, "Beatitude consists not in knowing something about God but in having Him within us."[14]

Vladimir Lossky summed up centuries of the Eastern church's experience when he wrote, "The Trinity cannot be grasped by man. It is rather the Trinity that seizes man and provokes praise in him. Outside of praise and adoration, outside of the personal relationship of faith, our language, when speaking of the Trinity, is always false."[15]

The Fathers of the church did not see themselves as carrying on the discussions recorded by Plato (427-347 BC) and taken up by Philo (ca. 20 BC–AD 50) and Plotinus (ca. AD 205-270). They did not see themselves as philosophers, though they used the language of philosophy, just as the Old Testament used the language of myth.

Let us be clear that the Old Testament tells the story of creation and salvation and that most of the story is historical. But Genesis 1-3, for example, makes use of mythical language, reorders it, and tells a new story by it—the story that God created everything and that the things like the sun and the moon, the sky and the earth, which people had worshiped as divine, are creatures, not gods. And we see traces of mythic language in references to Leviathan (Ps 74:14; Isa 27:1). Just as builders sometimes use stones or bricks from a demolished building, so Old Testament writers sometimes make use of terms from myths to build up a description of what God has done.

Kenneth Hamilton notes that "all language grows out of mythic thinking and still bears the marks of its origin....The Bible does not remove us out of the reach of mythic language, yet it allows us to avoid the untruth of myth."[16] Similarly, the theologians of the early church did not shrink from using words and concepts of philosophy, yet they wanted to avoid the falsehood of abstraction and they aimed at the relationship with God that comes only by faith, purity and worship.

St. Hilary (ca. AD 315–367) insisted that only God himself is a fit witness of himself in His Word.[17] Geoffrey Bromiley notes that Hilary always remembers that what is said about God is indeed said about *God*. Philosophy simply leads us astray when it subjects divine truth to creaturely logic.[18]

St. Basil (AD 330–379) began his book on the Spirit with a protest against using pagan logic, grammar, and philosophy in dealing with the Lord of all. His critics preferred his doxology "to the Father *through* the Son *in* the Holy Spirit" to his other doxology "to the Father *with* the Son *together with* the Holy Spirit." He protests, "it is these careful distinctions, derived from unpractical philosophy and vain delusion, which our opponents have first studied and admired, and then transferred to the simple and unsophisticated doctrine of the Spirit, to the belittling of God the Word, and the setting at naught of the Divine Spirit....We acknowledge that the word of truth has in many places made use of these expressions; yet we absolutely deny that the freedom of the Spirit is in bondage to the pettiness of Paganism."[19] Clearly, Basil has gone beyond philosophy to lay his foundations on revelation and particularly on Holy Scripture, even if his Old Testament was the LXX.

The most moving witness to the insights and the limitations of the philosophers is surely St. Augustine (AD 354-430), confessing his life to God,

> Thou didst procure for me...certain books of the Platonists.... And therein I found, not indeed in the same words, but to the selfsame effect, enforced by many and various reasons that "in the beginning was the Word, and the Word was with God, and the Word was God...." ...Furthermore I read that the soul of man, though it "bears witness to the light," yet itself "is not the light; but the Word of God, being God, is that true light that lights every man...." ...But that "he came unto his own, and his own received him not. And as many as received him, to them he gave power to become the sons of God, even to them that believed on his name"—this I did not find there.
>
> Similarly, I read there that God the Word was born "not of flesh nor of blood, nor of the will of man, nor the will of the flesh, but of

God." But, that "the Word was made flesh, and dwelt among us"—I found this nowhere there.... I read further in them that before all times and beyond all times, thy only Son remaineth unchangeably coeternal with thee, and that of his fullness all souls receive that they may be blessed, and that by participation in that wisdom which abides in them, they are renewed that they may be wise. But, that "in due time, Christ died for the ungodly" and that thou "sparedst not thy only Son, but deliveredst him up for us all"—this is not there.[20]

Lossky correctly declares, "Revelation sets an abyss between the truth which it declares and the truths which can be discovered by philosophical speculation."[21] He notes that it was through Origen that Hellenism attempted to creep into the church.[22]

He compares the mystical philosophy of Plotinus with that of Dionysius (ca. AD 500). For Plotinus, the realm of being is necessarily multiple and does not have the absolute simplicity of the One; to become one with the One you cannot regard the One as an object, for ecstasy means going beyond the distinction between subject and object to simplification, that is, reintegration into the One.

> Despite all the outward resemblances (due primarily to a common vocabulary), we are far removed from the negative theology of the *Areopagitica*. The God of Dionysius, incomprehensible by nature, the God of the Psalms "who made darkness his secret place [Ps 18:11]," is not the primordial God-Unity of the Neoplatonists.... Dionysius is aiming expressly at the "Neoplatonist definitions" when he writes, "He is neither One, nor Unity..." In his treatise *Of the Divine Names*, in examining the name of the One, which can be applied to God, he shows its insufficiency and compares with it another and "most sublime" name—that of the Trinity, which teaches us that God is neither one nor many but that He transcends this antimony, being unknowable in what He is.[23]

It is significant that, even without knowing that the Hebrew of Deuteronomy 6:4 for "one" was not the word for individual oneness (*yahidh*) but a word (*ehadh*) that was used for the oneness of man and wife (Ge 2:24),[24] the Greek-speaking Fathers realized that

God is more than a monad. Their guidance has a surer grasp of the biblical reality than contemporary scholars such as Knight have been willing to admit.

God: Static or Dynamic, Changeless or in Process?
A DYNAMIC GOD.

Do the Fathers have a fundamentally static view of God? We have already seen that the LXX is quite capable of picturing God as "very angry" (Ge 6:7). In their fidelity to the Bible, the Fathers did not teach a static monad, but rather a God so great as to be incomprehensible. Their apophatic or negative theology kept the remembrance of God as the holy One, whose thoughts are quite beyond ours (Isa 55:8-9) and whose being, rightly called Light, can only be found through the darkness (Ps 18:9-12).

St. Gregory of Nyssa's *Life of Moses* illustrates something of the patristic sensitivity to the dynamic of God. In the burning bush, Moses saw God in light, but on Mount Sinai,

> he enters the darkness, leaving behind him all that can be seen or known; there remains to him only the invisible and unknowable, but in this darkness is God. For God makes His dwelling there where our understanding and our concepts can gain no admittance. Our spiritual ascent does but reveal to us, ever more and more clearly, the absolute incomprehensibility of the divine nature. Filled with an ever-increasing desire the soul grows without ceasing, goes forth from itself, reaches out beyond itself, and, in so doing, is filled with yet greater longing. Thus the ascent becomes infinite, the desire insatiable. This is the love of the bride in the Song of Songs: she stretches out her hands towards the lock, she seeks Him who cannot be grasped, she calls Him to whom she cannot attain…she attains to Him in the perception that the union is endless, the ascent without limit.[25]

The God of love is not a static God.

Gerhart Ladner says that even though the mystic has a firm stand on the rock which is Christ, his condition is not *stasis* (stationary) in the ordinary sense; it is *kinesis* (movement), *tonos* (a tension that never slackens), and *prokope* (unceasing progress).[26] Considering

Paul's ascent to paradise (2Co 12:2-4) and his words, "forgetting what lies behind and straining toward what lies ahead, I press on toward the goal, for the prize of the heavenly call of God in Christ Jesus" (Php 3:13-14), Gregory comments,

> It is clear that even after the third heaven which he alone knew…and even after the ineffable hearing of the mysteries of Paradise, he still goes toward higher regions and never stops the ascent and never makes the good which he has grasped the end of his desire. He thus teaches us, I believe, that with regard to the blessed nature of goodness much means always that which is found; but infinitely more than that which is ever grasped is that which lies above it. And this happens continuously to him who participates [in God], so that there is increase of ever better things for those who participate through the whole eternity of aeons…. And neither does he who ascends ever stand still, for he exchanges one beginning for another, nor is the beginning of ever better things ever perfected in itself….[27]

The God of infinite love is not a static God.

A PROCESS GOD?

It appears that along with the insights of modern Hebrew scholars come also opinions typical of our age. We have seen that Professor Knight criticized the LXX and the church for holding to the view that God is unchangeable. He goes on to argue that "God is *not* an unchanging God, but a God who is progressing in fellowship with man in this world of space and time," and he calls this "a peculiarly Protestant, biblical approach to the doctrine of the Trinity."[28] Moreover, "while the OT reveals to us the same God as does the NT, while God acts with the same loving graciousness to Abraham and Jacob as He does to Peter and Paul and in consequence is the same God in 2000 BC as He is in AD 30, yet God has *gained* something throughout the centuries as a result of what has happened in the sequence of time; God has Himself grown in experience as a result of His gracious love for man." Knight has the grace to add, "Yet we must be careful. We must surely hold this concept as but one half of a mysterious paradox."[29] Yet Knight later says, "If we, then, are going to follow in the train of the Hebraic, biblical ways of thought, and discard all extra-biblical, static, Greek concepts about the Godhead, we must be prepared to postulate of God, of the Holy Blessed Trinity, this conception of growth within the compound nature of that Godhead."[30]

This concept of a progressing, growing God seems neither biblical nor Protestant. It reminds one of Voltaire's quip, "If God made us in His image, we have certainly returned the compliment."[31] While one might be prepared to discard all static concepts of the Godhead, one might think twice before discarding all extra-biblical concepts, wisdom, knowledge, and resources. The Bible itself records God's command to the Israelites to plunder the Egyptians (Ex 3:21-22; 11:2-3; 12:35-36). There is evidence that many Psalms are influenced by Canaanite and Egyptian prototypes.[32] Proverbs 22:17-24:34 parallels the Wisdom of Amenemope, an Egyptian sage. Isaiah 60 foresees the wealth of the nations coming to Jerusalem. St Augustine said that "every good and true Christian should understand that wherever he may find truth, it is his Lord's."[33] He also said,

> ...All the teachings of the pagans contain not only simulated and superstitious imaginings and grave burdens of unnecessary labor, which each one of us leaving the society of pagans under the leadership of Christ ought to abominate and avoid, but also liberal disciplines more suited to the uses of truth, and some most useful precepts concerning morals. Even some truths concerning the worship of one God are discovered among them. These are, as it were, their gold and silver, which they did not institute themselves but dug up from certain mines of divine Providence, which is everywhere infused, and perversely and injuriously abused in the worship of demons.[34]

The concept of the progressing, growing God seems incompatible with the numerous references to God as a rock (Dt 32:4, 15, 18, 30-31. Ps 18:2, 31, 46, etc.), not to mention Malachi 3:6, "For I the LORD do not change; therefore you, O children of Jacob, have not perished" (cf. Nu 23:19). God's faithfulness or stability is likewise a constant theme in the OT (Dt 7:9. Ps 89:1-2, 5, 8, 24, 33, etc.; Isa 25:1; 49:7). Rather than a God in process, the concept of a dynamic

God is closer to the OT witness. An unchangeable essence and will are not incompatible with being dynamic.[35]

It is quite improper for Professor Knight to call the concept of a growing God in any way a Protestant approach. The Lutheran *Book of Concord* states that the Father is *changeless* in His will and essence (*Solid Declaration*, XI, 75) (1577-1580). The Westminster Confession of Faith teaches that God is "infinite in being and perfection, a most pure spirit, invisible, without body, parts, or passions, *immutable*, immense, eternal, incomprehensible, almighty..." (C. II) (1647). The United Church of Canada's Basis of Union states, "We believe in one only living and true God, a Spirit, infinite, eternal and *unchangeable*, in His being and perfections..." (1925), I:35. (All italics added.)

Vladimir Lossky sums up the synthesis of Bible, Fathers, and Creed on this matter of process theology:

> There is no dependence in relation to created being on the part of the Trinity; no determination of what is called "the eternal procession of the divine persons" by the act of the creation of the world. Even though the created order did not exist, God would still be Trinity—Father, Son and Holy Ghost—for creation is an act of will: the procession of the persons is an act "according to nature."... There is no interior process in the Godhead; no "dialectic" of the three persons; no becoming; no "tragedy in the Absolute," which might necessitate the Trinitarian development of the divine being in order that it be surmounted or resolved. These conceptions, proper to the romantic tradition of nineteenth-century German philosophy, are wholly foreign to the dogma of the Trinity. If we speak of processions, of acts, or of inner determinations, these expressions—involving, as they do, the ideas of time, becoming and intention—only show to what extent our language, indeed our thought, is poor and deficient before the primordial mystery of revelation. Again we are forced to appeal to apophatic theology in order to rid ourselves of concepts proper to human thought, transforming them into steps by which we may ascend to the contemplation of a reality which the created intelligence cannot contain.[36]

Hellenism did not succeed in influencing the Fathers to become philosophers in the Platonic succession, or to believe that God is a static monad as in Plotinus, or to abandon the teaching of the Scriptures, even if they read the Old Testament in translation. The theological work of the Fathers in general and of the seven ecumenical councils in particular constitute a solid foundation on which we of the Twentieth Century can build. We do not have to re-invent the wheel. We do not have to invent the Christian faith, "that was once for all entrusted to the saints" (Jude 3; Gal 1:8-9). We are free to use all the resources of the ancient and modern worlds, just as the scribe trained for the kingdom of heaven brings out of his treasure both new and old (Mt 13:52).

Incarnation, Spirit and Trinity

The word "Trinity" is not found in the Bible. It is found first in St. Theophilus, sixth bishop of Antioch, whose Apology to Autolycus was finished about A.D. 181. The Greek word that he used is *Trias*. The Latin word *Trinitas* was first used by Tertullian (ca. AD 160–220) in his work *Against Paxeas*, written sometime after AD 213. The word "Trinity" is not found either in the Nicene Creed of AD 325 or in its final form promulgated by the Council of Constantinople in AD 381. It is, however, found in the Synodical Letter of the latter Council in AD 382.[37]

The textual seed of the doctrine of the Trinity is of course Matthew 28:19, where the risen Jesus Christ commissions His disciples to go and make disciples of all nations, "baptizing them in the name of the Father and of the Son and of the Holy Spirit." The singular of "name" indicates the unity of God; the three qualifying phrases indicate that God is one in these three. The authenticity of this passage has been called into question on the grounds of its being a late product of the church. In any case the passage is part of the canon of Holy Scripture and the virtually universal practice of the church in using this formula for baptism indicates its truth.

INCARNATION.

Vladimir Lossky declares that theology starts with the name of Jesus.[38] He finds the germ of all Trinitarian theology in the three affirmations of John 1:1, "In the beginning was the Word, and the

Word was with God, and the Word was God."[39] It is the incarnation of the Word of God which requires the doctrine of the Trinity for those whose faith seeks understanding. Without Jesus, the incarnate Son of God from all eternity, the doctrine of the Trinity would never have arisen. Because God revealed himself uniquely in Jesus—because Jesus was not only human but God, faith seeking understanding inevitably finds itself led by God to think of Him as the Three in One. And Lossky is right to say, "Between the Trinity and hell there lies no other choice."[40]

This is not a numbers game. If it were, we might be tempted to inflate three to seven, and seven to the ample pantheon of the Greek and Roman masses (or, contrariwise, to reduce the one to nothing, as the Culture of Death has).[41] Without the doctrine of the Trinity even philosophical monotheism stands only as a reduction of polytheism from many to one. That is why Dionysius can say that God is neither One nor Unity. It is logical and reasonable to reduce polytheism to monotheism, but no amount of logic or reason or pride will be able to build a tower to reach God. We depend on God to reveal himself, for He transcends both one and many. God has revealed himself, specifically to Israel and once for all through Jesus, the Christ of Israel, who baptizes with the Holy Spirit. God's transcendence over one and many is fittingly symbolized by the Trinity, the Three in One, but even this symbol is possible only because the Word of God was incarnate in the man Christ Jesus.

The controversies prior to the Council of Nicea related for the most part to the incarnation. The Council dealt chiefly with the eternal sonship of the man Jesus. It gave one short line to the Holy Spirit, "And in the Holy Spirit." Then came some anathemas against those holding certain Arian formulas.[42]

BASIL THE GREAT.

Between the Council of Nicea and the Council of Constantinople stands St. Basil the Great. His tract, *On the Spirit* (see Note 19), reviews the Christological doctrine before addressing the deity of the Holy Spirit.

He represents an advance in theological vocabulary over the prevailing terminology of Nicea, advanced though that was. It will be instructive to digest Basil's tract, for it deals with a number of important Trinitarian issues and it paved the way for the final ecumenical form of the Nicene Creed, promulgated two years after his death.

We have already seen that the occasion for his tract was the controversy over one of the two doxologies which he used in worship (the latter part of section one). Basil's second doxology makes it clear that the Father, Son, and Holy Spirit are equal, whereas his critics are in effect subordinating the Son and the Spirit. They appeal to 1 Corinthians 8:6, "…One God, the Father, from whom are all things…and one Lord, Jesus Christ, through whom are all things.…" Basil argues that such restrictive prepositions as his critics would assign to Father, Son and Holy Spirit have the effect of making the Father the only cause, the Son only an instrument or tool, and the Holy Spirit only a place or time.[43] Such a restriction renders the doctrine of the Trinity impossible.

Basil argues that 1 Corinthians 8:6 "are words of a writer not laying down a rule, but carefully distinguishing the hypostases." This language, "distinguishing the hypostases,"[44] would have been regarded as impious at Nicea, but the development of true doctrine required the use of this term and its differentiation from *ousia* or being. It was Basil most of all who initiated the use of the term *hypostasis* and its differentiation from *ousia*, though prior to Basil the terms were synonymous.[45]

BASIL'S CHRISTOLOGY.

Basil argues from Scripture that the Son is not after the Father and therefore inferior to the Father. John 1:1 says, "In the beginning was the Word." Basil says, "…Thought cannot travel outside 'was', nor imagination beyond 'beginning.'"[46] Christ is not on a lower level than the Father (insofar as Christ is the eternal Son of God) but is the power and wisdom of God (1Co 1:24), the image of the invisible God (Col 1:15), the brightness of His glory (Heb 1:3), etc. Moreover, Christ's glory is equal to the Father's glory (Mk 8:38; Jn 1:14; 5:23; 14:9, etc.).[47]

Basil says that a proper argument for glorifying Christ is the re-cital of His benefits and titles. He climaxes his recital noting "the mighty power and love to man (*philanthropia*) of the Savior, in that He both endured to suffer with us in our infirmities, and was able to come down to our weakness. For not heaven and earth and the great seas...so well sets forth the excellency of His might as that God, being incomprehensible, should have been able, impassibly, through flesh, to have come into close conflict with death, to the end that by His own suffering He might give us the boon of freedom from suf-fering." "We must not, however, regard the economy through the Son as a compulsory and subordinate ministration resulting from the low estate of a slave, but rather the voluntary solicitude working effectually for His own creation in goodness and in pity, according to the will of God the Father."[48]

Basil expands on this point in regard to Christ's words, "I do as the Father has commanded me" (Jn 14:31), saying, "It is not be-cause He lacks deliberate purpose or power of initiation, nor yet because He has to wait for the preconcerted keynote, that He em-ploys language of this kind. His object is to make it plain that His own will is connected in indissoluble union with the Father. Do not then let us understand by what is called a 'commandment' a per-emptory mandate delivered by organs of speech, and giving orders to the Son, as to a subordinate, concerning what He ought to do. Let us rather, in a sense befitting the Godhead, perceive a transmission of will, like the reflection of an object in a mirror, passing without note of time from Father to Son. 'For the Father loveth the Son and sheweth Him all things' (Jn 5:20 KJV)...."[49] In explaining John 14:9, "whoever has seen me has seen the Father," Basil refers to "the good-ness of the will, which, being concurrent with the essence, is beheld as like and equal, or rather the same, in the Father as in the Son."[50]

BASIL'S PNEUMATOLOGY AND DOCTRINE OF MONARCHY.

Having laid the Christological foundation, Basil proceeds to the doctrine of the Holy Spirit in chapters IX and following. He con-siders the common conceptions both from Holy Scripture and also from the unwritten tradition of the Fathers. He lists some of the titles of the Spirit and offers a lengthy definition, "an intelligent essence, in power infinite, in magnitude unlimited, unmeasured by times of ages…in essence simple, in powers various, wholly present in each and being wholly everywhere…."[51] To the pure, the Spirit like the sun shows in himself the image of the invisible. The Spirit lifts up hearts, bestows manifold graces and brings "joy without end, abiding in God, the being made like to God, and, highest of all, the being made God."[52]

In chapter X, Basil appeals to Christ's command to baptize all nations in the name of the Father and of the Son and of the Holy Spirit. "The Lord has delivered to us as a necessary and saving doctrine that the Holy Spirit is to be ranked with the Father." The heart of being Christian is our faith and the gateway of salvation is baptism in the triune name. Basil charges us "to preserve the faith secure until the day of Christ, and to keep the Spirit undivided from the Father and the Son, preserving, both in the confession of faith and in the doxology, the doctrine taught them at their baptism."[53]

Basil deals with various arguments which seek to reduce the divinity of the Holy Spirit. He distinguishes the Spirit from angels, who are sometimes enumerated with Father and Son but who never became incarnate for us.[54] He argues that baptism into Moses, which makes no mention of the Spirit, was a shadow and type of what was to come.[55] He argues that the water of baptism, which is a creature, fulfills the image of death but the Spirit gives us the earnest of life.[56] Everything in salvation (e.g., adoption, freedom, participation in the wonder of heaven) comes through the Holy Spirit.[57]

In every divine operation the Spirit is closely conjoined with, and inseparable from, the Father and the Son (Ac 5:3-4, 9; 1Co 12:4-6). The Spirit descended upon and remained with Jesus in His baptism, led Him into the wilderness, participated in His exorcisms, and was bestowed by Him when He breathed on His disciples after His resurrection.[58] The argument that the Spirit is subnumerated is without Scriptural proof, and it fails to take into account both that the names of Father, Son, and

Holy Spirit are ranked in one and the same coordinate series, and that nothing ever lost its own nature by being numbered.[59]

Basil's chapter XVIII is crucial in maintaining both the unity and the Trinity of God, by upholding the monarchy as well as the triune name invoked at baptism. "...Let the unapproachable be altogether above and beyond number.... We proclaim each of the hypostases singly; and, when count we must, we do not let an ignorant arithmetic carry us away to the idea of a plurality of Gods."[60]

> Worshiping as we do God of God, we both confess the distinction of the Persons, and at the same time abide by the Monarchy.... For the Son is in the Father and the Father in the Son; since such as is the latter, such is the former, and such as is the former, such is the latter; and herein is the unity. So that according to the distinction of Persons, both are one and one, and according to the community of Nature, one. How then, if one and one, are there not two Gods? Because we speak of a king, and of the king's image, and not of two kings. The majesty is not cloven in two nor the glory divided.... One, moreover, is the Holy Spirit, and we speak of Him singly, conjoined as He is to the one Father through the one Son, and through Himself completing the adorable and blessed Trinity....[61]

Basil turns to the question of the rightness of glorifying the Holy Spirit. The Spirit is described in Scripture as God, holy, good, upright, Paraclete, royal, Spirit of truth, and Spirit of wisdom.[62] Basil asserts that the Spirit existed, preexisted, and coexisted with the Father and the Son before the ages. The Spirit was everywhere associated with Christ from His advent to His resurrection. The Spirit commands the church (Acts 10:19-20, 13:2) with divine authority.[63] Scripture calls the Spirit Lord.[64] Like the Father and the Son the Spirit is unapproachable in thought.[65] As good, as knowledge of God, and as life-giver, the Spirit is God. It is no refutation to say that the Spirit is God's gift and therefore less than God, for Christ is also spoken of in Scripture as God's gift, and Christ is God.[66]

Commenting on John 4:24, Basil notes that Jesus said that worship ought to be offered in Spirit and in Truth, plainly meaning by the Truth himself. "As then we speak of the worship offered in the Image of God the Father as worship in the Son, so too do we speak of worship in the Spirit as shewing in Himself the Godhead of the Lord. Wherefore even in our worship the Holy Spirit is inseparable from the Father and the Son. If you remain outside the Spirit you will not be able even to worship at all; and on your becoming in Him you will in no wise be able to dissever Him from God;—any more than you will divorce light from visible objects. For it is impossible to behold the Image of the invisible God except by the enlightenment of the Spirit...."[67]

Basil appeals to tradition for the rightness of his doxology using "with" in regard to the Spirit.[68] He cites 1 Corinthians 11:2 and 2 Thessalonians 2:15 as scriptural authority for tradition.[69] He cites Irenaeus, Clement of Rome, Dionysius of Rome, Dionysius of Alexandria, Eusebius of Caesarea, Origen, Africanus, the hymn *Phos hilarion*, Athenogenes, Gregory the Wonder-Worker, Firmilian, and Meletius as those who glorified the Spirit with the Father and the Son.[70]

Implications of the Incarnation and of Sanctification
AFTER CONSTANTINOPLE (AD 381).

In this outline of Basil's tract we see something of the theological work that remained to be done after Nicea (AD 325). Even the Council of Constantinople, which benefited from Basil's work, did not complete the task. It remained for the Council of Ephesus (AD 431) to link the incarnation to personal, historical reality by ascribing to the Virgin Mary the title *Theotokos* (Mother of God)[71] as against Nestorius, who insisted that she was only the Mother of Christ, as if Jesus Christ and the eternal Son of God were only close associates. This concern was given definitive expression by the Council of Chalcedon (AD 451), which ratified Ephesus and condemned Eutyches, whose reaction against Nestorianism led him to confuse Christ's distinct natures (divine and human) and to argue that Christ's manhood was not consubstantial with ours. But if Christ was not consubstantial with us, how could His incarnation and death save us? What is not assumed cannot be saved. Chalcedon's definition is as follows:

We, then, following the holy Fathers, all with one consent, teach men to confess one and the same Son, our Lord Jesus Christ, the same perfect in Godhead and also perfect in manhood; truly God and truly man, of a reasonable soul and body; consubstantial with the Father according to the Godhead, and consubstantial with us according to the Manhood; in all things like unto us, without sin; begotten before [all] ages of the Father according to the Godhead, and in these latter days, for us and our salvation, born of the Virgin Mary, the Mother of God (*Theotokos*), according to the Manhood; one and the same Christ, Son, Lord, Only-begotten, to be acknowledged in two natures, inconfusedly, unchangeably, indivisibly, inseparably; the distinction of natures being by no means taken away by the union, but rather the property of each nature being preserved, and concurring in one Person and one Subsistence (*hypostasis*), not parted or divided into two persons, but one and the same Son and only-begotten, God the Word, the Lord Jesus Christ, as the prophets from the beginning [have declared] concerning him, and the Lord Jesus Christ himself has taught us, and the Creed of the holy Fathers has handed down to us.[72]

It should be emphasized that this is no hairsplitting exercise, for if the doctrine about Christ's incarnation is perverted, then the doctrine of our salvation is skewed and the gospel message nullified.

SANCTIFICATION AND DEIFICATION.

The Fathers' concept of salvation included not only the forgiveness of sins, the resurrection of the body and life eternal, but a logical interpretation of sanctification called deification. The young Athanasius (ca. AD 296-373) put it this way: Let the seeker "recognize the fact and marvel that things divine have been revealed to us by such humble means, that through death deathlessness has been made known to us, and through the Incarnation of the Word the Mind whence all things proceed has been declared, and its Agent and Ordainer, the Word of God himself. He, indeed, assumed humanity that we might become God."[73] We might shrink from such a bold statement, but even Calvin, commenting on 2 Peter 1:4, could say this much, "We should take notice that it is the purpose of the Gospel to make us sooner or later like God; indeed it is, so to speak, a kind of deification."[74]

Perhaps St. Gregory Nazianzus puts it in language that Protestants can appreciate. He says that man's condition was getting worse and needed a greater remedy, and this was...

> that the Word of God Himself, Who is before all worlds,...the Image of the Archetype, the Immovable Seal, the Unchangeable Image, the Father's Definition and Word, came to His own image, and took on Him Flesh for the sake of our flesh, and mingled Himself with an intelligent soul for my soul's sake, purifying like by like; and in all points except sin was made Man; conceived by the Virgin.... He came forth then as God, with That which He had assumed; one Person in two natures, flesh and Spirit, of which the latter deified the former. O new commingling; O strange conjunction! The Self-existent comes into existence, the Uncreated is created, That which cannot be contained is contained by the intervention of an intellectual soul mediating between the Deity and the corporeity of the flesh. And He who gives riches becomes poor; for He assumes the poverty of my flesh, that I may assume the riches of His Godhead. He that is full empties Himself; for He empties Himself of His glory for a short while, that I may have a share in His Fullness.[75]

Lossky comments,

> The Fathers of the "Christological centuries," though they formulated a dogma of Christ the God-Man, never lost sight of the question concerning *our* union with God. The usual arguments they bring up against unorthodox doctrines refer particularly to the fullness of our union, our deification, which becomes impossible if one separates the two natures of Christ, as Nestorius did, or if one only ascribes to Him one divine nature, like the Monophysites, or if one curtails one part of human nature, like Apollinarius, or if one only sees in Him a single divine will and operation, like the Monothelites. "What is not assumed, cannot be deified"—this is the argument to which the Fathers continually return.[76]

Similarly hold the Reformers on the doctrine of the Trinity, though they prefer to speak of sanctification. Lukas Vischer writes,

> The Reformers strongly emphasize the close connection between the doctrine of the Trinity and the salvation imparted to humanity in Christ. In their view, the ancient church doctrine is the precondition for being able to speak correctly of election, justification and sanctification. It therefore is binding in character because thereby confession is made of the same God who justifies and sanctifies the sinner. The doctrine of the Trinity is not a self-contained theme which could be dealt with separately from the proclamation of salvation in Christ. Theology does not enter a completely new field once it begins to deal with the appropriation of salvation. It is already basically concerned with this theme when it is developing the dogma of the Trinity. Conversely, the doctrine of justification and sanctification is unthinkable without the Trinitarian foundation: it is its necessary realization and application.[77]

Conclusion

By the grace of God, the Fathers have built a firm theological foundation for the whole church. They began their work on the only real foundation, which is Jesus Christ. Their faith was formed and fed by the Greek New Testament and the Greek Old Testament and by self-denial and prayer. They used their own language to articulate their faith and were willing to learn the language of the philosophers in order to think more clearly. When they spoke of God, they meant the God of Abraham, of Isaac, and of Jacob; the God and Father of our Lord Jesus Christ; the Father, the Son, and the Holy Spirit—one God. They ordered their lives to cooperate with God's plan to unite them to himself through Christ the God-Man. They challenge us not only to think our faith through but to pray continually, not only to worship corporately but in Spirit and in truth, not only to obey the commandments in love but to purify the heart, not only to do good works but to become holy, not only to do theology but to become theology.

Archimandrite Vasileios sums up this approach:

> The first Christians lived their theology totally and with the whole of their bodies, just as they were baptized with the whole of their body and soul into the new life.
>
> How frequently the Lord would stop people who wanted to start a 'theological' conversation with Him…. For He did not come to discuss, He came to seek out and save the one that had gone astray (Mt 18:11). He came and took on our whole nature. He entered into us, into the shadow of death where we are, and drew us to the light. We passed into His life: we live in Him.
>
> This life which is in Christ, and the expression of it, constitutes the true theology which is the one truth, because it speaks of and brings us to the one eternal life. Thus we realize that we cannot create theology by taking a piece of paper and writing down our ideas, which may very well be correct, theologically pertinent (as to their terminology) or socially useful. The material offered to each person to struggle with, to write theology with, and to speak about to the church, is none other than his own self, his very being, hidden and unknown.
>
> Our struggle to condemn sin "in our flesh" is at the same time our attempt to express our theology….
>
> How beautiful it is for a man to become theology. Then whatever he does, and above all what he does spontaneously, since only what is spontaneous is true, bears witness and speaks of the fact that the Son and Word of God was incarnate, that He was made man through the Holy Spirit and the ever-virgin Mary. It speaks silently about the ineffable mysteries which have been revealed in the last times."[78]

NOTES

1. See Dorothy L. Sayers, *Christian Letters to a Post-Christian World: A selection of essays*, ed. R. Jellema (Grand Rapids: Eerdmans, 1969), p. 24. Apophatic theologians might say that Sayers' contemporaries said better than they knew. See V. Lossky below.

2. See G.A.F. Knight, *A Biblical Approach to the Doctrine of the Trinity*, Scottish Journal of Theology Occasional Papers No. 1 (Edinburgh & London: Oliver & Boyd, 1953, 1957), p. 2.

3. See B. Hall, *The Cambridge History of the Bible: The West from the Reformation to the Present Day*, S.L. Gleenslade, ed. (Cambridge: Cambridge University Press, 1963), p. 56 .

4. See Knight, op. cit., pp. 8, 60ff.

5. See Knight, op. cit., p. 7. See also F. Büchsel, "eimi, ho on," in *Theological Dictionary of the New Testament*, ed. A. Kittel, tr. A.W. Bromiley (Grand Rapids: Eerdmans, 1964), vol. 2, p. 378 ff.

6. See Knight, op. cit., p. 8.

7. See R.H. Bainton, *The Cambridge History*, op. cit.

8. See Saint Augustine, *The City of God*, tr. M. Dods (NY: Modern Library, 1950), XVIII, 43, p. 652.

9. See Augustine, op. cit., XVIII, 44, p. 654.

10. See Knight, op. cit., pp. 6, 28.

11. See Knight, op. cit., p. 4.

12. See Alexander Schmemann, *Introduction to Liturgical Theology*, tr. A.E. Moorhouse (London: Faith, 1966), pp. 43ff. "The works of Oesterley, Jeremias, Dix, Gavin, Baumstark, Dugmore, and after them the study of the new material discovered at Qumran, have all shown clearly the general dependence of Christian

prayer and cult on the cult of the synagogue, and this in turn has begun more and more to attract the attention of Hebrew liturgiologists. This comparative study of Judaism, although it is by no means finished, leaves no doubt about the formal dependence of the former upon the latter" (p. 44).

13. See Gregory Nazianzen, Oration XXXII, 12, as quoted in V. Lossky, *The Mystical Theology of the Eastern Church* (Cambridge: James Clarke, 1957; Crestwood, NY: St. Vladimir's Seminary Press, 1976), p. 38.

14. See Gregory of Nyssa, "On the Beatitudes," Hom. 6, as quoted in Vladimir Lossky, *In the Image and Likeness of God*, ed. J.H. Erickson & T.E. Bird (Crestwood, NY: St. Vladimir's Seminary Press, 1967, 1985), p. 38.

15. See Vladimir Lossky, *Orthodox Theology: An Introduction*, tr. I. & I. Kesarcodi-Watson (Crestwood, NY: St. Vladimir's SP, 1978, 1989), p. 46.

16. See Kenneth Hamilton, *Words and the Word* (Grand Rapids: Eerdmans, 1971), p. 86.

17. Hilary of Poitiers, *Trinity*, I, 18. "For He whom we can know only through his own utterances is a fitting witness concerning Himself." As quoted in Calvin: *Institutes of the Christian Religion*, ed. J.T. McNeill, tr. F.L. Battles; Library of Christian Classics [LCC], Vol. XX (Philadelphia: Westminster, 1960), p. 79, n. 15.

18. Geoffrey W. Bromiley, *Historical Theology: An Introduction* (Edinburgh: T. & T. Clark, 1978), p. 88.

19. See *Nicene and Post-Nicene Fathers of the Christian Church* [*NPNFCC*], Second Series, Vol. VIII, *St. Basil: Letters and Select Works*, tr. B. Jackson (Grand Rapids: Eerdmans), pp. 4-5.

20. *Augustine: Confessions and Enchiridion*, tr. & ed. A.C. Outler, LCC Vol. VII (Philadelphia: Westminster, 1955); Confessions, VII, ix, 13-14, pp. 144-145. Limited space required omission

of Augustine's reference to Philippians 2:5-11 as not found in philosophy. His philosopher may be Plotinus, *Enneads*.

21.   See Lossky, *Mystical*, p. 49.

22.   See Lossky, *Mystical*, p. 32. Origen has an honored place in the history of scholarship; the recent *Catechism of the Catholic Church* cites him nine times. Pelikan cites Chadwich on Onigen's predecessor: "Clement is hellenized to the core of his being, yet unreserved in his adhesion to the Church" (*Emergence*, p. 55). Pelikan disagrees with Harnack that the dogma formulated by the Catholic tradition is in conception and development a work of the Greek spirit on the soil of the Gospel. Pelikan goes on to say, "Indeed, in some ways it is more accurate to speak of dogma as the 'dehellenization' of the theology that had preceded it and to argue that 'by its dogma the church threw up a wall against an alien metaphysic' (Elert)."

23.   See Lossky, *Mystical*, pp. 30-31.

24.   See Knight, op. cit., pp. 17, 47-48.

25.   As quoted in Lossky, *Mystical*, p. 35.

26.   See Gerhart B. Ladner, *The Idea of Reform: Its impact on Christian thought and action in the age of the Fathers* (New York: Harper Torchbooks: 1967), p. 104.

27.   See Ladner, op. cit., pp. 105-106.

28.   See Knight, op. cit., p. 60.

29.   See Knight, op. cit., p. 61.

30.   See Knight, op. cit., p. 68.

31.   Voltaire, *Le Sottisier*, xxxii.

32.   "While Gunkel seeks to make the biblical poets directly dependent upon Mesopotamian mythology, the Ugaritic myths and legends show that the biblical exegete need not go so far afield

to locate the source of Hebrew mythopoetic thought and expression" (Mitchell Dahood, *Psalms I*, Anchor Bible: Garden City, N.Y.: Doubleday, 1965, p. xxxviii). There are resemblances between Psalm 104 and the Egyptian Hymn to the Aton ascribed to Pharaoh Amenhotep IV. G. Nagel maintains that "it would be more prudent to envisage an indirect Egyptian influence through Canaanite mediation, more specifically through Phoenician intervention" (Dahood, *Psalms III*, p. 33).

33.   Saint Augustine, "On Christian Doctrine," *Library of Liberal Arts* (New York: Bobbs-Merill, 1958), tr. D.W. Robertson, Jr., II, xviii, 28, p. 54.

34.   Augustine, *Doctrine*, II, x1, 60, p. 75.

35.   T.F. Torrance writes of Athanasius, "Thus when associated with God's self-revelation in three distinct objective Persons or *hypostaseis* as Father, Son and Holy Spirit, Being or *ousia* signifies the one eternal Being of God in the indivisible reality and fullness of His intrinsic personal relations as the Holy Trinity. Far from being an abstract or general notion, therefore, *ousia* as applied to God had an intensely personal and concrete meaning" ("The Triunity of God in the Nicene Theology of the Fourth Century," in *Theological Dialogue Between Orthodox & Reformed Churches*, Vol. 2, ed. T.F. Torrance [Edinburgh: Scottish Academic Press, 1993], p. 11).

36.   See Lossky, *Mystical*, pp. 45-46.

37.   See *The Seven Ecumenical Councils, NPNFCC*, 2nd Ser., Vol. XIV, ed. H.R. Percival (Grand Rapids: Eerdmans), p. 189.

38.   See Lossky, *Orthodox*, p. 35. Cf. D.M. Baillie, *God Was in Christ: An Essay on Incarnation and Atonement* (Londer: Faber & Faber, 1961), 118-122.

39.   See Lossky, *Orthodox*, p. 36.

40. See Lossky, *Mystical*, p. 66. Cf. The Creed of Saint Athanasius (commonly so called): "Whosoever would be saved / needeth before all things to hold fast the Catholic Faith. Which Faith except a man keep whole and undefiled, / without doubt he will perish eternally. Now the Catholic Faith is this, / that we worship one God in Trinity, and the Trinity in Unity..." (BCP Canada, 1962, p. 695). The phrase "faith seeking understanding" was the original title of St. Anselm's *Proslogion*.

Calvin writes that God so proclaims himself the sole God as to offer himself to be contemplated clearly in three Persons. "Unless we grasp these, only the bare and empty name of God flits about in our brains, to the exclusion of the true God" (Inst., I, xiii, 2).

41. See Lossky, *Mystical*, p. 47. Lossky quotes Gregory Nazianzen: "When I say *God*, I mean Father, Son and Holy Ghost; for Godhead is neither diffused beyond these, so as to introduce a multitude of gods, nor yet bounded by a smaller compass than these, so as to condemn us for a poverty-stricken conception of deity, either Judaizing to save the monarchy, or falling into Hellenism by the multitude of our gods" (Oratio XLV, 4).

42. See Philip Schaff, *The Creeds of Christendom*, Vol. II (Grand Rapids: Baker, 1983), p. 60.

43. See Basil (*NPNFCC*), IV, 6, p. 5.

44. See Basil, V, 7, p. 5.

45. See Basil, p. 5, n. 4.

46. See Basil, VI, 14, p. 8.

47. See Basil, VI, 15, p. 9.

48. See Basil, VIII, 18, p. 12.

49. See Basil, VIII, 20, p. 14.

50.   See Basil, VIII, 21, p. 14.

51.   See Basil, IX, 22, p. 15.

52.   See Basil, IX, 23, pp. 15-16. See our section on "Sanctification and Deification."

53.   See Basil, X, 25-26, p. 17.

54.   See Basil, XIII, 29-30, pp. 18-19.

55.   See Basil, XIV, 31-33, pp. 19-21.

56.   See Basil, XV, 35, p. 22.

57.   See Basil, XV, 36, p. 22.

58.   See Basil, XVI, pp. 23ff.

59.   See Basil, XVII, 43, p. 27, cf. Note 41 above.

60.   See Basil, XVIII, 44, p. 28.

61.   See Basil, XVIII, 45, p. 28.

62.   See Basil, XIX, 48, p. 30.

63.   See Basil, XIX, 49, p. 31.

64.   See Basil, XXI, 52, p. 33.

65.   See Basil, XXII, 53, p. 34.

66.   See Basil, XXIV, 56-57, p. 36.

67.   See Basil, XXVI, 64, p. 40.

68.   See Basil, XXVII, 65-68, pp. 40-43.

69.   See Basil, XXIX, 71, p. 45.

70.   See Basil, XXIX, 72-74, pp. 45-47.

71.   The Leiden Synopsis of 1581 by John. Polyander, Andr. Rivetus, Ant. Walaeus, and Ant. Thyssius said, "What the Son of God

was by nature, the Son of man became by the grace of union. And hence Mary is called *mater Domini* [mother of the Lord] (Lk 1:35) and by the ancients *theotokos, deipara*" (XXV, 24-25), as quoted by H.L.J. Heppe, *Reformed Dogmatics: Set out and illustrated from the sources*, fwd. K. Barth, ed. E. Bizer, tr. G.T. Thomson (London: Geo. Allen & Unwin, (Ger. 1861) 1950), p. 418. Johannes Wollebius (1586-1629) wrote, "Mary ought not only to be called mother of Christ (as the Nestorians admitted), but also the mother of God" (*Compendium Theologiae Christianae*, I, xvi, 1626), in *Reformed Dogmatics: J. Wollebius, G. Voetius, F. Turretin*, ed. J.W. Beardslee III (New York: Oxford University Press, 1965), p. 94. Leonardus Riissenius wrote, "Concretely and specifically Mary is rightly called *theotokos* or *Deipara*, because she bore him who is also God..." (*F. Turretini Compendium Theologiae...*, XI, 17, 1695), as quoted in Heppe, p. 444. Karl Barth wrote, "To a certain extent it amounts to a test of the proper understanding of the incarnation of the Word, that as Christians and theologians we do not reject the description of Mary as the "mother of God," but in spite of its being overloaded by the so-called Mariology of the Roman Catholic Church, we affirm and approve of it as a legitimate expression of christological truth" in *Church Dogmatics*, Vol. I/2, *The Doctrine of the Word of God*, tr. G.T. Thomson & H. Knight (Edinburgh: T. & T. Clark, 1956, 1963), p. 138.

72.   See Schaff op. cit., pp. 62-63.

73.   See *St. Athanasius on the Incarnation: The treatise De incarnatio Verbi Dei*, tr. a Religious of C,S,M.V., intr. C.S. Lewis (London: Mowbray, 1963), VIII, 54, p. 93.

74.   See *Calvin's Commentaries: The Epistle of Paul the Apostle to the Hebrews and the First and Second Epistles of St. Peter*, tr. W.B. Johnston (Grand Rapids: Eerdmans, 1963, 1970), p. 330.

75.   See *NPNFCC*, second series, Vol. VII, *S. Cyril of Jerusalem, S. Gregory Nazianzen*, tr. C.G. Browne & J.E. Swallow (Grand Rapids: Eerdmans), p. 426. Oratio XLV (Easter, II).

76.   See Lossky, *Mystical*, pp. 154-155.

77.   See Lukas Vischer, "The Holy Spirit—Source of Sanctification: Reflections on Basil the Great's Treatise on the Holy Spirit," in *Theological Dialogue Between Orthodox and Reformed Churches*, Vol. 2, p. 102.

78.   See Archimandrite Vasileios of Stavronikita, *Hymn of Entry: Liturgy and Life in The Orthodox Church*, tr. E. Briere (Crestwood, NY: St. Vladimir's Seminary Press: 1984), pp. 29, 32-33, 35-36.

The Trinity in
The Nineteenth Century

Kenneth Hamilton

EACH century's ways of thinking are in reaction to those of the previous century—while also carrying over many of the presuppositions of the outlook now believed to be outmoded. The eighteenth century reacted sharply against the strong religious enthusiasms of the seventeenth century. *Enthusiasm*, indeed, became a word of reproach equivalent to *fanaticism*. The great watchword of the eighteenth century was *reason*, in the sense of reasonableness or good sense. In the nineteenth century this reasonableness seemed both ignoble and trivial as that century began to exalt the heroic dimension of the human spirit and the inner consciousness that went beyond reason.

The established churches up to the nineteenth century had remained staunchly Trinitarian.[1] But during the eighteenth century religious opinions that had previously been called Arian or Socinian took the name of Unitarian, and Unitarian churches became part of the scene in England and in the United States during the century's later years. Unitarianism fitted well into the desire for a reasonable Christianity,[2] allowing more emphasis upon Jesus as the unique teacher of God's commands than did the religious philosophy of deism which was influential in France, Germany and America. Both Unitarians and deists, however, rejected revelation as superfluous because reason could tell us all we needed to know about the Creator and His creation. What went by the name of *revelation* was pretty much the same as the dogmas invented by churchly authorities (including the incomprehensible dogma of the Trinity); and trust in authority instead of reason inevitably led to superstition.

The issue of authority, in fact, was the central issue for nineteenth-century churchmen and theologians. Even for Christian thinkers it seemed often necessary to establish the validity of religion in general before going on to speak of the content of Christian belief. This was because exponents of the Enlightenment (deists and allied thinkers) contended that priests and kings had invented religion to keep the masses in subjection through fear of authority. But those Dark Ages were now ending. The future belonged to enlightened minds believing only what their own intellects showed them to be undoubted and universal truths. If all religions were superstitions merely, then Christianity was already refuted.

A possible answer to the Enlightenment's attack upon all religion except "the religion of reason" was provided at the dawning of the nineteenth century by the Romantic movement in literature and the arts. For the Romantics, man was not simply a machine endowed with a brain, but a spirit moved by wonder, reaching out to the dimension of the infinite and things invisible. With this approach, religion could be shown to be no artificial social product but something as natural to the human condition as breathing and dreaming.

In 1799 the Berlin preacher and theologian Friedrich Schleiermacher published his influential *On Religion: Speeches to its Cultured Despisers*. He argued that religion was essentially "a sense and taste for the infinite." The various world religions had sprung from great individuals in whom the self-consciousness of being spiritual beings had been most highly developed. These individuals could be called "Mediators" because they helped others to realize that they too, though finite, were joined to the Infinite. The Founder of Christianity was the greatest in the long line of Mediators, for He did more than teach. He asked for faith in himself, which was to invite

His followers to share in that perfect consciousness of being at one with the Infinite which He possessed.

Schleiermacher reacted to the narrow rationalism of the Enlightenment, yet he shared with the rationalists the presupposition that authority in religion lay within ourselves. He simply enlarged the boundaries of human reason to include what he called "feeling." By "feeling" he meant more than emotion, although emotion was its accompaniment. He compared religious feeling with music in not being located in any of its constituent parts but in "a self-contained revelation of the world."

Later, writing as a Christian theologian in *The Christian Faith* (1821-1822), Schleiermacher spoke of God rather than of the Infinite as he wrote about the various traditional Christian doctrines. His starting point in self-consciousness of our oneness with the Infinite, all the same, remained unaltered. Thus, his treament of the Trinity was limited to an appended conclusion. Here he declared that Trinitarian doctrine "is not an immediate utterance concerning the Christian self-consciousness. "We have only to do," he wrote, "with the God-consciousness given in our self-consciousness along with our consciousness of the world."[3] In other words, he was reiterating his view of religion being a consciousness of the Infinite and of Jesus Christ being the first human fully to possess that consciousness. Our religious feeling was the sole authority required to give an understanding of ourselves and our world. In keeping with this assumption, Schleiermacher acknowledged no dividing line between revelation and inspiration. Both were as much natural as supernatural, being as they were an inward certainty.[4]

Where inward certainty was fully authoritative, everything pertaining to actual events in this finite world appeared to be of no religious value. Hence, Schleiermacher set aside as irrelevant the doctrines of Creation, the Resurrection, and Scripture as the primary authority for Christian belief.[5] Perhaps no more striking evidence can be produced to show how, when the centrality of Trinitarian doctrine is abandoned, other Christian doctrines fall like tumbling dominoes. For belief in the One God, Father, Son and Holy Spirit, is the recognition that Christianity is a revealed faith based on the authority of sacred Scripture.

Schleiermacher was sufficiently a child of the eighteenth century to distrust speculative thinking (the reason he gave for refusing to discuss the Trinity). On the other hand, his contemporary and fellow academic in Berlin, the philosopher G.W.F. Hegel, became the speculative thinker *par excellence*. Hegel had been educated in a theological seminary; he held that religion and philosophy are in substance identical, only differing in that religion used pictorial language while philosophy expressed itself in concepts. Like Schleiermacher, Hegel was strongly influenced by the Romantic movement—indeed his philosophical system has been called "Romanticism made rational." As with many of the Romantics, life (in the sense of what was dynamic as opposed to static) was Hegel's central preoccupation. He undertook to explain the universe as an endless process of becoming. In this he went far beyond Schleiermacher's understanding about the relation between the finite and the Infinite.

Schleiermacher had characterized this relation by saying that religion was the feeling of absolute dependence (upon God/the Infinite). Hegel retorted that, in that case, the most religious creature in Berlin was his dog. In place of the capacity of the finite to receive the Infinite he held God to be infinite Process. The Infinite gave rise to its opposite, the finite universe, and then proceeded to evolve in the direction of a union of the two in Absolute Spirit, the Universal. This triad of *thesis, antithesis,* and *synthesis* (which has been called facetiously "The Three Weird Sisters") may well have been derived by Hegel from the Christian Trinity. In any event, he took the doctrine of the Trinity to be the same as his threefold dialectic—though "merely pictorial."[6]

Schleiermacher and Hegel together cast a long shadow over the nineteenth century—and, indeed, over the twentieth also. Schleiermacher's definition of religion gave rise to the whole enterprise of basing faith upon "Christian experience" and therefore of considering doctrine to be of small importance. Samuel Taylor Coleridge and F.D. Maurice were among the first in England to adopt self-consciousness as the locus of faith. Both began as Unitarians but became Anglicans and therefore accepted the Trinity in principle. For them, doctrines could be accepted as revealed because they answered our intuitions. In America Horace Bushnell bent his New England Evangelicalism to accommodate Schleiermacher and Coleridge. He wrote of the Trinity in *God in Christ* (1849) and *Christ in Theology* (1851). Insisting upon the Father co-suffering with the Son, Bushnell agonized over whether God was threefold in himself or merely in relation to the finite consciousness.

Hegel's followers soon split into two camps. Left-wing Hegelians adopted first pantheism and then atheism.[7] Right-wing Hegelians thought that Absolute Idealism could be reconciled with orthodox Christianity. German Idealism was the inspiration of Ralph Waldo Emerson. His famous *Address* at the Harvard Divinity School in 1838 about a wholly interior deity scandalized even the Unitarians among whom he had been raised. Hegel was little known in England until the 1890s.[8] From then until the 1920s, Hegelianism enjoyed a renascence. The neo-Hegelian philosophers T.H. Green, F.H. Bradley, and Bernard Bosanquet profoundly influenced such leading Anglican theologians as W.H. Moberly and William Temple. This Hegelianized Christianity, all the same, was too rarified to make much impression upon the life of the churches. Only when Idealism spawned Process philosophy with Samuel Alexander and A.N. Whitehead did a wider awareness of the legacy of Hegel enter the consciousness of English Christians in the 1920s.

In the second half of the nineteenth century, two developments had a devastating effect upon church people at every level—the theological seminary, the church assembly, the pulpit, and the pew. These were the Darwinian theory of evolution and the historical criticism of the Bible. Both seemed to remove all authority from Scripture and thus to sweep Christian doctrine into the rubbish heap of outmoded beliefs. This situation was addressed by a newly influential German theologian, Albrecht Ritschl.

In the 1840s, Ritschl had followed the school of F.C. Bauer, who applied the Hegelian theory of progressive historical development to the origins of Christianity and the rise of the Christian church. But by mid-century Ritschl was repudiating speculative systems, and over the next forty years he wrote untiringly on what he believed to be the genuinely historical Christian faith proclaimed by Jesus. He cut away the ground of scepticism concerning the reliability of the Christian message of salvation by insisting that religion dealt in value judgments, and for Christian believers Jesus was valued as God. This did not allow us, of course, to posit a Trinity. Jesus, through His life and death, has fulfilled His vocation to reconcile us to God and to establish the church as the means whereby the kingdom of God, the true community, should extend to bring full social regeneration upon earth. Such is the special revelation acknowledged by Christians, and therefore God is known as the Father and Jesus Christ as the Son. God is known in the church through the same Spirit by which God knows himself. Beyond these statements we cannot go.

What commended the Ritschlian theology to many of his contemporaries was that his system seemed to be much closer to the New Testament than other theologies, whether traditional or modern. Its emphasis upon the kingdom of God especially, was welcomed. Ritschl himself believed that he had recovered the original message of Jesus more fully than even the Protestant Reformers of the sixteenth century, while meeting the objections to Christian faith raised by the modern mind. Nevertheless, looking back today, we can see that Ritschl produced one more variation upon the nineteenth-century theme of the authority of human consciousness.

Ritschl imagined himself to have broken free from both Schleiermacher and Hegel: from the individualistic "mysticism" of the former and from the speculative "metaphysics" of the latter. Unconsciously, though, he was dependent upon Schleiermacher's concept of "self-consciousness" (shifted to the sphere of moral consciousness, making value judgments authoritative) for his view of the validity of religion. And he took from Hegel the concept of history as an evolutionary process bringing all things to perfection.

His understanding of the kingdom of God as the progressive social regeneration of humanity had tenuous connections with the New Testament but accorded well with the belief in inevitable progress prevailing in the later years of the nineteenth century.

In his own lifetime, critics accused Ritschl of returning to an eighteenth-century view of religion as ethics—for instance, to that of Immanuel Kant's *Religion Within the Bounds of Reason Alone* (1793). The influence of Kant was gladly admitted by Ritschl, yet it was evident that he had broken through all the limits surrounding Kant's purely rational faith, commending Christianity as a revealed faith and being ready to accept the reality of miracles. At the same time, Ritschl's apparent willingness to uphold most of the central beliefs of traditional Christian faith was hedged about by the boundaries he himself had drawn. He was willing to speak of a special revelation in Christianity because he claimed that the aims of the Christian community surpassed anything found in other religions and because the Christian God was known uniquely as "Love."[9] Since these "revelations" were called by that name simply on the basis of our human value-judgments, however, there was little evidence that Ritschl's Christian faith was much more than a moral code buttressed by belief in God and immortality—which was Kant's religion. It has been pointed out frequently that Ritschl's central work, *Justification and Reconciliation* (1870-1874), reversed the order of Christ's saving work as traditionally presented, making our reconciliation with God the result of our own moral efforts.

Ritschlian theology dominated the last quarter of the nineteenth century and the first thirty years of the twentieth so thoroughly that when people spoke of "liberal Protestantism" it was really Ritschlianism they meant. Ritschl's followers, like Hegel's, split into a right and a left wing—although the division was not nearly so great but instead was a matter of gradations. Right-wing Ritschlians accepted fully the historical criticism of the Bible and, to some extent, Ritschl's stress upon the priority of the ethical element in Christianity, while adhering to the historic creeds as the necessary foundation for Christian belief. Left-wing Ritschlians, on the other hand, wished to abridge all doctrinal statements to what they thought to be the original teachings of Jesus himself. "Not faith in Jesus but the faith of Jesus," became their watchword. Adolf von Harnack, who wrote extensively on the early Church and the development of Church doctrine, argued that the elevation of dogma to become the defining element in Christian faith was the result of "the acute Hellenization" of Christianity. In his influential short work, *What is Christianity?* (1900), he identified the leading features of the preaching of Jesus with three themes: the Kingdom of God and its coming; God the Father and the infinite value of the human soul; and the higher righteousness and the commandment of love.[10]

In attempting to identify the essence of Christianity, Harnack used an image that was to appear again and again: the kernel and the husk. For him, of course, there could be no doubt that the kernel was the original ethical teaching of Jesus and the husk the doctrinal accretions of centuries of churchly teaching. This view became entrenched in the popular antithesis: the Jesus of history *or* the Christ of faith. (Here the supposition was that there was actually no alternative, since the Jesus of history was real and the Christ of faith a myth.) It was not until 1910 that such belief in the "simple" teachings of Jesus was made to look simple-minded by the appearance of Albert Schweitzer's *The Quest for the Historical Jesus.* While Schweitzer's portrait of Jesus as a self-deluded apocalyptist was highly questionable, it at least made the liberal-humanist Jesus appear to be the modern reconstruction it was. Yet the liberal viewpoint was so entrenched in most mainline Protestant churches that it lived on and still persists—overlaid, it is true, by so many contemporary ideologies that it is barely recognizable today as a branch from the Ritschlian tree.

At the turn of the new century, the Scottish theologians James Orr, James Denney, and P.T. Forsyth challenged the Ritschlian premises and called for a return to the dogmatic basis of Christian faith. Writing in the heyday of well-attended churches, Forsyth warned that these would soon be empty if the clergy persisted in catering to "the modern mind" instead of proclaiming a gospel having authority beyond subjective preferences. For these three Scotsmen, the Trinity was the necessary starting-point for all Christian doctrine, a conviction that was soon to be voiced powerfully by the young Swiss theologian Karl Barth.

The liturgical churches were better protected by their set forms of worship from doctrinal innovations than were the churches where worship was under the direct control of the pastor, and thus showed resistance to unitarian tendencies. During the nineteenth century, the Church of Rome manifested what amounted to a siege mentality. The cause was the French Revolution and subsequent turmoil in Europe when established religion seemed to be threatened with extinction. Rome's answer was to centralize all authority in the papacy, culminating in the First Vatican Council of 1870 where the doctrine of papal infallibility was overwhelmingly affirmed. Earlier, in 1864, Pius IX had issued a Syllabus of Errors. This detailed a long list of teachings which were to be repudiated by Catholics (among the "errors," Hegelianism was easily recognizable) as well as anything tending towards the separation of church and state. It ended by condemning the view that "the Roman Pontiff can and ought to reconcile himself to, and agree with, progress, liberalism, and civilization as lately introduced." Since the Syllabus was to represent the official mindset of Rome for almost a hundred years, clearly all thought of revision in existing Church doctrine was off limits for faithful Catholics during the nineteenth century.

The one area where a loophole was left for departure from tradition in Roman Catholicism was that of biblical scholarship. Being the preserve of the clergy engaged in teaching, it no doubt was considered safely under ecclesiastical control. But when radical biblical criticism arose in Germany in the 1840s, some Catholic scholars pursued similar paths to that of their Protestant counterparts. No serious challenge to ecclesiastical authority appeared, however, until what became known as Catholic modernism erupted during the 1880s in Germany, France, and England. Modernism advocated a free handling of Scripture under the same scrutiny as any other book, a subordination of doctrine to the conduct of life, and an estimate of the Church not based on its presumed founding by the historical Jesus but upon its effectiveness in answering the religious needs of its present-day members.

A leader of the modernist movement was Alfred Loisy, an Old Testament professor in Paris, who leaned strongly toward pantheism. In his *L'Evarigile et L'Eglise* (1902), a reply to Harnack's *What is Christianity?*, he reversed the German theologian's metaphor of the kernel and the husk. He argued that Christian origins were unimportant, for what mattered was what the church had become under the guidance of the Spirit. For the modernists generally, the Spirit moving in history was the supreme authority. The identification of this Spirit with the Third Person of the Christian Trinity was for the modernists more a convenience than a reality. The English Jesuit George Tyrell, for example, in *Christianity at the Cross Roads* (1909), envisaged Christianity as a path to a universal religion still to come.[11] In 1907, modernism was condemned by Pius X, who termed it "a synthesis of all the heresies," and its clerical advocates were excommunicated.

The Roman Church's refusal to admit the slightest inroad of "progressive" thinking into its fold during the nineteenth century (and, indeed, during the first half of the twentieth also) actually strengthened its position worldwide. To be a "Catholic" meant to belong to a community bound together by an unquestioned body of beliefs and by common practices embracing all aspects of daily life. The Romantic movement, which on one side had glorified the spirit of man as the self-sufficient source of unlimited freedom, on the other side had reacted against the arid rationalism of the Enlightenment and thus had seen the Middle Ages as a time of heroism and social solidarity. Rome benefitted from this revulsion against "soulless" modernity and consequent nostalgia for the Age of Faith. Many of the lapsed were won back and numerous converts made in the ranks of the intelligentsia. As the century wore on and the so-called fruits of progress were increasingly revealed to be hollow, the claim, "Europe is the Faith" (i.e., Western civilization is identical with Roman Catholicism) seemed justified. Meanwhile, as disadvantaged immigrants from Europe poured into North America, Catholics found in their church the means of preserving their identity in an alien culture.[12]

The established Church of England similarly expanded overseas during the nineteenth century and through its missionary efforts grew to become the widespread Anglican Communion. In its homeland, all the same, it did not fare so well. Its privileged position *vis-a-vis* the State largely disappeared when restrictions were withdrawn first from Nonconformists and then from Roman Catholics and Jews. The great influence of the evangelical wing of the church during the early decades of the century waned. The High Church Movement, which began in the 1830s, made a real impact. With its stress upon doctrinal orthodoxy and Anglican spiritual traditions, it brought about a notable revival. But when two of its most prominent leaders (John Henry Newman and Henry Edward Manning) went over to Rome, it suffered a permanent setback though remaining a potent force. That, which was called the Broad Church, was less a cohesive movement than the efforts of a few notables such as Thomas Arnold and Benjamin Jowett to make the Church of England a truly inclusive national church, doctrinally tolerant, and open to the issues of the times. As the century progressed, it was evident that the church generally was losing ground in spite of having produced many outstanding leaders.

Unlike Catholicism (which was expanding rapidly), Anglicanism in nineteenth-century England lacked followeers who gave it unquestioning loyalty—half the population, after all, belonged to Nonconformist congregations. The cynical called it, "The Conservative Party at prayer," and the fact that Nonconformists were mostly political Liberals gave point to the jibe. Churchgoing remained an accepted social ritual among the middle and upper classes until after the First World War, when it collapsed catastrophically. It was hardly accidental that the emptying of the Nonconformist Church also coincided with the near-extinction of political Liberalism.

Apart from Unitarianism and some fringe sects, the English churches, both Established and Free, remained doctrinally based throughout the century, with the Trinity as the unquestioned center of doctrine. Until the 1880s, Continental theology and biblical criticism impinged only slightly upon British thinking.[13] The dismissal of W. Robertson Smith from his Old Testament university chair by the Free Church of Scotland in 1881, however, brought the historical criticism of the Bible into the open. From then on, modernism was a raging issue in all the churches.[14] The Modern Churchmen's Union was founded in 1898 to encourage the revision of Anglican doctrine to accord with contemporary thinking. It made newspaper headlines occasionally yet had little direct influence. Ritschlian Liberal Protestantism became widespread only as the next century progressed. Then it became pervasive.

In Britain, the Church of England's historic role of taking up a mediating position between extremes had a moderating effect upon all the churches. In multi-denominational North America conservative and liberal churches tended to emphasize their differences. There, too, direct contact with European thinking had its effect. As the West was opened up, so came Continental Protestants as well as Catholic immigrants, and these were usually from conservative churches. When theological seminaries were established in the new American states, the practice long continued of bringing teachers from the Old Country. A parallel development was seen in Canada also. English-speaking Canadians had from the first looked to either England or Scotland for leadership and only gradually raised native-born scholars for their theological schools. After this happened, American influences increased and had some effect upon the spread of liberal ideas among the churches. By 1925, when the United Church of Canada was formed from Methodist, Presbyterian and Congregationalist denominations, post-Ritschlian liberal principles that played down doctrine and elevated practical issues of church organization made this early experiment in church union possible. These same principles, carried further, would open the way as well to a wholesale abandonment of doctrine and the importation of alien ideologies.

Looking back, we can see how all the ingredients found in the mix of contemporary theology and church life were contained already in the movements of thought born during the nineteenth century. The new theological systems and innovations in Christian practice have all been derived from elements brought to the fore in that era. What the Christian revisionists of the nineteenth century did not do—and what has been done today—was to introduce elements from other religions and pagan practices and to include these under the umbrella-name of Christianity. Yet even here the nineteenth century pointed the way by conceiving Christian faith to be a sub-species of the human enterprise of discovering religion within the human consciousness.

The fatal move by nineteenth-century thinkers was to remove the locus of authority in faith from the creedal basis of the Christian church to self-consciousness. P.T. Forsyth, who had studied under Ritschl, lived for fifty-two years in the nineteenth century and only twenty-one years in the twentieth. He feared for the life of the churches in the new century if they continued to overlook where the sole authority for Christians lay in the self-revelation of the Triune God as believed by the church on the basis of Holy Scripture. He wrote:

> We can sanctify Humanity only by the worship of One who is in but not of it. We can hallow society only by hallowing it within the society of the Church. And the Church can take and keep its spiritual place as the Church of the Living God only if by its living God we mean no glorified individual, but the Triune God who is the peculiar revelation of Christ. For the Christian God is not the Father, but the Father of our Lord Jesus Christ in the Spirit. It was such a God in such a revelation, such a self-donation of His in Son and Spirit, that created the Church; and no other God can sustain it.[15]

This statement answers every attempt of nineteenth-century thinkers to downgrade the importance of the doctrine of the Trinity, to abolish it or to turn it into a quasi-Christian speculation. And it does so out of concern for the continued existence of the churches calling themselves Christian in the future.

NOTES

1. English Presbyterian congregations, however, dissolved into Unitarian ones during the seventeenth century. The Presbyterian Church in England was refounded in the nineteenth century by members of the Church of Scotland.

2. The English philosopher John Locke had an extraordinary influence upon eighteenth-century thinking. His *Reasonableness of Christianity as Delivered in the Scriptures* (1695) admitted the supernatural and did not challenge any individual Christian doctrines but maintained that beliefs must be rationally acceptable.

3. F. Schleirmacher, *The Christian Faith*, ed. H.R. MacIntosh and J.S. Stewart Edinburgh: T. & T. Clark, 1928), pp. 735, 748.

4. Ibid., 51, 60.

5. For Schleiermacher, anything connected with historical aspects of life had a religious significance, since religion has to do with the impression we receive of our relation with the divine. Thus Creation signifies not an historical beginning of the world but an eternal relation of dependence upon God, the Resurrection signifies Christ's enduring influence upon us, and the New Testament is significant only as the "first member in the series" of presentations of faith in Christ. (The Old Testament, being the Holy Book of Judaism, has no essential connection with the Christ who founded a wholly new religion. It has been kept for historical reasons and has no normative passion in Christian faith.)

6. See G.W.F. Hegel, *Philosophy of Religion* (London: 1895) 3:12. Because evolving Spirit involved other "moments" besides the three fundamental developments, Hegel noted that this Spirit

might also be regarded as a Quaternity or even a Quintity (*The Phe-nomenologv of Mind*, London, rev. ed. 1931, 772).

7. David Friedrich (whose notorious *Life of Jesus* [1835-6] treated the Gospel narratives as pure myths), in his own development exemplified the transition from pantheism to materialism. Ludwig Feuerbach's *The Essence of Religion* (1841) took religion to be the external projection of the internal human consciousness. Feuerbach was regarded by Karl Marx as having given the final word on religion and thus prepared the way for his own substitution of Dialectical Materialism for Hegel's dialectic of Absolute Spirit.

8. German thought generally was almost ignored in England during the greater part of the nineteenth century. Scotland, however, had closer connections with the European mainland. In the 1820s and 1830s, Thomas Carlyle, who was educated at Edinburgh University, endeavored to make German philosophy known to the British public. He and Emerson were mutual admirers. Yet, in spite of his immense literary reputation, Carlyle's efforts achieved meager results. During the later years of the century many Scottish theological scholars went for studies at German universities. The Scottish Congregationalist A.M. Fairburn's *The Place of Christ in Modern Theology* (1893) was one of the early books to give a full overview of developments in German theology.

9. Some critics of Ritschl have expressed surprise that his system could allow him to posit a personal God. But Kant had supplied this basis for his belief when he maintained that there could be nothing good in the world (or out of it) except *a good will*. Only a personal Being could have a will, then, as Ritschl saw it. And the distinction between good and evil could be made only by beings having free will to choose between them—that was, to make value-judgments. God's will being wholly good meant that He was personal and completely loving.

10. Harnack was actually the founder of the Social Gospel movement on the European mainland; although the Social Gospel is usually associated with North America, especially with the work of Washington Gladden (*Social Salvation*, 1902) and Walter Rauschenbusch (*Christianity and the Social Crisis*, 1907; *A Theology for the Social Gospel*, 1917). In England, the Social Gospel built on the not-wholly-forgotten Christian Socialism of the mid-1800s as taught by Charles Kingsley under the inspiration of F.D. Maurice.

11. An influence upon Catholic modernism was the French Protestant theologian Auguste Sabatier. At first influenced by Schleiermacher and Ritschl, Sabatier came to view religion as having its origin in human psychology and having its impact upon all generations through its symbolic power. His *Religions of Authority and the Religion of the Spirit* (1903) set forth his mature convictions of the perennial religion persisting through all ages and developing new doctrines to suit the evolving self-consciousness.

12. The appeal of Rome to both cradle Catholics and converts lay very largely in its appearance of universality transcending national boundaries (as typified in the Latin mass) and also in the strong national traditions within the church giving it a cultural attraction. In addition, of course, unchanging doctrinal standards and traditional moral ones (reinforced by the Confessional) gave a feeling of security to the faithful. It is interesting to see how the reforms of Vatican II undermined that security. In the 1950s the Roman Catholic Church had never been more confident about its future, with expanding congregations and a plentiful supply of Catholics entering religious "vocations." All that changed only a few years after Vatican II and now even the survival of an undivided church has been seriously questioned.

13. See Note 8. The historical criticism of the Bible impinged upon the British consciousness with "the Colenso affair" in the

1860s. Bishop Collenso of Natal, South Africa published works on both the New and the Old Testament rejecting traditional authorships and suggesting the need for revised Anglican Church doctrine. As a result he was excommunicated. But Natal was far from England and the bishop was seen as an eccentric individual rather than as a portent of a coming threat to orthodox thinking in the Anglican communion.

14. The acceptance of the new biblical criticism in England was facilitated through such Anglican scholars as Brook Foss Westcott and Fenton Hort, who fully accepted the historical-critical approach but reached conclusions harmonizing with Anglican faith and doctrine. Thus the modernist/traditionalist issue was never so contentious as it was in America, and heresy charges were rare in any of the Nonconformist Churches.

15. See P.T. Forsyth, *The Principle of Authority in Relation to Certainty, Sanctity and Society* (London: Hodder & Stoughton, 1913), p. 259. Forsyth had been theologically liberal in his early days. He remained an avid reader of contemporary German theology always.

The Church Challenged: The Trinity and Modern Culture

Andrew Stirling

A rather forlorn and confused Sunday school teacher came to me for advice. Her predicament was that a student had confronted her with a most challenging question: how can God be three and one? As many teachers would do, she endeavored to answer the inquirer with the analogy of water manifesting itself as steam, ice, and running water, while still maintaining its essential properties and substance. She also referred to C.S. Lewis' concept of a three dimensional God in which one needs all three dimensions to fully appreciate God's reality.[1] Having not satisfied the inquisitive seeker with these analogies, she retreated to the last resort of most Christians and declared that the Trinity is a mystery.

It is precisely this dilemma of trying to explain God as three persons which causes many clergy and laity to avoid the mysterious doctrine of the Trinity. Rather than wrestling with the inner life of God, they opt for a vague form of Unitarianism in the hope that this will be a more palatable option. Indeed, on the surface it appears that a simple reconstruction of Christian doctrine which avoids the complexities and seemingly illogical disparities of Trinitarian thought, might provide a firmer foundation on which to base contemporary Christian thought. It is argued by some scholars that, by removing the Trinitarian definition of God, one avoids a dogma that obfuscates the theological enterprise. By so doing we can open the church to the simple faith of Jesus.[2]

Such a perspective is appealing to those who find difficulty with Trinitarian orthodoxy on the ground that it is essentially patriarchal and that to adhere to such an outmoded theology inhibits a meaningful encounter with the modern gender-inclusive world view.[3] It also resonates with some Fundamentalists who want a simple faith that is easy to promote among a "sound bite" generation. A total reconstruction of Trinitarian thought also finds support in those who seek to broaden our definition of God to include other religious perspectives. To them, the Trinity is a singular obstacle to those who want to develop a theology of religions and extend the domain and range of ecumenical dialogue.[4]

Is the Trinity, therefore, as egregious and restrictive as some would suggest, and is the current army amassed against its precepts correct in their analysis, that by removing this historical tenet we can revitalize the faith? I argue that the Trinity is essential for the distinctive nature of Christian proclamation and beneficial to those who seek a true understanding of the biblical God. It is an encouraging venture precisely because the Trinity has survived the vicissitudes of history, and neither the challenge of theosophical heresies, new cosmologies nor humanistic philosophies have provided an adequate replacement for this revealed doctrine. It is singularly amazing, and a testimony to its timeless truth, that the Trinity is still at the core of the Christian faith and is relevant at the beginning of the third millennium.

There are moments in history, however, that require a clear apologetic defense of its precepts, and that is why Donald Bloesch, Alistair McGrath, Ted Peters, Robert Jenson, and others have recently brought the issue of the Trinity to the forefront of the Christian tradition.[5] These books are particularly timely because the various attempts at theological reconstruction have caused the church in many areas to lose confidence in its message. It is precisely this lack of conviction which has contributed to the decline of most main-line Protestant churches in Western Europe and North America. Leander Keck, for example, argues that the Protestant church is suffering a malaise and is in need of a fourth Great Awakening.[6] But on what basis is this revival to be based? In response to such a crisis, some Christians are arguing that a structural and functional renewal take place. To accomplish this, many mainline churches are currently restructuring their organizational and decision-making procedures to make them more responsive to people's needs. The Church Growth Movement has also arisen in an attempt to revitalize the church's ministry. Through a plethora of statistical and sociological surveys to substantiate the need for renewal, some modern commentators have suggested that a profound change needs to take place in worship, programs, and service. Most of these suggestions revolve around stylistic changes in the presentation of the faith. What these schools of thought overlook, and this is evident from Keck's analysis, is that the problem facing the church is a challenge to the faith's substance as well as its form. That is why in addition to these movements there is a need to examine the extent to which a lasting renewal of the church is linked to a reawakening of the Trinity's importance. There is a clear connection between the church's adherence to that doctrine and its confidence in the gospel of Jesus Christ. The corollary of this is that no meaningful and substantial growth can take place in the church without a solid rediscovery of the Trinity's importance. Merely tinkering with liturgical changes will only bring a temporary respite to the church's woes.

Why the Need for a Reawakening?

Throughout history most revivals or awakenings have taken place in response to the preaching of the Word. While at present many theological Seminaries have moved away from an emphasis on preaching as a primary ministerial function, the vast majority of church attenders still look to the proclaimed Word and the sacraments as the principal expressions of Christian belief. Contrary to the opinion that the postmodern mind rejects the didactic nature of proclamation and would rather have a more inductive method of learning, rests the fact that vibrant and growing churches emphasize preaching. What lies at the heart of the current debate on the Trinity, therefore, is not whether preaching is important, but rather what its content should be. If, as Karl Barth suggests,[7] the purpose of theological inquiry is to inform the church's proclama-tion, there is a need to reconnect Trinitarian theology with Christian proclamation. I agree with Emil Brunner that "the Trinity is a theo-logical doctrine; it is not the biblical *kerygma*. It should not be preached."[8] I nevertheless believe that you cannot have authentic proclamation without a Trinitarian foundation. The early church, for example, did not preach the Trinity *per se*, but it still used it to promote its primary message that Jesus Christ is Lord. Most of the church Fathers recognized that the death, life, and resurrection of Jesus Christ was the locus of God's encounter with humanity. However, the only way to logically uphold this belief without cre-ating another god was to explain the relationship between Jesus, the Father, and the Holy Spirit in Trinitarian terms. The Trinity, therefore, became the lens through which the early church inter-preted the inner and outer life of God. It was also the means whereby it connected the *kerygma* with dogma. The former was the public proclamation of the gospel and the latter the symbolic language of the church, which sought a deeper meaning to the faith. While some Fathers, such as the Cappadocian St. Basil, emphasised the distinction between the two in his challenge with the Arians and the Pneumatomachi, the *kerygma* and dogma of the church clearly informed each other. After all, why would one need Trinitarian dogma if the *kerygma* were not true, and how could the *kerygma* be true if God were not triune?

It would be erroneous, therefore, simply to suggest that today we can preach the content of the Bible without it being informed by Trinitarian dogma. It is precisely for this reason that Barth com-menced his *Dogmatics* with an examination of this central and unique doctrine.[9] In so doing he rejected the anti-dogmatic subjec-tivism of nineteenth-century liberal Protestantism whose ideas are still pervasive in the church today. Barth also departed from many classical Protestants who believed in the Trinity, but who consid-ered it irrelevant to the main issues of faith and salvation.

The current crisis with regard to our confidence in the gospel, therefore, is directly related to the fact that in the latter part of the twentieth century, Protestantism moved away from Barth's conviction regarding the Trinity. In the church's search for relevance and social acceptance it has jettisoned dogma and has been driven by more expedient motives. This is manifested in the often vacuous nature of proclamation. The heart of the crisis is the content of proclamation, and if we relegate the Trinity to a simple matter of mystery we will have insipid sermons and dying churches. Ted Peters illustrated this best when he recounted the story of a Bavarian priest, who on the Feast of the Trinity announced to his congregation that, because it was so great a mystery, there would be no sermon![10] It is precisely this attitude which undermines the power of Christian proclamation and leaves it vulnerable to the vagaries and machinations of the human imagination which wants to reinvent God.

Singing the Lord's Song in a Strange Land
THE CHALLENGE OF SYNCRETISM.

A careful reading of the signs of the times (Mt 16:3) suggests that the church's reluctance to espouse Trinitarian dogma is related to profound changes which are taking place in Western culture. Apart from the fact that our culture has ceased to be based on the Bible, let alone its Lord, there are also popular trends which are causing us to move away from a distinctive understanding of God as Trinity.

The first of these is the impulse to adopt a form of cultural syncretism which seeks to create social and religious harmony by joining the world's religions into one voice or belief. Because the Trinitarian view of God is ostensibly associated with Western and European thought, those who desire a more inclusive and pluralistic cultural expression are willing to jettison the "old" understanding of God as Father, Son, and Holy Spirit. This movement is due in part to the expansion of worldwide information[11] and the phenomenon of international migration. These trends have broken down the barriers of cultural isolation and have exposed Western Christians to hitherto rarely known conceptions of the divine. In most urban centers in North America, Christians find themselves living and conversing with people of other faiths and traditions and find their old beliefs challenged by Islam's dogmatic monotheism and the godless beliefs of Hinduism. In a sincere attempt to find common ground on matters of faith, some Christians have strayed from their faith by overlooking the distinctive nature of their own belief. Some have even gone so far as to question its legitimacy.

Evidence of this is found in the popularity of Karen Armstrong's *A History of God*, in which she questions the so called "man made" doctrines of faith and seeks to create "a vibrant new faith for the twenty first century."[12] Armstrong takes the great themes of the monotheistic traditions (Judaism, Christianity, Islam) and then deconstructs them to the point of diminishing their peculiarities. This is a popular methodology, for it creates a form of syncretism which relativizes these historical expressions of God. It leads eventually to the belief that God is the product of our collective imaginations rather than emphasizing that we were created by God. Therefore, in such a method, Trinitarian expressions of God are seen merely as our attempt to explain God in the language and categories of Greek philosophy and are subject to change in the modern world.

If one adopts this view of the development of dogma, it naturally follows that all doctrinal statements are equally valid and that any differences are simply the product of cultural conditions. Such a belief is particularly palatable to those who ascribe to a belief that the principal thrust of history is directed toward the unity of humankind and the creation of a "one world" philosophy. The devotees of this perspective maintain that this was God's original intention as expressed in creation and that further religious developments (i.e., the call and election of Israel) were merely deviations from God's plan. This, of course, makes the doctrine of the Trinity redundant and in effect negates the imperative of personal faith. It also diminishes the importance of claims of truth and simply reduces them to personal opinions. This is exacerbated by the naive hope that lasting human unity can be created by denying the uniqueness of religious dogma.

THE RISE OF PAGANISM AND PANTHEISM.

The second trend in culture is the reemergence of what are euphemistically called "earth-based" religions. These have arisen primarily because of two forces. The first is the well meaning desire to have a closer association with native or aboriginal societies, some of which still hold on to "pagan" beliefs. Many Western (Christian) societies feel guilty for the way in which they colonized and oppressed the native community as they considered them to be less than full persons. Too frequently religious conversion went hand in hand with the imposition of colonial rule; the desire to convert the "pagan" to Christianity led to various forms of exploitation with force. Therefore, in an attempt to correct the errors of the past, our Christian society has adopted some of the aboriginal (pre-Christian) beliefs in an attempt to find a theological common ground.

The second appeal is in dealing with the environmental crisis. Because of the threat to our ecological system, there is a desire on the part of caring people to have a renewed understanding of nature's value. By emphasizing the spiritual value of creation and God's presence within it, environmentally conscious people are causing society to reevaluate its attitude toward the earth by stressing its divine nature. They believe that if one pollutes the world, one pollutes God.

These pantheistic movements essentially believe that there is only one substance in which everything exists and that God and nature are the same reality.[13] While there are clearly diverse expressions of this thinking, ranging from Wiccan spirituality to the heterogeneous movement called "New Age," the principle is still the same.

The doctrine of the Trinity clearly contradicts these positions precisely because it emphasizes the transcendent nature of God, who exists independently from creation. While it affirms that God created the world (*ex nihilo*), God is nevertheless above and separate from His creation. He does, however, reveal himself in creation in the person of Jesus Christ, whose sacrifice is celebrated in the sacraments.

THE RISE OF FEMINISM.

The third trend is the rise of a profound ideological movement called Feminism. This movement seeks to restore the balance of power between men and women in society. At the heart of its conviction is the belief that history needs to be revised so that we can reconstruct our understanding of the nature of humanity. By drawing primarily on feminine experience, it also reexamines the nature of God in an attempt to make the deity more gender-inclusive. Its exponents realize that the symbols and language of religion play a significant role in determining the structures of power in society. Because Christianity is the world's most prominent religion, and in the West its most influential, Christian feminist theologians have sought to deal with the greatest obstacle to their task, namely, the central figure of Jesus Christ. Because He was male and called God "Abba" (Daddy), and spoke in terms of *His* kingdom, feminists have tried to overcome the maleness of the language of the New Testament. Central to the task of dealing with this linguistic barrier is the reformulation of Trinitarian language. As Donald Bloesch explains,[14] feminists have replaced the traditional Trinitarian formula with a less ontological understanding by referring to God as "Creator, Redeemer, Sustainer," or as the United Church of Canada is exploring "Source of Life, Living Word, Wisdom of Creation."[15] A similar attempt is being made to separate the historical figure (Jesus) from the two other persons in the Trinity by replacing Father with Mother[16] and by claiming that the Spirit is female.[17] Sometimes, this same method is applied to Jesus himself by separating the two facets of Christ's name, Jesus and Christ. Pamela Dickey Young, for example, thinks that this can be useful:

> Here I refer to the identification of the Second Person of the Trinity as "Sophia," "Lady Wisdom." When we refer not specifically to the Jesus witnessed to in the apostolic tradition but perhaps to the presence of Christ among us, reference to the Second Person of the Trinity as "she" may serve a useful and meaningful function.[18]

Dickey Young can make this assertion because she sees the role of Jesus as the One who "re-presents God."[19] This is certainly a novel approach to Christology and finds neither support nor validation in the biblical text nor the Christian tradition. It is, in fact, the antithesis of incarnational theology and is a form of modalism.

We need to ask, therefore, whether the traditional male language for God necessarily leads to a corollary that it is *ipso facto*, oppressive to women. While it is true that throughout the Christian tradition, the maleness of the Godhead has been used to justify the subjugation of women, it was never meant to lead to oppression. Indeed, the God of the Bible is a liberating God[20] who relates to humanity lovingly as "Father, Son, and Holy Spirit." It is precisely the relationship among the three persons that constitutes not only the nature of the divine, but also the name of the divine. As the Cappadocians rightly pointed out, it is the relationship between the three persons of the Trinity that reveal to us the very being of God, and to tamper with that or speak of the second person as simply the "re-presentation" of God is to deny the essential unity of the Godhead. Denying the divinity of Jesus Christ and His union of substance with the Father, also serves to undermine the fact that the gospel of Jesus Christ was not only received by women as "good news," it was actively proclaimed as such by women who were hitherto social outcasts. The fact that they saw the very being of God in Jesus Christ enhanced their dignity as women. For example, when Jesus saved the woman caught in adultery from the wrath of self-righteous men, He was not only showing the forgiveness of His Father, He was also defending the value of a woman's life.

Toward a Renewed Appreciation of the Trinity's Relevance

If these forces are at work in the church and society, how can the church still hold on to Trinitarian doctrine while at the same time being relevant to modern society? Can we take seriously the condition of the ecosystem, the plight of aboriginal people and the liberation of women and still maintain our traditional view of God?

THE LOVE OF GOD.

A number of essential aspects of the Christian faith hinge on the validity of the Trinity, and without it they would lose their authenticity. The most notable is the concept of the love of God. The New Testament makes the constant affirmation that God is love. It does not, however, affirm this as a purely philosophical ideal, but rather expresses this conviction on the basis of God's self revelation. In Johannine literature, for example, the love of God is linked to the relationship between the Father, the Son, the Spirit and humanity. "God's love was revealed among us this way: God sent His only Son into the world so that we might live through him. In this is love, not that we loved God, but that he loved us and sent his Son to be the atoning sacrifice for our sins. Beloved, since God loved us so much, we also ought to love one another....We know that we abide in him and he in us, because he has given us of his Spirit" (1Jn 4:9-13).

Herein lies the implicit connection of the three persons of the Trinity and their loving nature. Because the biblical notion of love is not an ideal concept but a relational expression, the very nature of God's love is dependant upon an inner relatedness within the Godhead. How can we say that God is love if that love is not manifested in an outward and visible way? It is only mere speculation. And how can we experience and live this love if God does not reveal it to His creature in a way we can understand? What is more understandable than a man (Jesus) who continues to be revealed through His living Spirit? As Sydney Cave explains it,

> Love must have an object, and if God existed in solitude, then love would not be essential to His being. But if within the personal unity of God there be real distinction then the love of the Father can be interpreted as going out eternally to the eternal Son in the unity of the Spirit. Creation and redemption need no longer be conceived as arbitrary acts or processes, but as the external expression of the expression of the intra personal love of God.[21]

Such a belief gives love not only an objective foundation, but also a subjective content, for in our union with Jesus Christ we experience the inner love of the Trinity. Love, therefore, ceases to be a vague passionless concept and is transformed into a powerful relationship of faith. It is also one of the reasons why the Trinity has endured, for while Luther found it a problematic dogma,[22] it nevertheless became an essential ingredient in people's experience of faith. If we ignore the Trinity, we are in danger of losing the very love we desire to experience.

I fully realize, however, that for many people their experience of the Trinitarian God has been anything but loving. Because some exponents of the Christian faith have used this dogma to justify their abuse of power in the oppression of native peoples and women, some look with suspicion upon the God of the Trinity. However, it is not the Father, Son, and Holy Spirit who are unloving and oppressive. It is those who have used God's name to justify godless behavior. Surely any expression of the divine is subject to the same abuse. It is all the more important, therefore, to examine the true relationship among the three persons as witnessed in Scripture to experience the authentic love of God. It is precisely this relationship which should be at the heart of Christian proclamation and is summarized in John's gospel and the "True Vine" address: "As the Father has loved me, so I have loved you; abide in my love....This is my commandment, that you love one another as I have loved you" (Jn 15:9ff).

THE MISSION OF THE CHURCH.

Much has been written recently regarding the importance of "community" in the Christian faith. Both the liberal and conservative wings of the church affirm the importance of the need for fellowship (*koinonia*) especially in a society which is becoming increasingly isolating and individualistic. As John Stott argues,[23] the biblical warrant asserts that it is not good for man to be alone and that congregational life and fellowship is a means of addressing this vision within society. The human need to live in community, however, must find its genesis in God's original will and purpose for humanity. Alas! It was the disobedience of the Fall which gave rise to the sin of independence and isolation and the belief that humanity could live without God. The biblical testimony is that the story of salvation was God's attempt to restore that communion, and by means of a community of people (Israel) attempted to draw all of humanity into a covenantal relationship with himself. This mission was consummated and completed with the sending of His Son Jesus Christ who, through His resurrection and ascension, created a new community which expanded the covenant community to all people.

Therefore, the church of Jesus Christ was the means whereby people could live in communion with God, through the Son and in the bond of the Spirit. This community, however, was not only the avenue whereby God expressed His saving grace, it was also meant to reflect the means whereby God is personally known. Through the community of the church we become the *koinonoi*, "partakers of the divine nature."[24] This does not mean that the distinction between God and ourselves should be overlooked. I would not go as far as Catherine Mowry Lacugna and assert that "the divine (Trinitarian) life is also our life,"[25] for one does not have to tie the future of God with the future of humanity—God is always the "wholly other." On the other hand, Lacugna is correct in asserting that God has a living relationship with humanity and is always "God For Us." It is clear from Scripture that God desires for us to be one with Him in order that He may be (eschatologically speaking) "all in all" (Eph 4:6). In this sense, as Dietrich Bonhoeffer emphasizes, we were meant to live in communion with God and others. This fellowship is not an idealized human construction but "a reality created by God in Christ in which we may participate."[26] Therefore, our union with God through a covenantal community is a spiritual reality and is fed by surrendering "all power, honor and dominion to the Holy Spirit."[27] We know true community through the Father, Son, and Holy Spirit, and we celebrate it in the church.

It is the unity of the persons of the Trinity, however, which provides the impetus for the unity of the church. If we paint a picture

of the inner life of God as a disjointed connection of three independent persons, then it follows that the church to which they give birth
could be equally fragmented. The biblical revelation, however, paints
an entirely different picture. The Father and the Son are One and
they desire that the disciples become united in that oneness through
the Paraclete (Jn 17:21). This perspective was enhanced by the writer
of Ephesians who uses the analogy of the body to describe the church
and sees the unity of the Spirit as an essential ingredient in its mission. He concludes there is "one Lord, one faith, one baptism, one
God and Father of all" (Eph 4:3-5).

The ecumenical nature and the evangelical imperative of the
church are inextricably tied to the unity of the persons of the Trinity; divisive movements and heresies are an affront to God and
diametrically opposed to the unity of the Godhead. Those who desire
to create the unity of the church without the spiritual bond of the
three persons of the Trinity will ultimately be unsuccessful in reaching their goal. We see the signs of this all around us. The greatest
threat to the unity of the church comes from the spirit of Unitarianism which diminishes the place of the Second Person Jesus Christ.
Without the recognition that Jesus Christ is one with the Father
through the Spirit, there will only be discord, and the church will
cease to be not only Trinitarian but "Christian."

THE QUEST FOR LIBERATION.

The Christian tradition has been criticized for siding with the
powerful and affluent in society, and the so-called "Christian West"
is looked upon with disdain by many Third World theologians. This
is not surprising because many of the colonial systems used the
church to justify their conquests and hid behind the veil of religious
respectability. As a central tenet of the Western church's theology,
the Trinity has been reexamined by third world liberation theologians such as Leonardo Boff[28] in an attempt to remove the
hierarchical and monarchistic interpretations of the Trinity, which
they felt led to political oppression. Their critique is simply that the
traditional Trinitarian view of God as Lord leads to a "top-down"

method of social engagement where the people in power use their position to represent God and thereby impose His will on the masses. They have, therefore, tried to reconstruct the Trinity by using a social model where God's social inner life must be manifested on earth by similar egalitarian relationships. Using Jürgen Moltmann's "open Trinity,"[29] they have also tried to reconnect the suffering of people with the suffering of God and in so doing let destitute people know that God identifies with them. I applaud this method, for it is precisely in the crucified Christ that the poor of the earth know that God died for their freedom. While it is not our purpose to explore the finer points of their arguments,[30] the fact that they identify God with human pain is bold and helpful, for too often God was seen to be in His heaven and doing nothing.[31] This view of a detached God finds its origins in Greek philosophy, not biblical theology. It is only through a Triune God that the world and the divine are connected. Hegel referred to this as *infinitum capax finiti* ("the infinite encompassing the finite").[32] It is apparent, therefore, that those who espouse a unitarian understanding of God are unable to make this connection. Indeed, if God is a being about which we can only speculate, and not a revealed God incarnate in a person, then it is perfectly possible to assume that this deity does not care for the poor at all. Furthermore, if this God can only be known through observing the natural order, might we not assume that God is on the side of the powerful and rich and manifests His will through natural selection? The only viable option for those who truly believe in social justice is to have faith in the God who fully identifies with the poor and outcast and reveals the full nature of His love on a cross.[33]

POWER OF SPIRITUAL EXPERIENCE.

We are living in an age where the quest for spiritual experiences is becoming a social obsession. Many disillusioned people are turning to superstition, New Age cults, or even nature to find an authentic spiritual expression. They want transcendence and they look for it in mystical experiences and emotional fulfillment. Others are turning their attentions inward in an attempt to affirm their own experiences. It is precisely to such a generation that Trinitarian thinking should appeal, for it asserts that a true spiritual experience of God is found in the person of the Holy Spirit. Unfortunately, the third person of the Trinity often appears to be displaced[34] and put on the periphery of things. While one cannot develop an in-depth pneumatology here, suffice it to say that as the Bible affirms, the Holy Spirit is not only a gift (*charisma*) of God, He is also the One who reveals to us the will of the Father and bears witness to the Lordship of the Son. Experiencing and receiving the Holy Spirit means that one is experiencing God. To accomplish this we must look outside ourselves to a transcendent God who nevertheless becomes one with us through the Spirit. As Jurgen Moltmann points out, the Spirit forces us to ask the question which self-absorbed people often overlook: how does God experience us?[35] For it is the Holy Spirit who enables us to be conformed to God's image by convicting us of our sin and putting us in a right relationship with Him. The way in which we access this experience is not through simple introspection or a mystical union with the world, but by opening ourselves to the revealed power of God's Spirit. P.T. Forsyth poignantly supports this when he writes, "The essential thing is the object of faith, not the subject of experience." He goes on, "What we need is a theology that creates an obedient experience rather than experience that creates an interpretive theology."[36]

It is my contention that this authentic spiritual experience will be far more rewarding than any pagan substitute, for through our union with God in the Holy Spirit we know the Creator and not just His creation. Surely this is superior!

AN ENVIRONMENTALLY FRIENDLY GOD.

In humanity's desire to preserve the planet, the danger exists that we adopt a pantheistic understanding of God in which God loses His transcendence. The real peril of this position is that God and the universe become so interconnected that God ceases to be a transforming agent and is captive to the evolving processes of creation. When pantheists worship creation as if it were God, they are in fact nihilists, for God cannot be both the hope for creation and at the same time be creation itself. Ultimately, therefore, it is to a sound doctrine of the Trinity that environmentalists must turn if they seek the transformation and redemption of the world, for it is in the Trinity that God is at the same time both transcendent and immanent—both above creation, yet part of it. This relationship is paradoxical.

The biblical doctrine of creation affirms that God created something which was essentially good, but through the power of sin and disobedience, the cosmos fell from its ideal state. Therefore, creation needed to be liberated from its bondage to decay. The New Testament sees this liberation coming from the second person of the Trinity, who with the Father and Spirit, was present at creation and whose death and resurrection inaugurated a new era of redemption. Paul put it as follows, "Creation itself will be set free from its bondage to decay and will obtain the freedom of the glory of the children of God" (Ro 8:21). Dietrich Bonhoeffer believed that it was only through the Son that this is achieved, for in the Son God relates directly to the world,

> Thus only through Christ do we see the creator and preserver and the Lord of the whole world and in the world. Only through Christ do we see the world in God's hands.[37]

The value of creation, therefore, is seen through the Christ who came on behalf of nature. It is through our experience of the Holy Spirit whom Christ sends that we are united with Christ and are called to embrace the One who redeems the world. As His disciples we are obliged to continue this ministry of redemption by partaking of His sacraments and, as new creatures, participate in the ministry of Christ to the new creation. The fulfillment of this will only be achieved at the consummation of history. Nevertheless, it is precisely because God is Triune that we are called from our selfish and destructive needs to embrace the God of the future who will redeem everything by His grace.

Conclusion

The Trinity is an essential part of the modern church's proclamation. Despite the objections of those who want to reconstruct Christian dogma to suit their own political or personal agendas, the church must listen solely to the God who has revealed himself in history. The only way to truly understand the triune nature of God (the immanent Trinity) is by looking at God's encounter with the world through the life and work of Jesus Christ (the economic Trinity). In this, Karl Rahner's creed, "the economic Trinity is the immanent Trinity," is helpful, for it shows that the inner and outer life of God coincide.

However, there is a danger in taking this idea too far. God will always be sovereign and can never be constrained by our own apprehension of His works. We can never lose sight of the mystery of God, for the only way we can ever know God's plan and purpose is through His own self-revelation. This is precisely why the Bible speaks of Jesus Christ as the revelation of God's mystery (Eph 1:9). This does not mean that we should refrain from talking about God in Trinitarian terms, for it is the work of the Holy Spirit to illuminate our hearts and minds by confirming and bearing witness to God's sovereign acts in history through the cross and resurrection of Jesus Christ.

Just as important is the fact that all the things which trouble us most in the world can be addressed by such a living and vibrant God, without whom humanity and the world have no hope. May the church heed the warning of Richard Baxter against the dangers of idolatry and the creation of other gods. "Above all the plagues on this side of hell, see that you watch and pray against settling anywhere short of heaven, or reposing your souls on anything below God."[38] To this I say, "Amen."

NOTES

1. See C.S. Lewis, *Mere Christianity* (London: Collins, 1981), p. 138.

2. This was clearly evident in the theology of Adolf vonHarnack and was more recently restated by M.Durrant, *Theology and Intelligibility* (London: Rutledge and Kegan Paul, 1973).

3. One can see such a perspective in the theology of Pamela Dickey Young, who represents the more cautious wing of feminist theology. She speaks of Jesus as the one who re-presents God, thus avoiding the orthodox understanding of incarnation. She is also quite content to refer to the second person of the Trinity as "Sophia, Lady Wisdom," thus introducing a new character to the Trinity. See P.D. Young, *Feminist Theology/ Christian Theology: In Search of Method* (Minneapolis: Fortress Press, 1990), p. 104-105.

4. One finds this articulated by Matthew Fox, *Original Blessing* (Santa Fe: Bear & Co., 1983), pp. 215-216, who broadens the Trinity and speaks of it as a trinity of work, art, and play. Believing that orthodox Trinitarianism is "Christolotrous," Fox argues that we must primarily affirm God as Creator, and see ourselves as co-creators with God. In essence he deifies humanity, and in so doing opens the door for us to see the locus of the divine in creation and fellow human beings. In such a view, Christ becomes unimportant, for He only points to the divine within. Having removed Christ from the center of God-talk, Fox paves the way for an ecumenical, universalistic notion of God.

5. See Donald Bloesch, *The Battle For The Trinity* (Ann Arbor: Vine Books, 1985); Alistair McGrath, *Understanding The Trinity* (Grand Rapids: Zondervan, 1988); T. Peters, *God As Trinity* (Louisville, Ky.: Westminster John Knox Press, 1993); and R. Jenson, *The Triune Identity* (Philadelphia: Fortress, 1983).

6. Leander Keck, *The Church Confident* (Nashville: Abingdon Press, 1993).

7. For more on this, see Karl Barth, *Church Dogmatics: The Doctrine of the Word of God*, vol. 1:1 (Edinburgh: T&T Clark, 1990), pp. 71-87.

8. See Emil Brunner as quoted in S. Cave, *The Doctrine of the Christian Faith* (London: Independent, 1952), p. 266.

9. Karl Barth, *Church Dogmatics*, 1:1, pp. 295-489.

10. T. Peters, op. cit., p. 16.

11. For an excellent summary on this subject, see W. Knoke, *Bold New World* (New York: Kodanshe, 1996). For the implications for religion and faith, see pp. 296-299.

12. Karen Armstrong, *A History of God* (New York: Ballantine, 1993), p. 399.

13. See Spinoza as the father of this movement, *A Theologico-Political Treatise* (New York: 1951).

14. Donald Bloesch, op. cit., p. 51.

15. See *Voices United: Services for Trial Use* (Toronto: United Church Publishing House, 1996), p. 130.

16. Ibid., p. 129.

17. For more on this, see E. Schussler-Fiorenza, *In Memory of Her* (New York: Crossroad, 1984).

18. See Pamela Dickey Young, *Feminist Theology/Christian Theology* (Minneapolis: Fortress, 1990), p. 104.

19. Ibid., 105.

20. For an excellent summary of this perspective, see J. De Santa Ana, *Towards A Church Of The Poor* (Maryknoll, N.Y.: Orbis Books, 1979), p. 142-155.

21.   See S. Cave, *The Doctrine of the Christian Faith*, p. 276.

22.   Ibid., 266.

23.   See John Stott, *One People: Helping Your Church Become a Caring Community* (Old Tappan, N.J.: Fleming H. Revell Co., 1982).

24.   Ibid., p. 86.

25.   See C. Mowry-Lacugna, *The Trinity and Christian Life* (San Francisco: Harper & Row, 1991), 228.

26.   See Dietrich Bonhoeffer, *Life Together* (London: SCM Press, 1954), p. 18.

27.   Ibid., p. 19.

28.   See L. Boff, *Trinity and Society* (Maryknoll, N.Y.: Orbis Books, 1988).

29.   See Jürgen Moltmann, *The Trinity and the Kingdom of God* (London: SCM Press, 1981), 47.

30.   See T. Peters, op. cit., 103-110.

31.   Source unknown, but ascribed to Thomas Carlyle.

32.   See C. Braaten, *No Other Gospel* (Minneapolis: Fortress Press, 1993), 113.

33.   One of the criticisms against the belief that it was God who suffered on the cross is that it is similar to the third-century heresy of "Patripassionism," which finds its current manifestation in Panentheism. The problem with this heresy was its unwillingness to make clear distinctions between the persons of the Trinity. However, if we are willing to make clear distinctions between the Persons of the Trinity we can still affirm that "God was *in* Christ reconciling the world to himself" and thereby see the cross as God's identification with suffering people.

34. See David Watson, *One in the Spirit* (London: Hodder & Stoughton, 1973), 13.

35. See Jürgen Moltmann, op. cit., p. 3.

36. See P.T. Forsyth, *Revelation Old And New* (London: Independent, 1962), pp. 74-76.

37. Dietrich Bonhoeffer as quoted in E. Feil, *The Theology of Dietrich Bonhoeffer* (Philadelphia: Fortress Press: 1985), p. 70.

38. See L. Griffith, *What Is A Christian* (Toronto: Ryerson Press, 1962), p. 31.

The Trinity Against the Spirit of Unitarianism

Victor A. Shepherd

Faced with the cultural and religious pluralism of the twenty-first century, the church (at least in the West) appears extraordinarily anxious or extraordinarily accommodating, and perhaps extraordinarily accommodating just because it is extraordinarily anxious. The church, thinking its pluralistic setting to be novel, is tempted to fear the world and therein tempted to think it can preserve itself by isolating itself from the world; or else it is tempted in its bold engagement with the world to tailor itself to the world and therein to squander the "deposit" (2Ti 1:12) that it has been charged to guard. Those prone to anxiety are more likely to insist on retaining a doctrine of the Trinity, if only to preserve continuity with their forebears in faith and discontinuity with the mindset of modernity, not realizing that "if only" reduces the doctrine to an artifact, even a curiosity-piece, in the museum of intellectual history. On the other hand, those eager to meet challenges are more likely to jettison any doctrine of the Trinity as an encumbrance that inhibits the church in its witness to the gospel and its exemplification of the gospel amidst the common life of the world.

One issue facing the church, then, is this: is the doctrine of the Trinity baggage that is not only unnecessary but is actually a threat to the seaworthiness of the ship (church) as it appears to flounder in the storms of secularity? Or is it ballast in the ship's keel apart from which even moderate winds will blow the ship hither and thither, eventually to capsize it?

179

I submit that apart from the doctrine of the Trinity, "gospel" is rendered indistinguishable from religious aspiration or projection, while "Spirit" is reduced to a magnification of anything that the Fall-darkened heart and mind of humankind may conceive, and "church" becomes nothing more than one more social group (albeit in religious guise) which seeks to promote the agenda of its constituents. In short, without the doctrine of the Trinity the arch counter-miracle will occur: wine will be turned into water as the gospel is denatured.

In maintaining the doctrine of the Trinity to be essential to the faith I am not holding up as etched in stone the expression of any one thinker's understanding; neither Augustine's nor Aquinas's nor Calvin's nor Barth's. Nonetheless, I am convinced that just as these thinkers were impelled to speak on behalf of the triune God in order to forestall the acculturation of the gospel in their day, we must do as much in ours, all the while endeavoring to obey the fifth commandment; namely, to honor our parents (including our theological foreparents) in order that the days of the church may be long in the land which God gives us.

Scriptural Building Blocks of the Doctrine

True, a fully-articulated doctrine of the Trinity is not found in Scripture. Nonetheless, the building blocks of the doctrine incontrovertibly are. Consider the following:

> Go therefore and make disciples of all nations, baptizing them in the name of the Father and of the Son and of the Holy Spirit (Mt 28:19).

> This Jesus God raised up....Being therefore exalted at the right hand of God, and having received from the Father the promise of the Holy Spirit, he has poured out that you both see and hear (Ac 2:32f).

> The grace of the Lord Jesus Christ, the love of God, and the communion of the Holy Spirit be with you all (2Co 13:14).

> For through [Jesus Christ] both of us have access in one Spirit to the Father (Eph 2:18).

> There is one body and one Spirit, just as you were called to the one hope of your calling, one Lord, one faith, one baptism, one God and Father of us all....But each of us was given grace according to the measure of Christ's gift (Eph 4:4-6).

> ...God chose you as the firstfruits for salvation, through sanctification by the Spirit and through belief in the truth. For this purpose he called you through our proclamation of the good news, so that you may obtain the glory of our Lord Jesus Christ (2Th 2:13),

> ...chosen and destined by God the Father and sanctified by the Spirit to be obedient to Jesus Christ and to be sprinkled with his blood (1Pe 1:2).

Throughout its consistent attestation of the incursion of the Word, Scripture constrains us to understand God as eternally triune. A doctrine of the Trinity makes explicit what is everywhere implicit in the "the faith that was once for all entrusted to the saints" and for which faith, the apostle tells us, we must ever "contend" (Jude 3).

Oneness of Divine Being

Christian faith is rooted in the oneness of being between Jesus Christ and God the Father. In the gospel, God has revealed himself to us as Father, Son and Holy Spirit. (Without the divine activity of the Holy Spirit we should not *know* of the deity of Father and Son.) In this self-unveiling God has revealed himself in such a way as to disclose that what God is in himself, God is toward us, and what God is toward us God is in himself, throughout His saving acts in history. In other words, what God is eternally in himself, that is, in His internal relations as Father, Son, and Holy Spirit, God is in His activity toward us through the Son and in the Spirit.

If the oneness in being between Jesus Christ and God the Father is cut, then the substance and heart of the gospel is lost. For if what Christ does is not what God does, then *before God* humankind's predicament is unrelieved. Again, if God himself has not come among us in the Incarnation, then God's love for us (despite God's good intentions!) stops short of *God's* full identification with us sinners; in truth it is not finally love (or at least it is woefully deficient and defective love) and the redemptive activity of God is finally ineffectual.

The oneness in being among Father, Son, and Holy Spirit, however, does not imply any oneness in being between the Creator and the creation. In fact there is no intrinsic ontological similarity between the eternal being of God and the contingent being of creatures. The two spheres of being—divine and creaturely—are ontologically distinct and are joined only by grace. Scriptural monotheism is never to be confused with philosophical monism. Awareness of the foregoing, it must be noted, is a predicate of the triune God's self-disclosure *as* triune. In short, knowledge of God (with all that this implies with respect to knowledge of the relationship of divine to creaturely being) is the work of God himself, never the work of rational inference or philosophical speculation. To say the same thing slightly differently, faith in this Triune God arises only as God himself generates it; only as God himself attests and interprets (the activity of the Holy Spirit) God's own Word (the activity of the Son). This can only mean that the fact of faith, that is, the presence of men and women who believe, testifies to the utter priority of God over all thought concerning Him. We can think correctly about God at all only because God includes us in His self-knowing.

In conjoining "Spirit" and "Holy," Scripture insists that God is the only fit witness to himself; only God can disclose God. And since God has given himself to us in the person of the Son or Word, then Spirit and Son (Word) are inextricably linked. Or in the idiom of the written Gospels, Jesus Christ is the unique bearer and bestower of the Holy Spirit. This is but to say that one cannot pronounce "Spirit" except in reference to Jesus Christ. (In this way the apostles insist that while Christless spirits do indeed abound, they can only be less than holy!) This point is reinforced by scripture's depiction of the Spirit as being sent from the Father in the name of the Son, never in the Spirit's own name; the Spirit speaks only of the Father and of the Son, never of himself. Put simply, the Spirit is like floodlighting. Floodlights are positioned in such a way that one does not see the floodlight itself, only that which it lights up and to which it therefore directs attention. (Recall our Lord's words, "He (i.e., the Spirit) will glorify me" (Jn 16:14). The Spirit imports no new substance into faith's knowing, but rather facilitates faith's knowledge of the Son, who is the substance of the Father.

Operative Unitarian Doctrines

While the foregoing is formally espoused throughout the church catholic, it is materially contradicted frequently in the various "unitarianisms" found at all levels in all denominations. (While the stated theology of any Christian body is Trinitarian, the stated or official theology should not blind us to the operative theology that tends to characterize the denomination or at least aspects of it.) Several of these operative unitarianisms are outlined briefly below.

A UNITARIANISM OF THE FATHER.

This popular "unitarianism" certainly preserves the truth that God is exalted, "high and lofty"; that God's thoughts are not our thoughts nor our ways God's ways (Isa 6:1; 55:8). God is the sole, sovereign, eternal one. God is not an aspect of His creation-at-large (the cosmos) nor an aspect of His creation-at-small (humankind). While by God's permission, invitation, and facilitation we may genuinely *apprehend* God (in both senses of "apprehend": *understand* the nature of God and *seize* Him as we are first seized by Him), we never *comprehend* God. We never grasp God so as to master Him, domesticate Him, render Him an object. The one who is irreducibly subject never gives himself over to us (while always giving himself for us and to us!), never allows himself to be that upon which we can perform those operations which bend natural objects, for instance, to our purposes and our control. God is inviolably GOD, never a tool that we may deploy, never one with whom we may trifle.

However, the God who is *only* "high and lofty," without differentiation, tends to be so exalted as never to humble himself, so far beyond us as not to render himself accessible, sovereign with more than a suggestion of severe, unknowable in the sense of arbitrary, a creator who is also (or may be) capricious.

Eighteenth-century deism portrayed God as the Creator who fashioned the universe and then effectively absented himself from it. Here God was "high and lofty" so as to be inaccessible. On the other hand, seventeenth-century Protestant scholasticism portrayed God not so much as remote in himself but as inaccessible with respect to His "ways." The notion of double predestination, for instance, could only render God ultimately capricious in His activity on behalf of humankind. God, it was said, foreordained elect and reprobate *as such* even before they were born, and therefore before they even had opportunity to sin. When confronted with the arbitrariness of the twofold decree (all alike merit condemnation, even as some are condemned prior to their being able to merit anything, while others are recipients of a Spirit-facilitated gospel-pronouncement that the reprobated are never permitted genuinely to "hear") its proponents insisted that its irrationality was only seeming; God has His "reason," and to this reason no person is privy. The "reason" is hidden inscrutably in the innermost recesses of God. Therefore it is not our place to enquire, only our place to adore. While all Christians would admit that it *is* our place to adore the Holy One whose ways are not our ways (Isa 55:8), it is not our place—i.e., it is never God-honoring to "adore" an absurdity. The more the hidden justice of this arbitrariness and irrationality was advanced, however, the more apparent the injustice of it all was to many. In view of the unqualified remoteness of God, or the arbitrariness of God, or the injustice of God that a unitarianism of the Father seems to imply, this particular unitarianism, paradoxically, ends in the denial that God is parent in any sense.

A Unitarianism of the Son.

Undifferentiated transcendence is overcome as Jesus Christ is acknowledged to be God-with-us. So far from disdaining the complexity and sin, anguish and frustration of the human situation, God has identified with it all in its variegated multi-dimensionality. Jesus Christ is bone of our bone and flesh of our flesh, is tempted at all points as we are (Heb 4:15), even becoming one with sinners, as His baptism attests, by being made sin for us (2Co 5:21). In the same manner He is subject to the principalities and powers; He can restore a creation now groaning in its futility (Rom 8:21-22) just because He identifies himself fully with it.

At the same time, to *collapse* God into God the Son distorts even the truth of the Incarnation. For the Christian understanding of Incarnation, it must be remembered, is not to be confused with pagan incarnations wherein the deity collapses itself into the creaturely in such a way as to forfeit transcendence. In such a subtly paganized "unitarianism of the incarnate one" the nearness of God the Son is affirmed at the expense of God's holiness; affirmed, that is, at the expense of God's very Godness. Here God-with-us is demeaned as pal. This saccharine Jesus finds no paradigm in Scripture. No one who met Jesus Christ in the flesh ever spoke of Him in this manner or found Him cozy. The written Gospels, rather, customarily depict Him as One whom people do not understand and cannot tame. Even disciples, newly made aware in His presence of their systemic sinnership, can only plead with Him to leave them alone. The apostles never confuse proximity with presumption. So far from being the grand aider and abettor and guarantor of human schemes, Jesus is the One who does *not* supply answers to questions, always refusing to endorse whatever understanding the people before Him have brought with them. Throughout the written Gospels, Jesus refuses to answer the questions put to Him, preferring instead to reply with His own questions. Plainly, He will not underwrite the standpoint or the perception or the purpose of the questioner; plainly, He will not endorse the questioner's question as a legitimate question. In disallowing the question put to Him, in insisting on interrogating the questioner so as to change the latter from aggressor to defendant, He shows the speaker to dwell in spiritual unreality (i.e., suffer from spiritual psychosis). In the same way, He does not lend himself to the schemes and dreams of those who think that their piousness concerning Him supplies the boost that is needed to ensure the full-flowering of their plans for themselves. And lest we think this to be an insignificant over-subtlety, the apostolic discernment that makes the stories of Simon Magnus, plus Ananias and Sapphira, normative for Christian understanding should correct us!

A Unitarianism of the Spirit.

It is the Spirit who imparts vitality and vibrancy in believer and congregation alike. It is the Spirit who supplies zeal, warmth, boldness, effectiveness. It is the Spirit whose gifts equip the congregation for ministry and whose fruits adorn the gospel, in all of this exhibiting the truth of God as the power of God and not mere ideation.

One New Testament word for the Spirit, "*arrabon*," a "down payment" or "pledge" (in modern Greek it means a woman's engagement ring), plainly means that there is more to come. While the Spirit satisfies the restless human heart, the satisfaction it yields never satiates; believers, contented as never before and nowhere else, are nonetheless "hungrier" than ever even as they know that one day they will be fed so as to leave them hungering no more. The entire experiential aspect of primitive Christianity—e.g., the question in Galatians 3:2 that asks, "did you receive the Spirit by works of the law or by hearing with faith?" plainly directs the attention of the readers of the epistle to an identifiable experience—is much undervalued in most expressions of the church today.

Notwithstanding, when the Spirit is magnified disproportionately and experience put forward unnormed, then "Spirit" ceases to be the power in which Jesus Christ acts himself and that He pours forth on His people. "Spirit" instead lends itself to frenzy, the suspension of the intellect, and the identification of God with that which is indistinguishable from the intrapsychic proclivities and pressures of the devotees themselves, as well as from the supra- individual forces that thrive amidst institutions, ideologies, images, and diverse "isms."

It appears that whenever the Trinity is denied through the aforementioned unitarian view of redemption, the heart of Scripture is denied as well. In the first instance, God's transcendence is upheld in such a manner as to render God remote, distant, inaccessible, with the result that the creation is left unaffected. The older discussions of God's impassibility had the same result: the God who is beyond suffering is scarcely able (or willing) to do anything for those whose suffering is as undeniable as it is inescapable. In the second instance, God is so identified with the creation as not to transcend it so as to be free for it. This was surely the problem with Schleiermacher and his theological descendants, indeed with the liberal school of theology that accepts the world's self-understanding as the presupposition for humankind's understanding of God. In the third instance, God is identified with human intra-psychic processes so as to deify them.

It is the triune God who alone saves, for it is the triune God who alone can. Only that God can save who transcends the world and is therefore free from it so as to act for it; who also loves it and identifies himself with it so as not to forsake it in any respect; and who also invites the beneficiaries of His love to know *Him* in such a way as to distinguish themselves from Him, and their psycho-physical immediacy from intimacy with the One who ever remains "other."

Modern Denials of the Trinity
Separating the Son from the Father.

In many areas of the church catholic today, the doctrine of the Trinity is denied not merely materially but formally as well. Such a denial occurs whenever, for instance, the deity of the Son is impugned. In Scripture, the phrase "son of" has the force of "of the same nature as"; to modify it to mean "of a similar nature" is to deny what the church has always confessed in terms of the Incarnation.

Here we must recall the cruciality of Athanasius's triumph over Arius at the Council of Nicaea. While both Athanasius and Arius spoke of Jesus as "Son of God," Athanasius' insistence on *homoousios* (the *same* nature or substance) over against Arius's *homoiousios* (a *similar* nature or substance) was nothing less than the preservation of the gospel. For if the Father is not *essentially* identified with the activity of the Son, then all that the Son said, suffered, and did is without saving significance; devoid of redemptive significance, it is also without revelatory significance. (Those who are impatient with this discussion and others like it, speaking disdainfully of the controversy over an iota, the smallest letter of the Greek alphabet, must be reminded that there is no little difference between asking others to "run" your business for you and asking them to "ruin" it!)

Formal denial need not be blatant; in fact it is no less a formal denial for being subtle. Whenever the question, "Is Jesus the Son of God?" is answered, whether waggishly or sincerely, "Of course He is; all of us are sons and daughters of God," the Incarnation is denied and therefore the Trinity as well. And because the being of God is intrinsically related to the knowledge of God, any departure from acknowledging the Tri-unity of God imperils the knowledge of God. The current preoccupation with "Creation Spirituality" is such a subtle yet formal denial.

"Who is God?" is a question that Scripture answers only indirectly. It answers this question by first asking and answering two others: "What does God *do* (outside of us, yet for our sake)?" and "What does God *effect* (in us)?" We can know who God is only as we first learn what God has done on our behalf, for our sake in the Son (and learn this *from* God), and also only as we become beneficiaries of this work on our behalf through the power of the Spirit. In sum, we know God as we are included in God's work for us and as we are illumined concerning this work. To become acquainted with the living God, then, is to be drawn into God's own life and be made a participant in God's self-knowing; it is to overhear God talking to himself as we are permitted to listen in on Him and therein have answered our question, "Who is God?"

An unavoidable implication of this is to understand that the creation is not God. It is too frequently overlooked that the non-divine status of the creation has to be *revealed,* or else why should the creation not be assumed to be divine, as in fact it often is? As it is only by grace (i.e., by the action of God himself) that we learn that the triune one is God, so it is only by grace that we learn that the creation is not God but rather is creaturely. Creation Spirituality, on the other hand, is predicated on the postulate that the creation either is God or mediates God. Biblical prophets and apostles reject this postulate consistently. Because God is God and we are but creatures of God, the order or logic of revelation generates the order or logic of our knowledge of God. And because the creation does not reveal the triune God, the creation (itself fallen and in bondage to death) is not the vehicle of that life which the Spirit (who is God) alone effects.

Any diminution of the Son as one with the being of the Father is an explicit denial of the Trinity. Such diminution of the Son invariably fosters an idolization of the creation. And idolatry, everywhere in scripture, is not merely ignorance of God (in the sense of lack of information about Him) but rather an estrangement from Him the consequences of which are unimaginably deleterious.

SEPARATING THE SPIRIT FROM THE SON.

Any sundering of Spirit from Son is a similar denial with similar consequences. Sundering the Spirit from the Son means that the Spirit ceases to be holy, ceases to be intrinsically related to the Word (as the reformers, following the apostles, were careful to note), and becomes instead the religious legitimation of human fancy or fantasy. Since, as was seen above, it is only through the truth that truth is known and non-truth recognized and only by reality that illusion is discerned, then only through revelation can we gain proper perspective on and understand assorted claims to truth, reality, godliness, and goodness.

These modern attempts to deny the Trinity can have destructive consequences. Despite its apparently ascendant secularism, our era is startlingly religious. It is assumed that religion is good and that Christianity is religious. Christianity may indeed be, but is *faith* religious? Prophets and apostles attest that the gospel exposes religion as non-gospel, non-faith (i.e., unbelief). Elijah on Mount Carmel does not suggest to the Baal spokespersons that they are religious, he is religious, and therefore they should all pool their religiosity, seeking out a common denominator, maximizing convergence and minimizing divergence. On the contrary, Elijah maintains that shortly Yahweh will act in such a way as to expose Baalism for what it is. This is not to say that Israel's faith remained free of religion; the prophets continually deplore the religious invasion of Israel and continually recall Israel to the God, who displayed His outstretched arm in delivering them from slavery, and formed them as His people at Sinai, and now nurtured them like a mother with her child at her breast.

It seems that the church today thinks itself to be meeting religious pluralism for the first time, when in fact the faith of Israel and of Israel's greater Son came to birth and had to survive in the context of competing religious claimants. To be sure, this pluralism always encroached upon the faith of God's people, threatened to dissolve them, and therefore had to be resisted as grace freed faith to be irreligious. Significantly, while Paul begins his sermon on Mars Hill (Ac 17:19ff) by acknowledging the phenomenon of religions (the Greek word he uses, *deisdaimon*, also means "superstition"), he quickly moves to an unambiguous declaration of Jesus Christ, His resurrection, and the coming judgement. Nowhere do the apostles counsel seeking commonalities with contiguous religious manifestations.

Unless the church recovers its discernment of how revelation discloses itself as distinct from religion, how will the church be able to recognize and repudiate the religious accretions to the gospel, and even the most subtle (yet no less spiritually harmful) psychoreligiosities that attach themselves to our own believing and attempt to transmogrify faith? How will it distinguish between the truth that God, for the sake of His glory and our salvation, has freely justified us of His own free grace, and the religion which attempts to justify ourselves before a god whose mercy and pardon we plainly doubt?

Again, as soon as Spirit is sundered from Word (Jesus Christ is the *one* Word of God we are to hear and heed in life and in death, according to the Barmen Declaration), the Spirit is co-opted as the legitimization and even the divinization of culture. Aesthetic riches with their concomitant delight are then spoken of as "spiritual experience." All experiences of the creaturely order in its own mysterious depths are denoted as spiritual because *genuinely* mysterious (i.e., non-reducible in terms of psychology, sociology or biology) are confused with the work of the Holy Spirit of God. The obvious conclusion from this confusion is that cultured people are spiritually superior and that culture saves.

The Germans, as usual, have a polysyllabic word for it: *Kulturprotestantismus*. The culture-religion which had permeated the German church left people unable to distinguish between God himself and the awesome depths of God's creation; between having "God's love...poured into our hearts through the Holy Spirit that has been given to us" (Rom 5:5) and being moved by natural beauty or artistic talent. When *Kulturprotestantismus* went beyond viewing aesthetics as the vestibule to the kingdom and affirmed culture and kingdom to be synonymous, the nazification of the land of Goethe, Schiller, Beethoven, not to mention the world's leading medical research, demonstrated that culture can readily cloak the conflict between Holy One and evil one. It demonstrates too that *Kulturprotestantismus* supplies neither the ability nor the urge to remove the cloak.

The spectacle of most television religious programing, replete with references to "God," "Holy Spirit," and "faith," raises the issue of narcissism. Narcissism is preoccupation with oneself, preoccupation with one's own comfort, advantage, recognition, advancement, and reward. Narcissistic people look upon themselves (however unconsciously) as the focal point of the universe and the measure of it as well. The televised "gospel" enhances this more often than not. It is only as the Spirit is known to be always and only the Spirit of Him who had nowhere to lay His head, of Him who appoints would-be followers to leave all and shoulder a cross; it is only as the Spirit is known to be the Spirit of Him to whom all judgement has been given (Jn 5:22), that the self-preoccupation of pietistic self-measurement is identified as the narcissistic counterfeit of faith.

In the same way, once the Spirit is divorced from the One who is the guarantor of the kingdom (i.e., the creation healed), once pneumatology is separated from Christology, people are theologically/spiritually defenseless against psycho-religious pathology. Jonestown need not be recalled; suffice it to recollect those whose "faith" has rendered them ill, or rendered them more ill.

Less dramatically, once pneumatology is separated from Christology, once the Spirit is (falsely) identified with "religiously-tinged" interiority, there appears to be little or no ground for distinguishing between neurotic and real guilt, little or no help for disentangling them or for seeing how the neurotic may cloak the real or the real obscure the neurotic.

In short, once pneumatology is separated from Christology it becomes difficult to see how pastoral psychology can be genuinely pastoral: how it subserves a "cure of souls" and not merely a "cure of psyches."

Hope of Restoration

When Jesus Christ is confessed as the unique bearer and bestower of the Spirit; when the Spirit is known as the power in which Jesus Christ acts, to the glory of God the Father, then distortions that bedevil the church are avoided and Trinitarian doctrine preserves proper balances.

Reference has already been made to the question Paul put to the Christians in Galatia, "Did you receive the Spirit by doing the works of the law or by believing what you heard?" (Gal 3:2). The question directs his readers to recall and reflect upon an aspect of their life in Christ, which they cannot deny, an event (however protracted), moreover, which is so common as to provide an indisputable beginning-point for his subsequent reasoning with them.

As the church today recovers its experience *of God* (for experience of God is the only experience the Spirit of Jesus Christ facilitates), the theological content of the gospel will no longer be arid intellectualism. It is the Spirit who prevents the gospel (so-called) from becoming the preserve of the intellectually gifted, from degenerating into a western philosophy that happens to employ a religious vocabulary. The gospel must not become one more abstraction to be assessed along with other "worldviews," when in truth the gospel, ultimately, is the presence and power of the living Lord Jesus Christ in His person. Doctrine, indubitably, is necessary, or else we have renounced all notion of truth and any suggestion that we can apprehend truth (however fragmentarily) and articulate truth (however provisionally). Yet in the light of the Spirit's repudiation of intellectualism, faith can never be reduced to the grasp of doctrine.

When the Spirit is honored as the power of God which renders Jesus Christ forever contemporaneous, then living faith will always triumph over traditionalism. "I'm a Lutheran," when uttered in the apparent absence of throbbing faith in the living Word, usually means that the Lutheran Church is the one someone stays away from! The same phenomenon is seen in those whose Protestantism consists in their anti-Catholicism.

Faith's triumph over traditionalism in no way belittles the place of tradition. Tradition, as G.K. Chesterton reminds us, allows the dead to vote! Permitting the dead to vote is crucial, since a church without tradition resembles an amnesiac. The most ominous feature of those afflicted with amnesia isn't that they cannot remember where they have left their umbrella; rather, it is that they have no identity, and therefore cannot be trusted. A church disdainful of tradition is a church not to be trusted.

When "Spirit" and "Word" are acknowledged to imply each other then institutionalism will not supplant adventurous discipleship. No longer subserving itself or an un-gospel agenda, the institution will subserve the community which lives for the praise of God's glory. The institution will resist calling for that obedience which is owed God alone. Neither will it attempt to forfend criticism by accusing dissidents of disloyalty. In trusting the promise that the powers of death shall not prevail against Christ's people, it will soberly remember that institutional remains litter the landscape of history even as God's peculiar treasure is safeguarded unto the day of its vindication.

Where the Spirit is recalled as the Spirit of Him who insists that harlots and tax-collectors enter the kingdom of God ahead of the "righteous" the placebo of moralism will be detected and dropped. The Christian life will not be impoverished until it becomes precisely what the world misunderstands it to be: conformity to a code, success at which breeds self-righteousness while failure precipitates despair. Because Jesus died for the ungodly and not for the immoral, morality will be seen for what it is: the barricade behind which people attempt to hide from God rather than the vestibule to God's kingdom. Evident instead will be glad obedience to the living Person of Jesus Christ, motivated by gratitude for deliverance from the sin of moralism.

Where the Spirit is trusted to lend effectiveness to proclamation in Christ's name evangelism will not give way to assorted techniques for proselytizing or garnering adherents. To evangelize is to set forth the gospel of the Son in reliance upon the God whose Spirit is sufficient to empower the saints' testimony. In other words, the outcome of our evangelism can be left in God's hands.

A church that does not trust the Spirit to honor witness borne to the Son is a church that confuses evangelism with conversion; which is to say, a church which cannot distinguish between its work and God's work. Moreover, a church that thinks that conversion (rather than witness) is its responsibility is a church that coerces; the harassment can be physical, social or psychological, but it remains coercion. Paradoxically, the church that thinks that *it* has to generate the fruit of its diligent "God-talk" announces to the world that it does not believe in God, since it cannot trust God to vivify God's own Word! To trust that the Spirit is the Spirit of the Son or Word is to be freed from anxiety concerning the results of mission and therein spared the fear of failure and the concomitant temptation to coerce.

As the Spirit brings women and men to faith in the crucified, the Son's cross will be recognized as the limitless vulnerability of the Father, and the Son's resurrection as the limitless triumph of this vulnerability. Trusting the triumph of God's vulnerability, God's people can allay all anxiety concerning the prosecution of the Christian mission, even as they forego the seeming shortcut of strong-arm tactics.

The Trinity and the Church's Mission

A recovery of the doctrine of the Trinity would do ever so much to assist mainline denominations with respect to the catholicity of their mission. Despite mainline Protestantism's protestations that it sides with the victimized, the marginalized, the oppressed, and those disadvantaged in any way, it remains almost exclusively an occurrence within the ascendant middle class. That segment of the socio-economic spectrum from which the mainline draws its people is becoming smaller as it also becomes more affluent: we are attracting fewer and fewer people, virtually all of whom are more and more wealthy. We attract no poor people, even remarkably few who are not upwardly socially mobile.

In times of economic turbulence, the rich are cushioned against material misfortune and remain rich; the poor are not cushioned, but neither do they have anything to protect, with the result that they remain poor. The rising middle class, however, is unrelievedly vulnerable. In times of economic dislocation, it is precipitated downwards. It collapses into that segment of the socio-economic spectrum with which mainline denominations have no credibility at all. In other words, simply as a result of uncontrollable economic convulsions they would be deprived of their constituency. A recovery of Trinitarian faith, especially with respect to the self-appointment of God in the person of the Son, would commission us to re-examine our socio-economic exclusiveness. After all, the Word of God is baptized in dirty water at the hands of someone who will be forever out of place among the socially slick. The pronouncement heard at this baptism, "You are my Son the Beloved; with You I am well pleased" (Lk 3:22) is a conflation of Psalm 2 and Isaiah 42. Psalm 2 is God's appointment of the Royal Ruler, the One possessed of genuine authority. Isaiah 42 speaks of God's approval of the Servant of the Lord, commonly known as "the suffering servant," the One who was despised and rejected by humankind...and we esteemed him not (Isa 53:3). The mission of God himself in the Son will ever be effective (God *is* sovereign), but its effectiveness will materialize through a servanthood that entails hardship and sacrifice and social rejection. Then to be Christ's follower is to be commissioned to a ministry of service, not domination; of self-forgetfulness, not personal advantage; even of social rejection rather than public congratulation. Would not a new appreciation of the Son's mission, when the Son is one with the Father himself, be the recovery of our identification with the Son who cherished the very people to whom the mainline churches cannot relate? In that Son who is of the same substance and nature as the Father, God effectively loved the world entirely, not merely one aspect of the world (i.e., social aspirants whose psycho-social needs are apparently served through church affiliation).

The recovery of the doctrine of the Trinity will foster the recovery of Trinitarian faith; this in turn will mean a return to the catholicity of the gospel. And such a return will spell recovery of mission and service on behalf of *all* the "far off" who have been "brought near by the blood of Christ" (Eph 2:13). For "through him both [Jew and Gentile, which is to say all human beings equally, despite apparently insurmountable barriers] have access in one Spirit to the Father" (Eph 3:18).

The tetragrammaton, יהוה, contains no vowels. Lacking vowels, it is unpronounceable. Because it is unpronounceable it is untranslatable; for this reason there can be no substitute for it. There can be no substitute for the name of the God who has named himself Father, Son, and Holy Spirit. To know God, honor and obey and adore God, is to find that the doctrine of the Trinity is neither the museum-like security-blanket of the nervous nor the jettisonable baggage of the naive. The doctrine of the Trinity rather will ever orient us to the living God whose love for a dying world commissions us to love it no less.

Called To Be One: Worshiping the Triune God Together

Edith Humphrey

> Nourished by the sacraments and formed by the prayer and teaching of the church, we need seek nothing but the particular place willed for us by God within the church. When we find that place, our life and our prayer both at once become extremely simple.[1]

Thoughts in Solitude seems an odd point to begin a discussion of unity, worship, and the Trinity. This particular thought of Merton may seem an even stranger place to begin, given our late twentieth century context, and its inhospitable attitude towards obedience and "place." Yet, it is probably wise, in the midst of baffling complexity, to return to simplicity. "Alone" with God, Merton speaks of the "we" and the church, of what (or who) nourishes and forms us, of praying and living with singleness of heart. To read Merton beyond this brief quotation is to discover that the quest for our particular place in the church comes not through a popularly-styled "search for the self" but through a focus upon and adoration of the One who is "the Center to which all things tend, and to whom all our actions must be directed."[2]

So it is in our "quest" for unity in the church. If we are truly "called to be one" and this is not a humanly-directed or corporately conceived project of unification, then our unity must spring from our steady gaze upon the One who "gives life to the dead and calls into existence the things that do not exist" (Ro 4:17). Indeed, our unity springs not from our efforts (not even the effort of worship), but from that very One himself, as we gaze upon His image and are transfigured from glory to glory through the Lord (who is the Spirit). Our talk about the vocation of the church to worship as one is bound up with our corporate invocation of the One who is and who first called us. In making sense of our unity, we are thrust back to the Source and foundation of unity; in making sense of our diversity, we must go first to the triune One in whom and from whom diversity generously springs. To truly begin, it seems that we must reverse the proposition, "called to be one" and begin with the Caller, rather than with our calling.

I am well aware that in doing this reversal, I am rejecting the advice of numerous theologians who argue that it is a counter-intuitive move. Many have argued that to begin thinking about our salvation and about our humanity (or even talk about the Trinity itself) with talk of the triune God *in se* is not only counter-intuitive, but arbitrary. So, in a particularly coherent but simple statement of the problem, Migliore warns: "If talk of the triune God is not to be wild speculation, it will always find its basis and its limit in the biblical narration of the love of God for the world."[3] It is quite clear that Migliore and others of his mind are intent to avoid a myriad of evils attendant upon arid speculation; we may also be sympathetic to their departure point, that is, the biblical narrative. However, while it is evident that the basis of our thinking about the triune God is to be the biblical story of God's love for us, we need not follow in Migliore's plea that this is to be our limit. For it seems that part of Jesus' calling of His followers as no longer servants, but friends (Jn 15:14f) involved (and involves) the disclosure of mysteries beyond our own situation. Trustworthy knowledge about God does indeed come through the salvation narrative, which offers a picture or icon of God's incarnate Word; yet we may not limit what it is that Jesus intended (and intends) to teach to His new community. There are several points in Scripture where the apostles, and through them, we ourselves, are invited beyond the immediate realm of instruction in our salvation to think about the mystery of the relationship between the Father and the Son—one thinks immediately about the Johannine Last Supper discourse.

John 13:31-John17:26, in fact, provides an excellent locus for a discussion of worship, unity and the mysterious nature of God. In beginning here, we will be following in the footsteps of many church fathers who meditated upon this passage in order to understand and illuminate the mysteries of the Trinity and the church. Moreover, we will be, in a parallel way, exploring the ongoing basis for hope, as expressed by our Roman brothers and sisters, *ut unum sint* (Jn 17:21). In beginning with the gospel, and in the knowledge of traditional interpretation, we can hope to shed light on problems of worship and language which are confronting us today, and make godly decisions that will confirm us in the first and fourth "marks" of the church: our unity and our catholicity.

Beginning at the Beginning: The Triune God

We must begin by acknowledging that there is no fully-developed doctrine of the Trinity outlined even in these chapters of the "theological" gospel. If this were the case, the church would not have labored under the difficult discussions that preceded Nicaea and Chalcedon, nor would some sects or individuals which divorce the Scriptures from their traditional interpretation continue to express quasi-Arian theologies. Nevertheless, this passage, among others, was essential in the later articulation of the Trinitarian mystery. Our purpose here is not to inquire into the understanding of the first-century Christian communities, nor to exegete the original "intent" of the writer of the fourth gospel; rather, it is to see our place within the entire tradition of the church, including the credal formulations to which we lay claim, and by which we are informed. With a full awareness that other types of questions may be asked of this passage, we fruitfully read it for an intimation of the Trinitarian faith which we embrace.

Jesus begins, after announcing His impending departure, by calling His disciples to the new rule of love (Jn 13:34); He closes His teaching by praying for their unity (Jn 17:21-26). The vision of true love and unity therefore envelopes this passage, and characterizes or names the community for which Jesus is praying—both the immediate historical community of the disciples, and those who will believe because of their word (Jn 17:26). The basis of this love is made clear both within the intricacies of the teaching (chapters 14-17), and in the final summary: "I made your name known to them, and I will make it known, so that the love with which you have loved me may be in them, and I in them" (Jn 17:26). Many studies have been written, of course, on the significance of the "name" in the fourth gospel and in the ancient biblical world in general. We do well to remember that the gospel begins by speaking of those who, " received him who believed in his name" (Jn 1:12) and so are made children of God: the parallelism here, plus the high importance of the "name" and "naming" in Hebrew and ancient Christian culture, demonstrate that the word "name" refers to the whole person, to the nature of the one so evoked. It is not that Jesus had divulged to His disciples a secret or code name for God, so that they could live as an esoteric community, although this is the spin that Gnostic writers in the past and present-day witnesses have put on John 17:26. This manipulative, literalist or magical view of the Name's invocation is far from the text. Rather, Jesus has revealed God's nature, and the person of God, and promises that this revelation will be made even more full. In so knowing God (which includes knowing about Him but extends beyond this to a growing knowledge of God *himself*), divine love will be created within His followers.

When we ask what it is that has been shown, and what promises to be shown by Jesus so that this love may be created, we begin, however, with the "names" of Father, Son and Spirit that are given and explained in this discourse. Jesus speaks continually here of "my Father" but implies throughout that the link between the Father and Him will be extended to include others. This, of course, becomes explicit in the resurrection appearance to Magdalene: "Go to my brothers[4] and say to them, 'I am ascending to my Father and your Father, to my God and your God'" (Jn 20:17). The message is clear: it is on the basis of Jesus' right to call God Father that believers are given this name, for they have become God's children. Moreover, in thinking about this mystery, we are pushed back beyond the "human" experience of Jesus (if it is even sane to make such distinctions!): the bond between Father and Son and their relationship One with the Other is no mere temporal condition. As Jesus suggests in His high-priestly prayer, His glory, which He is about to fully receive, and pass on to the disciples, is a glory that He had in the presence with the Father before the world existed (17:5). The Father is in the Son, and the Son in the Father; the Son glorifies the Father, and the Father will glorify the Son; even left "alone," the Son is in the company of the Father; the Son comes from the Father and the Son goes to the Father; the Son does as the Father commands, to demonstrate His love for the Father; the Father and the Son will come to those who love the Son, and make their home with them. These are only a few of the chords sounded in Jesus' words. Our filial bond to the Father springs from the ineffable, eternal and fruitful bond of identity and relationship between Father and Son. In Christ, and not destined to be orphans, we are adopted by God as true children. Out of that status, brothers and sisters together, we forge true love, or indeed, have forged within us the love that comes from the inner being of God.

The creation of this love between us moves us directly to the third Name disclosed by Jesus. Jesus speaks, in personal terms (contrary to the grammatic neutral gender demanded by *to pneuma*) of the "other Advocate" or "Spirit of Truth" or "Holy Spirit" *who* proceeds from the Father and *whom* the Father will send in the Son's name. In concert with the Father, the Spirit will glorify the Son; in concert with the Son, He will not speak on His own but will witness to the divine will. Through His coming, what is the Father's, and therefore the Son's, will be given to the disciples (Jn 16:14-15). We are to share in the nature of God! Bound up with the gift of the Spirit is the keeping of the commandment of love, the ability to abide in God, the teaching of greater mysteries, the ability to do great things, the remembrance of the Son's words, and the imparting of divine peace. As the church fathers were later to describe this, it is out of the inner "dance" (*perichoresis*) of the Father, Son, and Spirit (who share glory One with the Other) that our glory as children of God springs.

One of the greatest mysteries to note here is that the "dance" and mutuality do not exclude the notions of obedience and self-effacement. The Son goes to the Father who is, in one sense, "greater" than He (Jn 14:28),[5] and demonstrates His love through obedience (Jn 14:31). Some commentators, in fear of losing the divinity of the Son, have softened the implications of this passage by reference to *economia* and the filial subjection of the "human" Jesus. Such an interpretation does not seem, however, to do justice to the ongoing and assertive present tense of the passage. Moreover, it is not only here in the New Testament that we are troubled by an enigmatic reference to an extra-temporal ordering of the Father and Son. Equally problematic are Paul's words about the *eschaton* in 1 Corinthians 15: 24-28:

> Then comes the end, when he hands over the kingdom to God the Father, after he has destroyed every ruler and every authority and power...When all things are subjected to him, then the Son himself will also be in subjected to the One who put all things in subjection under him, so that God may be all in all.

Alongside assertions of a high Christology (a Christology which would issue in the full-blown doctrines of the Trinity and the two natures of Christ) both the fourth evangelist and Paul assert an order. Adrienne von Speyer, in commenting upon the Johannine passage, does not skirt the "subordinist" problem, but explores its meaning within an unmitigated Trinitarianism,[6]

> Here the immense mystery begins. He, a man, goes as God to God...[P]rofound depths of truth lie in this word of the Son: *The Father is greater than I*. No human person says this or could say it, nor is it a word of the Father, who would not say it; rather, it is a word that only the Son's love and humility can utter.[7]

The Son demonstrates His obedience to the Father; similarly, the Spirit proceeds from the Father, and does not bear witness alone. Nevertheless, Father, Son, and Spirit are duly given glory and worship. This tension between order and mutuality, while difficult to grasp, may be helpful in understanding the complex roles which we fulfill in our human but divinely conceived community: mirroring the Godhead (or better, sharing in its nature) our family will include both order, and equal glory or honor. As St John Chrysostom puts it, "if you love, you ought to submit to the one you love."[8]

The Problem of Language: Our Corporate Worship

So, then, when we begin with the story of the Gospels, we find that our names of Father and Son (together with the more shadowy person of the Spirit) come from Jesus' own way of referring to himself, and the language used by the Gospels and letters in referring to God. While the Old Testament uses metaphor to speak of God as a father, it is not until the New Testament that we find the word used consistently as a kind of name, a name that goes beyond a mere picture. Jesus, the Son of God, taking up in himself the role of Israel as God's Son, but also transcending it because He is the uniquely begotten Son, addresses His Father personally. "Abba, Father," He says. As Pannenberg notices, "On the lips of Jesus, 'Father' became a proper name for God. It thus ceased to be simply one designation among others."[9] Until recently, there was no question about this characteristic and family manner of thinking about and referring to God. Of course, other titles and names were used to speak of the One who is not to be contained. Yet, those who were in Christ considered it a privilege and a glory to call upon the Father in God-given boldness, *parresia*, and considered that this particular invocation rested upon the revealed character of the Father. This was no Johannine aberration, but a name and relationship found generally enough in the New Testament to inform later thinkers on Trinitarian theology: "No one knows the Son except the Father; and no one knows the Father except the Son and anyone to whom the Son chooses to reveal him" (Mt 11:27). Let us leave, for a moment, the rich implications of such language, and turn to the challenge that has been directed toward this peculiarly Christian way of naming God, based on the link between Father and Son.

In fact, a very different story of origins has now been urged in the church and academy, and accepted by many. "Role-model theology"[10] has convinced not a few that every religion projects social values onto the figure of God to construct a picture of a god[11] after which we can confidently pattern ourselves. Since hierarchy and patriarchalism are in the late twenty-first century undesirable, our picture of God should avoid gender terms, or use both equally. Metaphor, then, is seen as our way of seeking to name the unnameable, and good theology should use appropriate and (enlightened) pictures, or society and the church will suffer. A creative and vocal spokesperson for this view is the hymnwriter and thinker Brian Wren, who is well known for encapsulating the "patriarchalist" view of God (enshrined in the culture-bound Scriptures, and from which he hopes the church will be liberated) in the acronym KINGAFAP ("King and Father All-Powerful").[12] Here the original metaphors are seen within their (inadequate) biblical narrative and traced throughout several theological moments in church history. For Wren, even the distinction between double and single procession is incidental, although he is taken with the Augustinian depiction of the Holy Spirit as the "love-link" (*De Trinitate*, 7:3-6, 8:10-14, 5:19-37) without realizing the difficulties which this picture (compounded by the *filioque*) may have caused or may cause in our full acceptance of the Spirit as a person.[13] Though he makes use of the Augustinian view,[14] his major point is that Eastern and Western theologians alike accepted and continued in the twentieth century to accept "the sequence given in the KINGAFAP system."[15]

Wren's experimental renaming and creative re-narrativization of the Christian story is, interestingly, often right in what it affirms, but wrong in what it denies. The same may be said, it seems, of more nuanced and "traditional-friendly" deliberations, such as those of Jane Williams.[16] Williams is content to retain the names of Father and Son; Wren seeks "more adequate" terms. On one major point, however, both are in agreement. As Williams states, "To call God "Father" is not to evoke the 'patriarch'.... 'Authority' and 'headship' are not characteristic of God's fatherhood, in the biblical tradition;"[17] Wren concurs, "In keeping with the biblical record, 'Father' is Abba, and the 'kingdom' of God is marked not by hierarchy, but by freedom."[18] While Wren revises, and Williams qualifies, both see mutuality and freedom as incompatible with headship and obedience. Thus, Wren faults Moltmann for his depiction of the Son as responding in submission (although this is in concert, as we have seen, with both the fourth gospel and Paul). Again, he cites with approval the dancing metaphor of C.S. Lewis' *Perelandra*, while totally missing Lewis' own emphasis on subordination as inherent in the dance![19] Wren rightly characterizes the dance as "not a solo performance, but a communal enterprise, like an eightsome reel, a square dance, or barn dance."[20] Lewis would, while agreeing with the "communal" aspect, also point out that the dance is courtly, with a leader, and key players, not a free-for-all or a mere line-dance. The drama is not to be tamed by the conflation of leader and follower: yet there is freedom and mutuality!

With other Trinitarians, Wren, in hymn, celebrates "every kind of unity/...[which] begins with God, forever One,/ whose nature is Community."[21] This "Community" is, however, re-formed along contemporary egalitarian lines, in agreement with other theological and exegetical moves that are being made today, such as "the brokerless Kingdom," the egalitarian "Q community," or the picture of "God as Friend." At this point, several questions demand a hearing: What is at stake in "correcting" the root biblical metaphors and story? What is lost in reducing the tension between the liberty offered, and the submission required, by the rule of God? The new vision, and new dance affirm the first (liberty), while denying the second (submission). This is no mere squabble about arbitrary metaphors or appealing names. Rather, we are in the realm of root issues: metaphorical theology urges us to "try out new pictures"[22] more suited to the *Zeitgeist* of the day; traditional theology continues to cry out "Abba, Father!" because it sees itself in solidarity with Jesus, the humble One who has made the Father known.

We do not need to remain naive or rigid at this point in order to remain faithful. The apophatic tradition of the church rightly reminds us that no name comprehends the living God, and that we must also murmur, "Neither is this thou." However, to speak of the limitation of human words, images and concepts is not an open door to the complete relativization of all words, images and concepts. To recognize that we do not fully comprehend God, even in the pictures and ideas that He has given us, is not the same as saying that we can substitute more palatable images or terms. There is the initial difficulty in knowing what constitutes the essence and what the separable vehicle in a theological symbol: no human mind can be entirely sure, when naming a mystery, about what is "like" and what is totally "other" in contrasting the symbol with its referent. We would have to be outside of our own world, and able to compare this (independently) with the greater reality, in order to be certain.

Careful thinking about the ways in which the names are used will nonetheless free us from the inevitable imprisonment suspected in the complaint, "If God is male, then the male is God."[23] It is helpful here to contemplate the *shape* of the biblical story. When the story speaks about a Father and Son, how does it use these pictures? We do well to remember that the Bible (and subsequent Jewish as well as Christian thought) have never spoken of God as *male*, although they have pictured God in masculine terms. The Anglican 39 Articles declare, "There is but one living and true God, everlasting, without body, parts or passions."[24] Second, the Christian story presents us with a very unusual turn of events. In the words of Garrett Green,

> This God does not jealously hoard His power. As a husband He does not beat His unfaithful wife but cries out with the pain of a jilted lover and redoubles His efforts to win her back (Hos 2). As Father He "did not spare his own Son but gave him up for us all" (Ro 8:32). As Son He did not claim the prerogatives of power and lord it over His subjects but "emptied himself, taking the form of a servant...He humbled himself and became obedient unto death, even death on a

cross" (Php 2:7-8). As Spirit He incorporates us into the mystical body of Christ, in whom "there is neither slave nor free, there is neither male nor female" (Gal 3:28). As king He does not isolate himself in heavenly splendor but wills to dwell with His people, to "wipe away every tear from their eyes" and to deliver them from all that oppresses them, even from death itself (Rev 21:4).[25]

Here is a poignant reversal of the all-powerful One who yields all, even dying for those whom He loves. This masculinely-pictured God is neither male nor oppressive, but overturns our presuppositions. The historical Christian faith, then, is a revealed religion, which uses masculine imagery for God in a very surprising way. God, if you like, takes up our human metaphors, but uses them in a way we never could have expected. The names of Father and Son function iconically, but also iconoclastically, affirming order, but also disrupting our fond ideas of what that order might mean. We might venture to say that hierarchy, which includes both grandeur and tenderness, is affirmed, but hierarchial*ism* is squarely judged.

Our First and Fourth Mark: One and Catholic

This affirming and disorienting vision of Father, Son, and Holy Spirit must be faithfully and reverently maintained if we hope, as a communion, to retain our God-given birthright of unity, and if we hope, along with our sister communions, to express ever more fully our catholicity. We need the name of Father, Son, and Holy Spirit, to safeguard the characteristic idea of our faith, the idea of "otherness in relation." To put this less functionally, it is by mirroring the ordered and communicative reality of the Trinity, as revealed to us in Scripture, and expounded to us in the church, that we find our own life. This does not mean that other names may not be used in reference to the One we adore; many names and even the action of not-naming have been faithfully employed within our Christian family as a reminder that our God may not be contained. Nevertheless, many of the new projects of re-naming seem, at root, to spring from the assumption that we *know better*[26] than our forbears (even the witnesses in Scripture!). Where renaming is conceived as a substitutionary endeavor, or as a way of marginalizing the normative Trinitarian name, there is inevitable fallout. Loss of particularity, functionalism, depersonalization, panentheistic interconnection with the creation and sexualization are some of the vicious possibilities encountered in the well-meaning attempts at revision.[27] Even those who work diligently to avoid such problems fall prey: Wren, for example, is concerned to give the Holy Spirit a more descriptive definition than he perceives in the traditional name, but in adopting the term "Mutual Friend" makes the Spirit's role wholly determined by her (*sic*)[28] relation to the first and second persons of the Trinity.

A better route would be to affirm the scriptural and apostolic witnesses, alongside careful teaching about the key Player(s): the inter-relationship of the persons of the Godhead, and God's unfathomable love for humankind. The problem is not with the story. The problem is not with the pictures or the Name. The problem is not in hearing the story, in not explaining the Name well enough. God is self-revealed to us in history and in the name of Father, Son, and Holy Spirit. To hastily alter that name is to abandon the truth to ideology and political correctness, is to risk a subtle or even decisive change in our story and our knowledge of God, and to endanger our catholicism. If we follow the course of one of our sister communions in Canada (which has allowed, in some jurisdictions, baptism into the "name" of "Creator, Redeemer, and Sustainer") we not only risk serious rupture with present apostolic communions, but we effectively cease integral connection with the historic church. There is no way that the "intent" of the officiant to baptize into the name of the Christian Trinity can be assumed if such a reformulation is used.[29] Such distancing from the church might even be accomplished were the traditional formula to be made simply *pro forma* at "high occasions" such as baptism, without reflecting the normal and natural use of our community. (We may, in fact, be on the way to this divorce, with the growing preference for substitutions at the prayer before the homily or at the dismissing benediction). Nor would such suspicions about catholicity be arising simply on a formal or technical basis. For it is reasonable to suppose that where other considerations relegate the traditional Trinitarian name to the antiquarian past, that that community will eventually no longer be formed by the Father, informed by the Son, and conformed by the Spirit,[30] the triune Source of perichoretic unity. Already, a primary mark of the Son, His humility, is finding little room in our communities, even as a desired virtue: independence has supplanted it. Together, we learn a different way of being from the Trinity. For the One upon whom we call is the One who calls us into being. Let us therefore cleave to Father, Son, and Holy Spirit in our adoration, but explain the drama of the salvation story, as well as the free and humble "dance" which that Name enacts, evokes, engenders and brings to birth.

All language is, of course, insufficient to comprehend the Living God. Yet, paradoxically, God has made himself known in the One whom we call the Word, and who spoke to us about himself as Son, as well as about the Father and the Spirit of Truth. What we can know, as yet by far, of our triune God, is truly if not exhaustively represented in the names of Father, Son, and Holy Spirit. These names speak first of all about God's own nature, and second, of God's intimate relationship to us. In times of controversy and struggle, even over principle issues such as our mode of worship, and the names that we use, we can take courage from the church's past and remember that it is out of such difficult times that rich theology may come to light. Remembering that we do not ask alone, but with the whole of the church, and in concert with the Spirit, who prays in us, let us pray that these names will not become a barrier in our communion, but that they will continue to be the effective token of our reconciliation. For the Son is our peace, and through Him we have access to the Father by one Spirit.

NOTES

1. Thomas Merton, *Thoughts in Solitude* (New York: Farrar, Straus and Giroux, 1958) 52.

2.   Ibid.

3.   Daniel L. Migliore *Faith Seeking Understanding* (Grand Rapids: Eerdmans, 1991) 61.

4.   It is essential to note here that although Jesus is sending a message first to the apostles, whom He terms "his brethren," this is a message that is first heard and mediated by the female disciple given the title "Equal-to-the-Apostles." Moreover, the word about "your Father" is an inclusive one that is passed on by the apostles to the church, including males and females. Jesus is not calling the apostles *alone* His brethren, but implying that all believers now have this new standing with God. This is consonant with the assurance and promise made in 14:7, 16:15, and 17:20.

5.   It does not seem adequate here to explain this away in terms of Jesus' "human" subordination to the Father, since the Johannine thought speaks in the present tense of the ongoing relationship between Father and Son. While this verse is challenging to Trinitarian thought, it is not idiosyncratic in the Scriptures. See also the eschatological ordering of 1 Corinthians 15:24-28, where Paul explains the Son's glory in terms of the Father's super-order. Paul and John seem to hold to the equality of Father with Son alongside a certain subordination. If the former (the equality) is doubted, see the reconstrual of the divine "name" of Isaiah 45:23 in Philippians 2:5-11, or the reconfiguration of the Shema in 1 Corinthians 8:6. I owe this insight of Paul's implicit "binitarianism" to the teaching of the Rev. Dr. N.T. Wright. Typically commentators have noticed the subordination, without heeding the exaltation of the Son; inversely, "conservative" theologians have highlighted the exaltation, without knowing what to do about the ordering. The patristic view, continued in the Eastern tradition, and now reclaimed by the ecumenical removal of the *filioque* holds both together, in that it speaks of

perichoresis alongside filiation and procession. There is a true triangle, but it may not be inverted.

6.   The balance between high Christology and ordering in the Johannine and Pauline passages would seem to affirm the kind of Monarchianism *within* Trinitarian thought displayed by the Cappadocians, rather than either Marcionite or dynamic monarchianism which were excluded from orthodox thinking. Monarchianism *within* Trinitarianism sees the Father as eternally the font of the other Persons (filiation and procession) while affirming the equal divinity and power of the entire Godhead. It is of course true that some Western theologians continue to affirm double procession while consenting to the removal of the *filioque* as a charitable strategy. There is, unfortunately, no time here to debate the difficulties cited by Moltmann *et al* (in defense of double procession), where they reclaim the Anselmian principle of a necessary consonance between the inner relation of the Trinity and divine self-disclosure. Nor is there space to present (as a counterargument) Lossky's compelling restatement of the Palamite distinction between the essence and energies of God. On all accounting, we are on mysterious ground at this point; sooner or later analysis must cease, as we simply stand in awe, watching the unconsumed bush burn.

7.   Adrienne von Speyer, *The Farewell Discourses; Meditations on John 13-17*, tr. E.A. Nelson (San Francisco: Ignatius Press, 1987) 152, 155.

8.   John Chrysostom, *Commentary on St. John the Apostle and Evangelist, Homilies 48-88* in *The Fathers of the Church, A New Translation*, tr. Goggin (New York: Fathers of the Church Inc., 1960) 283.

9.   Wolfhart Pannenberg, *Systematic Theology*, I, tr. G.W. Bromiley (Grand Rapids, Eerdmans, 1991) 262.

10. Here I adopt the terminology of Garrett Green, in his interaction with Sallie McFague. See "The Gender of God and the Theology of Metaphor," in *Speaking the Christian God; The Holy Trinity and the Challenge of Feminism*, ed. Alvin F. Kimel, Jr. (Grand Rapids: Eerdmans, 1992) 44-64.

11. See, for example, the argument that "Father," etc., are "our images, not pictures of God in the reality and fullness of the divine being," *Commentary on Prayer Book Studies 30* (New York: The Church Hymnal Corporation, 1989) C-8. This view is actually taught in one of the hymns of the proposed Canadian Hymnbook, where role-model theology is ascribed to Jesus himself. In Hymn 283, option for March 19, St. Joseph's day, the relationship of Joseph and Jesus is described in this manner:

> All praise, O God, for Joseph
> the guardian of your Son,
> who saved him from King Herod,
> when safety there was none
> He taught the trade of builder,
> when they to Nazareth came,
> and Joseph's love made "Father"
> to be, for Christ, God's name.

12. Brian Wren, *What Language Shall I Borrow? God-Talk in Worship: A Male Response to Feminist Theology* (New York: Crossroads, 1990). See especially p. 196.

13. It is interesting to note that while the Eastern tradition did not use this language to refer to the *hypostasis* of the Spirit, there is to be found in Palamas, for example, an analogy of love directed towards describing energy of love *common* to the three persons of the Godhead.

14. The Spirit becomes, in His reformulation, "The Mutual Friend" (210): a rather dependent, or relative, role!

15. "A KINGAFAP sequence with the King-Father giving orders to His Son and the spirit being sent by the Father alone or Father and Son together," ibid, 198.

16. Jane Williams, "The Fatherhood of God," in *The Forgotten Trinity; A Selection of Papers presented to the BCC Study Commission on Trinitarian Doctrine Today,* (London: BCC/CCBI Interchurch House, 1991) 91-101.

17. Williams, 96.

18 Wren, 198.

19. Lewis' protagonist Ransom describes the great dance thus: "Yet the former pattern not thereby dispossessed by finding in its new subordination a significance greater than that which it had abdicated." In Wren, 213.

20. Wren, 212.

21. Ibid.

22. Sallie McFague, *Models of God: Theology for an Ecological, Nuclear Age* (Philadelphia: Fortress Press, 1987) xii.

23. Mary Daly authored this phrase, since become a motto, in *Beyond the Father: Toward a Philosophy of Women's Liberation* (Boston: Beacon Press, 1973) 19.

24. We may, of course, want to question the totalizing concept of an impassive God, in the light of the drama of the Incarnation, and in the knowledge that such language owes much to classical philosophy as absorbed by church tradition. Nevertheless, the citation demonstrates the intent of Anglican (and Christian) theology to eschew the notion of a male god.

25. Green, "The Gender of God and the Theology of Metaphor," 60.

26.   See, for example, the self-congratulatory mood of Wren's con-
      clusion to "Naming Anew," p. 214, where he shows the
      advantages of "Beloved, Lover and Mutual Friend" over the
      traditional triad.

27.   Particularly strong is the plea to picture God as Mother. How-
      ever, this may well suggest a religion in which God is not personal
      and transcendent, that is, separate from the creation, but inter-
      connected with the creation which has proceeded from the
      womb of the Goddess. The implication is particularly strong
      when God is invoked as Mother, but not usually when a simile
      is used, disclosing the mother-like characteristics of God . Such
      similes, but never a maternal name, are also used in Scripture.

28.   Wren uses the feminine pronoun as a "move away from
      hierarchy…recognizing that both *she* and *he* are inadequate"
      (210). He also attaches *sic* to those who refer to the Spirit as
      "he." The question inevitably arises: "inadequate" to what?
      For while "he" may be problematic to some revisionists, it is
      the surprising pronoun used in the Fourth Gospel. Wren and
      others find themselves *sic*ing not only the traditionalists, but
      the evangelist!

29.   Interestingly, "Creator, Redeemer and Sustainer" found ap-
      proval from a Jewish friend outside of the Christian communion
      who did not, obviously, accept the doctrine of the Trinity: His
      God was equally a creator, redeemer, and sustainer. Paul Minear
      offers this anecdote in "The Bible and the Book of Worship,"
      Prism 3 (1988) 52-53.

30.   I adopt these terms as an extension, and re-formulation of
      "institution" and "constitution" suggested by Karl Rahner, *The
      Trinity* (1970) and *passim* as cited by John Zizioulas, "The
      Doctrine of God the Trinity Today: Suggestions for an Ecu-
      menical Study," in *The Forgotten Trinity,* 28.

The Trinity and Liturgical Renewal

Daniel Meeter

I N this essay, we will examine some of the implications of the doc-trine of the Holy Trinity for liturgy, especially for liturgical renewal. At stake is not only the vitality of what we do on Sunday morning, but also the validity of the church's mission to the world. Whenever we address liturgical questions we need to remember that "one can't tug at a finger of liturgy without immediately getting the whole hand of theology."[1] A number of important Trinitarian concerns lie under most of the apparently practical questions of liturgical direction and style.

At the outset, a truly Trinitarian theology is a Christocentric theol-ogy. In other words, the one God who was confessed by Israel (Dt 6:4) is made known to us fully only in Jesus Christ, in and around whose life and passion the three persons of the Trinity have been re-vealed. Our relationship to the one God is therefore also Christocentric it is "in Christ" (Eph 1:3) and this has important implications for worship. At the same time, because the person of the Holy Spirit is also fully God, I will try to open up some fresh pneumatological per-spectives which also have implications for worship. I will depend upon the late Dutch theologian A. A. Van Ruler, who drew the lines of what he called a "fully developed Trinitarian theology" which would do justice to both Christology and pneumatology.[2] We will suggest how Trinitarian theology offers to liturgical renewal not only necessary correctives and discipline but also pregnant opportunities.

Some preliminary definitions are in order.[3] First, Christian worship is what happens when God comes to have a meeting with us in Christ.[4] Of great importance in this definition is that God is both present and active in our worship, and that God's activity is primary. Also important is the word "meeting," and the connotations of a business meeting are not to be avoided. God comes to have such meetings with us in order to accomplish certain business. In biblical history, these business meetings took the form of covenantal transactions.[5] They were covenantal, first, in that through them, God established and maintained lasting relationships built around specific promises and mutual obligations; second, that within them, God ordained certain signs, symbols, and procedures in which the promises and obligations were comprehended, and to which God vowed to be faithful; and third, that God's people were faithfully to carry out the covenantal obligations and procedures as the means by which they would enjoy God's promises.

In our own day, God makes use of the worship service to meet with us, to create faith in us, and to stimulate and strengthen that faith.[6] The purpose of the meeting is that God's people be converted.[7] The means that God uses to accomplish this purpose are the various activities in the worship service, the "agenda" of the business meeting.[8] The church, by the very act of participating in God's meeting and sharing in God's activity, offers God true worship. The church exercises its faith, and responds to God in confession, praise, and thanksgiving. The covenantal character of worship continues in that God has ordained certain signs and symbols, the sacraments, which comprehend God's promises, to which God is faithful, and by means of which the church enjoys God's promises.[9] This means that the worship service is designed to be an actual salvation event. It also means that if the church wants to offer true worship to God, it needs to make use of God's divinely ordained means of salvation and to pay heed to biblical norms for worship. To do otherwise is to put the congregation outside of God's chosen way of working, and to deny it the proper enjoyment of the promises of God.

Liturgy is the shape which the church has given to its meetings with God. Here the human element comes to the fore—human freedom and human creativity. The church has both the right and the responsibility to give thoughtful shape to God's meetings. This right comes as a result of the outpouring of the Holy Spirit on Pentecost, and this responsibility comes from the fact that the New Testament itself does not prescribe a specific pattern of worship.[10] But the church's freedom and creativity are not to be understood as a general license. Any liturgy which calls itself Christian must be a celebration of the passion and resurrection of Christ, because Christ's passion was not only the focus of all God's promises to humanity, but also the central and definitive meeting which the one God has had with us.

The Worship of the One God

We understand the Holy Trinity to be the three persons of the one God confessed by Israel (Dt 6:4). We begin our Trinitarian understanding of worship by looking at the great covenantal meeting which the one God had with Israel at Mount Sinai. God called Israel out of Egypt into the desert in order to have this meeting with them (Ex 3:12), and this meeting became Israel's definitive experience of worship. The purpose of the meeting was that Israel should be converted from their slavery into being "a priestly kingdom and a holy nation" (Ex 19:6). God began this conversion by graciously and unilaterally delivering Israel from judgment by means of the sacrificial blood of the Passover lamb, and then delivering them from Egypt through the death and resurrection of the Red Sea. God called them together at Sinai, where they prepared themselves through washing and abstinence. Then God spoke to them directly from the mountain, and continued to communicate with them through the medium of Moses, laying out the terms of the covenant, to which the people responded, "All the words that the Lord has spoken we will do" (Ex 24:3). Moses then set the covenantal terms to writing. The next morning Moses built an altar and twelve pillars, where the young men of Israel made sacrifices (the first since the Passover night), and he sprinkled half the sacrificial blood on the altar. Then he read the Book of the Covenant, and again the people responded, "All that the LORD has spoken we will do, and we will be obedient" (Ex 24:7). Moses sprinkled the remainder of the blood upon the people and said, "See the blood of the covenant that the LORD has made with you in accordance with all these words." Then the seventy-four leaders of the people ascended the mountain, saw God, and ate and drank (Ex 24:8ff). The covenant was ratified, sealed, and celebrated, real business was accomplished, Israel had been constituted as the kingdom of priests and a holy nation.

The rest of the Torah, the laws and ordinances of the Books of Moses, the system of Levitical sacrifices, and even the architecture of the tabernacle were meant to deepen and extend this basic covenantal meeting at Sinai. The laws and rituals were designed to reveal and teach and celebrate God's character, God's mighty acts, God's relationship to creation, the truth about humanity, and Israel's vocation. The laws and rituals also provided the means for Israel to maintain its vocation and the integrity of its relationship with God. Israel was to be a distinguished people with a mission of witness to and priesthood for the world ("Indeed, the whole earth is mine," Ex 19:5), and the laws and sacrifices were engineered to develop a working holiness and righteousness that revealed God's nature and led to the offering of appropriate praise. When the tabernacle was replaced by the temple in Jerusalem, these designs and patterns remained essentially the same.

The glory of the covenantal relationship was that God would dwell among His people. God promised, "If you follow my statutes and observe my commandments…I will place my dwelling in your midst, and I shall not abhor you, and I will walk among you, and will be your God, and you shall be my people" (Lev 26:3-12). The sign of God dwelling in the midst of Israel was the cloud that covered the tent of meeting and the glory that filled the tabernacle (Ex 40:34). The same cloud of glory filled the temple of Solomon (1Ki 8:11). After the destruction of Jerusalem and the exile, Ezekiel prophesied the restoration of the temple and the return of God's glory, for God would reside among the people of Israel forever (Eze 43:1-7).

Christocentric Worship

In this light, we can see how important it was that when the infant Jesus was brought into the temple by His parents, the ancient Simeon identified Him with the "glory" of Israel (Lk 2:32). In the person of the incarnate Christ, the one God was recapitulating His dwelling among His people and walking in the midst of Israel.[11] In Christ as the Son of God, God was keeping the covenant. But also in Christ as the Son of Man, God found a true covenant partner, who was recapitulating Israel's corporate experience of the Passover, Exodus, and Mount Sinai in His own passion and resurrection experience. When we look at the meetings that our Lord had with His disciples before and after His passion, we see that His words and actions made strong reference to the Passover and Exodus. For example, in the upper room, during the Passover meal, when He said, "this is my blood of the covenant" (Mt 26:28), He was obviously referring to Moses' words at Mount Sinai, "See the blood of the covenant" (Ex 24:8), after which the elders went up to eat and drink with God.[12] Our Lord was prophesying that His sacrifice would recapitulate both the Passover sacrifice and the sacrifice at Sinai, which ratified the covenant.[13] He was announcing that the old covenant was being fulfilled and replaced by a new one (Heb 8:13; 9:15). But this new covenant, as the apostolic writers recognized, had essentially the same goal as the old, that God should have a people, drawn from every tribe and tongue, who are a kingdom of priests and a holy nation (1Pe 2:9; Rev 1:6; 5:10).

When we put Christ's passion in the context of the Passover and Mount Sinai, it becomes clear that Christ's crucifixion was in itself an act of worship, indeed, the great act of worship. The sacrifice of His body was a Levitical act, Christ was both the victim and the priest, and the hill of Calvary became the true temple (the veil was rent) with its own court of gentiles (the soldiers) and court of women in attendance. As the High Priest, Christ offered absolution from the cross ("Father forgive them" and "Today you will be with Me") and sang Psalm 22 ("My God, my God"). The crucifixion was the great act of worship that constituted the new people of God just as the meeting at Sinai had constituted Israel. The epistle to the Hebrews argues that the ascended Christ continually offers the liturgy of the crucifixion to His Father, eternally pleading the once-for-all sacrifice as the principle of God's reconciliation of the world and the means of our incorporation into the people of God.[14] By faith we participate in Christ's work for us, and God creates faith and nourishes it through the preaching of the gospel and the use of the sacraments, God's covenantal signs. That is the business of every meeting that God has with the congregation every week. The purpose of the liturgy, therefore, is to communicate, extend, and celebrate this new covenant, which Christ, on our behalf, has made with the one God through His blood.

It is unfortunate that so much Protestant worship (without necessarily denying the divinity of Christ), lacks a Christocentric character. The service is not understood as a covenantal transaction used by God to create and strengthen faith. The result, in the mainline churches, for example, is often a worship style which amounts to a bland unitarianism, where God is spoken of in very general terms, apart from the confession of Israel, and where God is approached without an awareness of the necessity of the blood of Christ. There is little sense that the Sunday morning service is meant to remember and celebrate the biblical history of salvation in Israel and the gospels, and even less sense that the service is meant to be an appropriation of the covenantal sacrifice of Christ by which we are reconciled to God. Thus, no conversion is expected, in any sense of the word, and very little seems to be at stake. God is distant, and the talk is mostly about God, rather than to God or from God. The prayers are minimal and formal (even when they're not written out) and the sacraments convey neither the vital presence nor the active work of God. Since there is no expectation that God comes to have an actual meeting with us, the liturgy usually functions to make a point or reinforce an idea, and the worship leaders feel free to be very creative, expressive, or inventive with liturgical form and language.

On the other hand, what we find in the more conservative, evangelical, or fundamentalist churches amounts to what we might call "Jesusism." The passion of Jesus Christ is heartily confessed, and the Trinity is officially honored, but the fullness of God in the confession of Israel is generally underplayed, and the emphasis is on what Jesus means to the individual believer rather than on how we are reconciled with the one God. The language is fixated on a narrow kind of conversion, rather than on the congregation becoming a "royal priesthood and a holy nation." Conversion is understood to be something which the individual does in response to the message presented by the worship leaders, and not something which God accomplishes by means of the agenda of the service itself. The sacraments are regarded as ordinances to be obeyed for the expression of faith rather than as means of God's sovereign activity. There is little expectation that in the worship service God actually comes to have a meeting with us and to transact business according to a covenantal agenda, and therefore the form of the liturgy is incidental. There are ways in which this kind of service ends up being similar to the more liberal service. It is not designed to remember and celebrate the biblical history of salvation in Israel and the gospels nor to appropriate the covenantal sacrifice of Christ by which we are reconciled to God. Although there is a sense of the presence of God, it is a generalized presence, and so, while there is as much talk to God as about God, there is little actual talk from God. Here too what liturgy there is usually functions to make a point or reinforce an idea, and the worship leaders freely modify liturgical form and language according to their particular message for that week.

By contrast, Christocentric worship would require every Sunday morning service to be built around the appropriation and celebration of Christ's passion and resurrection, making use, week by week, of the richness of salvation history. An underlying confidence in God's activity through God's divinely ordained means of grace would allow the worship leaders to give room for the liturgy to do its work, and conform their speech to Scripture, so that their talk might be not so much about God as from God. The Bible itself would provide most of the language of the service, not slavishly quoted, but digested, processed, and appropriately recast as prayers, hymns, and responses, in order to give the congregation entry into salvation history. Because the goal of the service would be the continuing conversion of the people into God's "royal priesthood and chosen nation," and because Christ "gives knowledge of salvation to his people by the forgiveness of sins" (Lk 1:77), the service would include important moments of reconciliation, including confession of sin and absolution. Important to the service would be the proclamation of the promises of God in Jesus Christ, as well as the claiming and enjoyment of those promises, especially through the sacraments, God's covenantal signs. Indeed, it is in Holy Communion that we are both to remember our Lord's passion (Lk 22:19) and to recognize His living presence (Lk 24:35).

It is apparent that the Christocentric perspective provides discipline for the practice of liturgy. There is an objective "once-for-all-ness" to the everlasting gospel which needs to be heard and believed in again and again; there is a sense in which it is always news, even to believers. Worship leaders, under less pressure to be relevant or creative, would be able, in a real sense, to get themselves out of the way of the exchange between God and the congregation. Indeed, the worship leaders would have less control over the service, and there would be no need to build the whole service around a chosen theme. The service can be more open-ended, giving full play to a multiplicity of themes, full and partial, from the richness of the history of salvation. The creativity can be entrusted to the congregation, in its response to the gospel interaction, and in the weekly rehearsal of its priesthood.

Fully Trinitarian Worship

We have already shown how the crucifixion of Christ is the Son's worship of the Father; this inter-Trinitarian worship is the great fact that is at the center of Christian worship. We too have an entrée into the Trinity, for we worship the Father inasmuch as we are incorporated into the Son; we have become "members of Christ" and corporately "His body, the church." But our relationship with God does not end with the second person of the Trinity that we are "in Christ." It goes one step further to the Spirit. Christ is not the whole, He is the means; He is the center, but the center is not the end.[15] Christ speaks beyond himself, to the Father and the Spirit (Jn 15). The Spirit comes after, "whose outpouring and indwelling is a new act of God of comparable significance to the incarnation," in which the believer becomes the "bearer and image of God's savings acts,"[16] which, as our Lord said, would be even "greater works" than His own (Jn 14:12).

This means that the full Trinitarian movement is bi-directional: toward God and back toward humanity. First, in Christ, we are reconciled to the Father, and then, in the Spirit, God fully dwells amidst the church as God's people. The Christian community "grows into a holy temple," with Christ Jesus as the cornerstone, that it may be a dwelling place of God in the Spirit (Eph 2:20-22). This dwelling of God among us is the benefit of the ascension of the crucified and risen Christ (Eph 1:18-23).

A fully Trinitarian theology recognizes that each movement in salvation can be looked at from both the Christological and the pneumatological perspectives,[17] and what is proper to the one perspective may be improper to the other.[18] How does this work? When we look at the Holy Trinity itself (the immanent Trinity), we see that within it, each of the three persons is distinguished by a specific and irreducible identity. "The Father alone is Father and not the Son. To beget is properly the work of the Father and not the Son, and so forth."[19] But when we look at the activity of God toward us (the economic Trinity), we see that the acts of God are indivisible. In other words, all of the works of God "are the works of the full Trinitarian being of God in His three persons."[20] This means that we need to examine the meeting of God with us in Christ from both a Christological and pneumatological perspective, neither one of which should be collapsed into the other.[21]

Viewed from a pneumatological perspective, therefore, the purpose of Christian worship, is to announce, effect, and celebrate the

Trinitarian relationship in which, by God's grace, we participate. The interaction in this relationship also has a bi-directional movement. The first movement is on God's part, to have established the covenant of promise in Christ, once for all, and also to continually communicate the Word of that covenant to us by the witness of the Holy Spirit. The word that the Spirit speaks is never the Spirit's own, but Christ's, as He taught His disciples in John 16:13-14,

> When the Spirit of truth comes, he will guide you into all the truth; for he will not speak on his own, but will speak whatever he hears, and he will declare to you the things that are to come. He will glorify me, because he will take what is mine and declare it to you.

This is an important corrective for those churches that seek to have new revelations from the Holy Spirit within their meetings. The Spirit works to bind us to Christ, and to accomplish the mystical union we have with Him.

But the second movement in this relationship is on our part, which is to respond in faith, believing the promises. But even this faith is a work of the Holy Spirit, "who creates it in us by means of the preaching of the Word, and strengthens it by our use of the Holy Sacraments."[22] At this point we can refine our opening definition by saying that when God comes to have a meeting with us, it is in the mode of the Spirit. By this we do not mean that only one of the persons of the Trinity comes to meet us, but that the whole God, the one God, Father, Son, and Holy Spirit, comes to meet us in the Spirit.

Therefore we can also say that the contents of the Christian liturgy are the means and forms that the Holy Spirit uses to do the business of converting us, incorporating us into Christ that we might, in Him, be reconciled to the Father, but also forming us into the dwelling place of God in the Spirit. The congregation of God's people becomes in itself the living temple in which God's glory dwells.[23] And it is precisely because of the indwelling that the Spirit makes sovereign use of the liturgy which the church, in all of its culturally-conditioned humanity, has developed to give form to God's meetings with us.

It is on this basis that we can joyfully embrace the idea that there is a "real presence" of God in Christian worship. But we must understand this real presence in fully Trinitarian terms. The ascension and Pentecost are irreversible. When Simeon received the baby Jesus in the temple, God was dwelling in Israel by means of the incarnation. But now that the incarnate Christ has ascended bodily to the right hand of the Father, there is a real sense in which He is removed from us.[24] Since Pentecost, it is by means of the outpouring of the Spirit that the church is the dwelling place of God.[25] The church is the body of Christ as a pneumatological reality, and not as a matter of incarnation, which is unique to the person of Christ.

FOUR CHARACTERISTICS.

There are certain characteristics of this indwelling that we need to establish. First, it is wrong to divide the world up into "nature" and "supernature," with the assumption that the latter is the realm of the Spirit, or that what is "spiritual" is somehow less real, less physical, or less down to earth. Psalm 104:30 says, "When you send forth your Spirit, [the creatures] are created, and you renew the face of the ground." As Van Ruler says, "It is thus characteristic of the Spirit to grasp us in our concrete reality."[26] This means that the Spirit enters into the down-to-earth reality of human existence, of human culture, and even of institutions, and that the goal is eventually to transform them into being fit for the kingdom of God.[27] It is not the goal of the Spirit to make us less creaturely, less physical, less historical, or less cultural, but to "fully honor us in our characteristic humanity," and in our humanity make us presentable to God.[28] The church is the firstfruit of the new creation, and the concern of the Spirit is as wide as creation.

This has important implications for mission, which must be regarded in full Trinitarian light. The Christian story does not end with redemption, but with the final fulfillment, when God will be "all in all" (1Co 15:28). Christian worship may not ignore the whole scope of God's creation nor the institutions of daily life as the arena of God's concern. God called Israel to be a kingdom of priests and holy nation precisely because "the whole earth is Mine" (Ex 19:5). The final consummation will be even larger than creation, incorporating the results of human culture, judged and purified.[29] The purpose of mission is not the salvation of only individual souls, but of "nations" (Mt 28:19).

Second, the indwelling and work of the Holy Spirit is characteristically expressed in diverse ways, by contrast to the Christological perspective, which emphasizes the unique singleness and once-for-all-ness of Christ. The Apostle Paul declares that he wants to "know nothing…except Jesus Christ, and him crucified" (1Co 2:2). But Paul goes on in the same chapter to introduce the theme of wisdom as the work of the Spirit, which suggests a richness of growth, experience, and knowledge. The pneumatological perspective recognizes the great variety and diversity of particularities. Each individual person is a discrete and eternally valuable individual, whose individual identity is never merged into a larger being (as in the case of Hinduism or Buddhism), but who learns to say "I" in proper and joyful relationship to God. The place of the individual person within salvation is precisely a matter of pneumatology.[30] This is not to give the lie to humanistic individualism. For the indwelling of the Spirit is a corporate reality, and the church is the body of Christ in a way that the individual is not. Yet it is the Spirit that allows each person to learn to say "I."

A third characteristic is a corollary of this. Christ's person and work was manifestly visible, to be seen and recognized by all, and not to be confused with any other. But the person of the Holy Spirit is hidden in our own persons, and the Spirit's work is mixed with ours, and it is provisional, partial, diverse, and characterized by plurality and multiplicity. "To put it in other words: in the Spirit, there is no unity of being but a unity of love."[31] This means that there will be a whole number of diverse cultural expressions of the Spirit's indwelling, none of which ought to be identified as the single best or final expression. This, obviously, has great importance for liturgy, although it should not be taken as license for pragmatic relativism, which would be to ignore the Christological perspective.

A fourth characteristic of the Spirit's indwelling is that the physical body of the individual Christian becomes important. As Van Ruler says,

> God the Holy Spirit dwells in the highest part of human reason but also in the depths of our hearts. He dwells in the entirety of our hearts, but also in human souls and in human feeling. Furthermore, also the human body, including the body that awakens and produces life, is a temple of the Holy Spirit. The entire mystical, bodily, moral existence of human beings is God's dwelling place.[32]

The effect of this indwelling, it must be remembered, is still provisional and often hidden. Furthermore, the goal of the Spirit's work in the body is not to make us something other than natural or creaturely, and therefore its signs will be natural and creaturely.

SIX IMPLICATIONS.

A number of liturgical implications of a Trinitarian theology balance an orthodox Christology with a richer pneumatology. First, it is these terms that should determine our understanding of how the communion elements are no less than the "true and natural" body and blood of our Lord.[33] Debates about the elements have been hampered by a narrow Christological focus which ignores pneumatology, and by the general use of the word "spiritual" to mean something essentially unreal and non-physical. Fortunately, the liturgical churches are taking important steps in the right direction by incorporating the epiclesis (invocation of the Holy Spirit) into their Communion prayers, by emphasizing the real presence in the whole action, rather than only the elements, and by reclaiming the priesthood of the whole congregation. Ironically, the evangelical churches "believe in miracles" but are afraid to credit the sacraments with any miraculous significance.[34] What is needed is a fully Trinitarian approach. A richer Christology learns to see the sacraments as covenantal signs by which we are incorporated into Christ's passion and resurrection. A richer pneumatology breaks down the barriers between what is regarded as miraculous and what is regarded as ordinary, natural, and institutional.

When the miraculous is kept out of the sacraments, some groups will come up with substitute sacraments (though they do not call them that) where the miraculous is celebrated and the Spirit is claimed. Outstanding examples of substitute sacraments are speaking in tongues (which is a substitute sacrament for baptism) and healing (a substitute sacrament for communion). These practices emphasize the presence and work of the Spirit, but in a way that is narrowly personalistic. Their implied pneumatology is separated from Christology, for these substitute sacraments are not designed to incorporate us into our Lord's passion and resurrection. Further, they bypass the concern of the Spirit for all of creation and the whole kingdom of God. By contrast, the sacraments of baptism and the Lord's Supper fully embrace all these realities. They offer a disciplined sensuality, a communal participation, a clear relationship to material creation, and an eschatological significance. Not only is Holy Communion the means by which we celebrate our mystical union with Christ, it is also the reality of God's union with us in the Spirit. The worship service needs to give room for the congregation to enjoy the sacraments, even the elements themselves, and the words of the liturgy need to employ, over time, the full historical and covenantal imagery of Scripture to which the sacraments connect us.

Second, the liturgy cannot be one-sidedly objective, but must give place to the subjectivity of self-awareness, so that I, the believer, might come to know myself, body and soul, as an eternal covenant partner with God. This also means that the Spirit's use of the Word is not only to communicate the covenantal promise of salvation, but also to rebuild the believer into "the measure of the full stature of Christ" (Eph 4:11-15). The more evangelical churches, especially the Pentecostal churches, can instruct others in this regard. In any case, the service needs to give room for the confession of faith, not only in the form of corporate creeds, but also personal testimonies (although the Apostles Creed is intended as such). The most edifying means to such self-awareness, however, is probably well-structured silence.

This leads directly to a third consideration, the place of the human body in worship. Apart from the sacraments, just how sensual should worship be? The orthodox Protestant churches have traditionally restricted their sensuality to hymnody, in contrast to the rich objective sensuality of Roman Catholicism and the aggressive subjective sensuality of the charismatic movement. I have no simple answers for this, but a balanced Trinitarian theology can help. For example, I have argued that the liturgy needs objectively to proclaim and celebrate the once-for-all reconciliation we have in Christ. But, as the Apostles' Creed reminds us, the forgiveness of sins is the Spirit's work, and so each individual needs also subjectively to appropriate forgiveness. Doesn't that happen, not only by believing the promises, but also by giving full rein to the Spirit's indwelling, even in terms of the emotions and the physical body, where reconciliation may even be worked out as healing? Can the liturgy give room for this, if not every Sunday, then at least occasionally, and intentionally? The development of sacramentally-oriented healing services is a positive step in this direction. A fully Trinitarian approach would honor the experiential side of regeneration, including emotional and physical healing, as the fruit of the Spirit's indwelling, while avoiding the trap of locating the certainty of salvation in our experience.

The remarkable shortcoming of the charismatic movement is that, even in its sensuality, it fails to honor the fullness of the work of the Spirit and the totality of its indwelling in us. The charismatic manifestations are typically regarded as supernatural works of the Spirit apart from our ordinary creatureliness. Speaking in tongues, for example, is understood as supernatural heavenly speech rather than as the Holy Spirit praying along with the believer's deepest inner thoughts, which are bound to be extremely emotional, pre-rational, and only partially in the believer's own awareness. There are real opportunities here, but they require careful discipline. When a service celebrates sheer physicality through the encouragement of laughing, shaking, and falling down, abuses may result if psychological and anthropological realities are ignored.[35] But these realities cannot be ignored, because the Spirit deals with our concrete humanity. These realities are not antithetical to the Spirit, but precisely where the Spirit brings salvation into creation.

The liturgical sensuality of the Spirit's indwelling should never be disconnected from the discipline of Christology. Instructive here is the advice of the Apostle Paul in Colossians 3:16,

> Let the word of Christ dwell in you richly, teach and admonish one another in all wisdom; and with gratitude in your hearts sing psalms and hymns and spiritual songs to God.

Does "richly" go so far as to include the sensual? Probably. But the Spirit has no words of its own apart from the Word of Christ. Furthermore, the chief manifestation of this rich indwelling is wisdom. Wisdom does not deny the rational, but includes it and goes beyond it. Wisdom suggests a wholeness that includes emotional healing but does not require physical healing.

This means that the liturgy itself must give room to wisdom. This is done in at least two ways. The first is the kind of long term wisdom that is stored up in the psalms and the great hymns. It is especially through singing psalms and hymns that the congregation enriches itself with the experience of the whole church catholic in time and space. This means that doctrinal content and poetic integrity are important matters. It also means that the hymns should have sufficient weight and gravity to be long-lasting. At the same time, Paul not only recommends psalms and hymns, but also spiritual songs. No doubt these were the songs of a more popular nature that made an immediate appeal to the emotions, and these are necessary. But they hardly contribute to wisdom. The second way of giving room to wisdom is to allow for silence in the service. The individual must have a liturgical place as an individual.

A fourth consideration comes from the fact that the Spirit dwells in the church corporately. The Spirit's use of the Word is not only to communicate the promise of salvation, but also to edify and build up the congregation as a place of fitting spiritual beauty, just as the Torah gave shape to the tabernacle. In the worship service itself the congregation is the temple, where God is "enthroned on the praises of Israel" (Ps 22:3). This means that the liturgy can never be utilitarian and pragmatic, because as service to God, it needs no external justification. The matter of relevance is not always important.

On the other hand, we can never go so far as say that the liturgy exists for itself, apart from the world. The service is where the congregation exercises its priesthood, offering service to God (Ezr 6:18; Ro 12:1) for the sake of mission to the world. There is a real work of the Spirit in the congregation's bearing fruit, the firstfruits of the greater harvest of the whole world. Thus there must be room in the service for communal interaction and mutual service. This can happen through the frequent celebration of the Supper in ways that are more suggestive of an actual meal. But it also happens through the ministry of prayer. These prayers must be not only for the congregation itself, however, but for all the world, for that is the import of the church's identity as the priesthood for all the world. This needs especially to go beyond the Sunday service. Those who participate in daily common prayer, for example, discover how the simple reading of the psalms and prayers together can develop community. Perhaps this is because it is in prayer that Christ most powerfully takes form in us, and the priesthood of Christ takes form in the priesthood of all believers together. Indeed, why should the service not always include the Lord's Prayer, for doesn't the indwelling of God mean that Christ himself is praying with us, and that the church, as the body of Christ, provides the corporate mouth through which He prays His own prayer?

Fifth, the purpose of the worship service is not, as such, to save souls or to win people for Christ. Of course, conversion (as defined above) is always a purpose of the liturgy, and this can give room to decisions for Christ and confessions of faith. Mission must be part of the service, because it is an integral part of the church's exercise of its priesthood. But as noted above, the calling of God's people is as a priesthood for all the world, and the concern of the Spirit includes human culture, tradition, and the institutions of daily life. The liturgy needs to address these matters in the preaching and the prayers, but even more, in order to build up the body of Christ as the new humanity, the liturgy needs to be open to the incorporation of the fruits of human culture as part of the "living sacrifice" (Ro 12:1). The liturgy is one of the key places where the gospel interacts with culture, as expressed in art, music, and drama. When it does this, it offers to God the firstfruits of the reclamation of the whole of the world. At the same time, Christological discipline means that the liturgical music, for example, is not meant to call attention to itself, but to be the means by which the whole of the human person and culture is opened to the reconciliation of God. It also means that its concern for culture never be a preoccupation with the currents of contemporary society, which are always under the judgment of the cross. We are still looking for the final consummation. The present indwelling of the Holy Spirit is not final. There is a greater end to come. "The promised Holy Spirit…is the pledge of our inheritance toward redemption of God's own people, to the praise of his glory" (Eph 1:13-14).

Sixth, a full pneumatology finds a suitable place for liturgical tradition.[36] The church has given form to the gospel in its prayers, hymns, and liturgical orders. The ecumenical creeds, for example, represent the church's communal digestion and confession of the promises of the gospel. A fully Trinitarian approach to liturgy is willing both to gain spiritual wisdom from the liturgical tradition and to judge all liturgical tradition according to the Christological discipline. For example, the pattern of the Eucharistic Prayer, which the church has developed over the centuries, ordinarily provides the best means for a congregation to be fully biblical in its celebration of communion. At the same time, since the work of the Spirit is so diverse, the church must not seek to control everything through too much commitment to the written tradition. The golden age of the church is not behind us, but before us (Heb 12:18-29).

Our Lord told the Samaritan woman at the well that the days were coming when we would worship the Father in Spirit and truth (Jn 4:23). "Spirit" signifies the new and exciting movement of God across the face of the earth beyond the boundaries of Israel and Samaria. "Truth" signifies covenant faithfulness. In other words, no matter in what new ways the Spirit moves, God will always hold to the ancient covenant promises, and so must we. But "Spirit" also means the dwelling of God within the heart, out of which "shall flow rivers of living water" (Jn 7:38). We worship the Father in Spirit and truth, and that signifies the bi-directional direction in the liturgy, always toward Christ's once-for-all passion and resurrection, and always toward our life in this world, which, after all, is God's.

NOTES

1. Gerardus van der Leeuw, *Liturgiek*, 2nd. ed. (Nijkerk: Callenbach, 1946), 9.

2. A.A. Van Ruler, *Calvinist Trinitarianism and Theocentric Politics: Essays Toward a Public Theology*, John Bolt, ed. and trans., Toronto Studies in Theology 38 (Lewiston, NY: The Edwin Mellon Press, 1989), especially Chapter 1: "The Necessity of a Trinitarian Theology," Chapter 2: "Structural Differences Between the Christological and Pneumatological Perspectives," and Chapter 3: "Grammar of Pneumatology." These chapters are simply selections from a much larger corpus of many books.

   A.A. Van Ruler (1908-1970) was Professor of Theology at the University of Utrecht, the Netherlands, from 1947 until his death. He was a leader in the post-war renewal of the national Netherlands Reformed Church. His work is well known in German circles, especially for his influential monograph on *The Christian Church and the Old Testament* (English translation by Geoffrey W. Bromiley, published by Eerdmans, 1971). He came to have strong differences with Karl Barth, especially on the matter of pneumatology. It was Van Ruler's audacious judgement that the Christian church had not yet produced a fully Trinitarian theology. He considered his own work as but an attempt to show the need and point the way. *Trinitarianism*, 1.

3.	The following definitions reflect Reformed theology as expressed in the confessional documents of the Sixteenth Century, especially the Heidelberg Catechism of 1563, which is a doctrinal standard of the German, Dutch, and Hungarian Reformed churches, and the Belgic Confession of 1561.

4.	I do not mean to detract from the thoroughly human character of worship, but to put it in perspective. This is a dogmatic (doctrinal) definition, rather than a phenomenological one, which would have its own validity, beginning with what human beings do in worship. This definition is my own, although I have since discovered a somewhat similar one in Robert Webber's introduction to liturgy for evangelicals, *Worship Old and New*, Ministry Resources Library (Grand Rapids: Zondervan, 1982), p. 11.

5.	For the covenantal character of worship, see Hughes Oliphant Old, *Worship that is Reformed according to Scripture*, Guides to the Reformed Tradition, John H. Leith and John W. Kuykendall, editors (Atlanta: John Knox Press, 1984).

6.	Heidelberg Catechism Question 65: "Since then faith alone makes us share in Christ and all his benefits, where does this faith come from? Answer: From the Holy Spirit, who works it in our hearts by the preaching of the gospel and strengthens it by the use of the sacraments."

7.	"Conversion" is used here as the Heidelberg Catechism defines it in question 88: "What is true repentance or conversion? Answer: It is the dying away of the old nature and the coming to life of the new." Thus, conversion is simultaneously once-for-all and continuous, as well as both individual and corporate. In this light, we can certainly say that conversion is one of the goals of every worship service.

8.	The word *agenda* ("things to be done") was typically used as the title of liturgical books in Central Europe.

9. Heidelberg Catechism 66, Belgic Confession 33-35.

10. Reformed worship is biblical in the sense that the Bible is the only rule (*regula*) or yardstick of practice, rather than the only source of practice, which was the Anabaptist and later Puritan sense. Such Reformers as Bucer, Calvin, and Bullinger held that the tradition of the church could be accepted so long as it passed the strict judgment of Scripture. They did not expect the Bible to provide the precise models for worship. Calvin identified his own published liturgy as being "after the model of the early church," not after the model of the New Testament church.

11. The Gospel of John makes a similar point about the incarnation when it says that "the word became flesh and dwelt (lit. *tabernacled*) among us, full of grace and truth, and we beheld his glory" (Jn 1:14). The reference to the "glory" filling the tabernacle in Exodus 40 is unmistakable. The word "recapitulate," as we are using it, means to repeat a past action in a new way which harmonizes with, fulfills, expands upon, and deepens the past action.

12. At the Passover, the sacrificial lamb was eaten by the family, thereby establishing the basic pattern of the sacrifice consummated by the meal. The principle is that the virtue of the sacrifice was communicated to its beneficiaries by means of the meal. Certain of the Levitical sacrifices climaxed in the worshippers eating of the sacrifice (Lev 6:14-18, 7:16, 23:1-43) within the precincts of the tabernacle, as in the case of Elkanah and Hannah (1Sa 1:3-9). Solomon's temple included, around the central chambers, three tiers of "upper rooms" for the sacred meals, so that the people might eat and feast "before the Lord" (1Ki 6:5-6, 8:65-66, 1Ch 28:11). The eschatological temple of Ezekiel's vision included similar tiers of rooms, plus a number of other rooms in the outer walls (Eze 41:5-11), and these were also for the purpose of eating the

sacrifice in the presence of the Lord (Eze 42:13). This is doubt-less what Jesus was referring to when He told His disciples, "in my father's house [temple] are many rooms" (Jn 14:2), and why Jesus celebrated His last Passover in an "upper room" (Mk 14:15, Lk 22:12). The disciples were eating of the sacri-fice in the presence of the Lord. The post-resurrection meal at Emmaus (Lk 24:31) must also be seen in terms of the meal on Sinai, for, like the seventy elders, the two disciples "saw God, and ate and drank."

13. Thus, the wonderful irony of God's grace when the people cried out to Pilate, "His blood be on us and our children" (Mt 27:25).

14. See especially Heb 2:17, 5:7-10, 7:18-28, 9:1-10:18.

15. Van Ruler, *Trinitarianism*, 46, 65.

16. Van Ruler, *Trinitarianism*, 6.

17. "...the pneumatological vantage point in the doctrine of atonement or redemption...is undoubtedly a different per-spective than the Christological one, yet equally important, at least if one wants to think in a Trinitarian way. God is not only *in Christo*, He is also in the Spirit *(en Pneumati)*. Neither of course can be without the other. That God is *en Pneumati* is something different than His being *in Christo*. God not only dwells near us in Jesus Christ, but we also become 'a dwelling place of God in the Spirit' (Eph 2:22)." Van Ruler, *Trinitari-anism*, 2.

18. Van Ruler, *Trinitarianism*, 28-9.

19. Van Ruler, *Trinitarianism*, 2.

20. Van Ruler, *Trinitarianism*, 2. One reason we cannot replace the formula of "Father, Son, and Spirit" with one like "Cre-ator, Redeemer, and Sustainer" is that these works of God are done by all divine persons, not by one each.

21. Our Trinitarian analysis has been emphasizing the Son and the Spirit. Can we say that we have any direct experience of the Father? Or must we say that we experience the Father only in the Son through the Spirit? It certainly seems right to address the Father directly in prayer, as we do in the Lord's Prayer. So the Father is properly the objective goal of our worship, just as, conversely, the Father is the subjective source of all that is. As the Father generates the Son and gives procession to the Spirit, so, in reverse order, we give worship to the Father in the Spirit through the Son. If this is the case, then we apparently do not experience the person of the Father directly in worship.

22. Heidelberg Catechism 65.

23. In order to safeguard the doctrine of justification by faith, the Reformers taught "imputed righteousness" rather than Rome's "infused righteousness." A fully Trinitarian theology offers both an imputed righteousness, in Christ, and an "indwelling" righteousness, in the Spirit, which remains a righteousness *extra nos*.

24. The Heidelberg Catechism, in answer 47, on Christ's ascension, states that "With respect to His human nature He is no longer on earth, but with respect to His divinity, majesty, grace, and Spirit He is never absent from us." This, of course, was at issue between the Lutherans and the Calvinists.

25. Because the outgoing works of God are indivisible, we are correct to speak of the "Spirit of Christ." Yet the unaltered Nicene Creed reminds us that the Spirit proceeds from the Father. The indivisibility of God's work also means that it is the fullness of the one God who comes to us in the Spirit.

    The ecumenical creeds present the Holy Catholic Church, baptism, and the communion of saints as pneumatological rather than incarnational realities. This is not to deny that

Christ takes form in the church, that we are conformed to His image, and that we enjoy a mystical union with Him. But this is all a work of the one God in the Spirit. *Trinitarianism*, 39, 42, 86. Van Ruler argues that the incarnation is a category which is best reserved for the unique hypostatic union of Christ's person. The implication of this is that we have overextended the doctrine of the incarnation in order to compensate for an underdeveloped pneumatology. *Trinitarianism*, 30-34, 74.

26.   Van Ruler, *Trinitarianism*, 82.

27.   Van Ruler, *Trinitarianism*, 72, 76, 85.

28.   Van Ruler, *Trinitarianism*, 58.

29.   The final dwelling of God with humanity takes place in a city rather than in a garden (Rev 21-22). The city represents the expansion of God's creation by human culture. Into this city "kings of the earth shall bring the glory and honor of the nations" (Rev 21:24-26). Human history and culture count for something in eternity.

30.   Van Ruler, *Trinitarianism*, 30, 33.

31.   Van Ruler, *Trinitarianism*, 77-8. The context is a discussion of the cultural and institutional expressions of the gospel, which Van Ruler calls "salvation realities." He should not be understood as denying the unity of God's being.

32.   Van Ruler, *Trinitarianism*, 54.

33.   Belgic Confession 35.

34.   Undoubtedly the most important reason for this is the enduring anti-Catholicism of Protestantism, although the influence of rationalism cannot be underestimated.

35.   For example, the "Toronto Blessing" (or "Airport Vineyard") services attempt to do psychological healing through ecstatic

liturgical experiences rather than through responsible counselling and patient pastoral care.

36. "The poured-out Spirit remains dwelling on earth after Pentecost, particularly in the church. There is a continuity in this once-for-all-ness which is also found in the church, in its tradition, and in the historical, apostolic, mission activity." Van Ruler, *Trinitarianism*, 38.

The Doctrine of the Trinity and the Renewal of the Church

David Curry

THE round window in the gable of Little Sands United Church in the Canadian Atlantic Province, Prince Edward Island, circumscribes two equilateral triangles, the apex of the one pointing heavenward, the apex of the other toward the earth. As described in Kim Ondaatje's photographic ramble *Small Churches of Canada*,[1] it is not (simply) the Star of David. It represents, instead, the "Double Trinity."

The "Double Trinity"? Surely "three-in-one and one-in-three" is enough of a mystery without being compounded. But, in fact, it seems this image of a church bearing a symbol of the Trinity brings us face to face with two inseparable mysteries: the mystery of the Trinity and the mystery of the church.

That there is an ambiguity about the symbol requiring explanation suggests, too, that the church is a mystery which is at once hidden and revealed in the mystery of God. We are confronted with something about which we have to think. The renewal of the church revolves around the necessity of thinking about the Trinity.

The Trinity is not something immediate to our senses; it requires reflection upon what is revealed. Just so the symbol in the window requires reflection upon what is seen. Is it the Star of David or something else?

Yet because the triangles are equilateral and because they are circumscribed within a circle, the figure is not, properly speaking, the

242 • The Trinity: An Essential for Faith in Our Time

six-sided symbol of the Star of David, the six sides of which are not all of equal length. The Star of David *can* be formed by two equilateral triangles but it *cannot* be circumscribed in a circle. In Christian iconography, however, the Star of David also signifies the Trinity. The suggestion here is its further elaboration as a symbol of the Double Trinity: God in relation to himself in the transcendence of heaven and God in relation to us in the economy of salvation. This is suggested by the equality of the triangles within the unity of the circle. The mystery of the church, it may be suggested, essentially belongs to this double relationship of God to himself and God to everything else. In the mystery of the church, this means the principle of proclamation and the principle of participation.

Proclamation

That the Trinity and the church are inseparable mysteries does not mean that they are equal. The one exists for the sake of the other: the mystery of the church for the mystery of the Trinity. Augustine gives classical expression to this teaching in the *Enchiridion*.

> Therefore the true order of the Creed demanded that the church should be made subordinate to the Trinity, as the house to Him who dwells in it, the temple to God who occupies it, and the city to its builder.[2]

In mentioning the Trinity in the context of the Creed, Augustine signals the church's proclamation of God. The church exists for the praise of God and finds the understanding of her being in what she is given to proclaim: "Go therefore and make disciples of all nations, baptizing them in the name of the Father and of the Son and of the Holy Spirit, and teaching them to obey everything that I have commanded you. And remember, I am with you always, to the end of the age" (Mt 28:19-20). The mission is in the proclamation: "I made your name known to them and I will make it known" (Jn 17:26). For in proclamation the church points primarily to God. He alone is praiseworthy precisely because in the freedom of His eternal being He does not need our praises. The proclamation of the

Trinity is the acknowledgment of the perfect self-sufficiency of God alone upon which everything else depends. Yet in proclamation the church is also most free. The God who does not need our praises is freely praised. For however much humanity *needs* to praise God, our praises are not praises if they are forced. Praises belong to the highest order of human freedom; they connect us to God's own freedom. Thus, the principle of proclamation brings to light the second principle of the church, the principle of participation. "Father, I desire that those also, whom you have given me, may be with me where I am, to see my glory, which you have given me because you loved me before the foundation of the world" and again, "I made your name known to them...that the love with which you have loved me may be in them and I in them" (Jn 17:24,26).

Participation

The church participates in what she proclaims. Fundamental to any renewal of the church is the acknowledgment that the church exists for the praise of the Trinity and that the church is the form of our participation in the life of the Trinity. This means that the church is shaped and formed by what she is given to proclaim. And by her proclamation the church shows herself to be the chosen vessel giving shape and form to the faith of individual believers in what is essentially to be believed.

The Spirit of God is given at Pentecost to be the Spirit of the church. The Holy Spirit gives shape to the life of God in us through the patterns of prayer and praise in the ordered life of the church. For instance, the Word and Son of the Father is heard and received in the Spirit. It is "by the power of thy Holy Spirit," [the Spirit of the Father and the Son, that] "all...who are partakers of [the] Holy Communion [are] fulfilled with Your grace and heavenly benediction."[3] In short, we participate in the life of the Trinity through the church. The church is where we "live for the praises of his glory" (Eph 1:12) so that we all may become "dwelling place[s] of God in the Spirit" (Eph 2:22). Again, Augustine states the understanding. "The temple of God, then, that is, of the Supreme Trinity as a whole, is the holy church, embracing in its full extent both heaven and earth."[4] The mystery of the church signifies the mystery of our proclamation of the Trinity and the mystery of our participation in the Trinitarian life of God.

Mystery

The word *mystery*, perhaps, disquiets and misleads us. We are apt to think of it in terms of "unsolved mysteries," a perplexity in human affairs that is yet to be unraveled, a puzzle where the pieces don't seem to fit; in short, something hidden from view. Actually, it means the exact opposite. Mystery in Christian theology is not what is concealed but what is revealed, it comprises what is made known and the medium by which it is made known.

Mystery has another but related sense as well. *Mystery* refers to our entering into and being joined to what is revealed. Thus, mystery as revelation connects with proclamation; mystery as incorporation connects with participation. The Holy Mysteries, for instance, are the sacraments, principally, baptism and the Eucharist, in which we participate in what is essentially revealed.[5] What is essentially revealed is the Trinitarian life of God. The church is the mystery in which, through the Holy Mysteries, we participate in the mystery of the Holy and Blessed Trinity.

TRANSFIGURATION AND THE TRANSFORMATION OF UNDERSTANDING.

The connection between the mystery of the church and the mystery of the Trinity, between proclamation and participation, is dramatically illustrated in the sequence of teachings that culminate in the story of the Transfiguration of Christ.[6] It suggests, moreover, that mystery as what is essentially revealed speaks to the understanding. It shows, in other words, the necessity of doctrine. Doctrine, we may say, is the shape which the mystery gives itself through our thinking upon it. It is not simply a product of our human understanding but our entering into a divine understanding.

On the Mount of Transfiguration we are told "from the cloud, a voice" (Mt 17:5). What does it mean to see what is heard? It means an understanding—a divine understanding articulated through our human understanding. Hearing and seeing are the biblical senses of understanding. To behold a voice is the language of revelation.[7] It means that the images are substantial; that is to say, they convey an understanding and are themselves part of the understanding they convey. They belong to the understanding which they communicate.

The Transfiguration of Christ is an epiphany of the Trinity which complements the epiphany of the Trinity in the Baptism of Christ. For yet both, there is a beholding of what is heard. "This is my Son the Beloved, with whom I am well pleased" (Mt 3:17) and again "This is my Son the Beloved; with him I am well pleased; listen to him" (Mt 17:5). The Baptism inaugurates the way of the obedience of Christ for us; classically, this means the principle of justification. The Transfiguration commands the way of the obedience of Christ in us; classically, this means the principle of sanctification.[8] Hence there is the added charge, "listen to him." In short, we participate in what is proclaimed.

The voice is the Father's voice. To hear that voice in the biblical sense of acting faithfully upon what *we* hear is to enter into the way of understanding through the revelation of God in Jesus Christ. The sequence of teachings which precedes the Transfiguration (Mt 16:13-17:1) illustrates just how hard and yet how necessary that way is. "Who do men say that the Son of Man is?...Who do you say that I am?" Jesus asks his disciples (Mt 16:13, 15). Peter answers, "You are the Messiah, the Son of the living God" (Mt 16:16).

Jesus' response shows that what Peter understands, he understands from God. "Blessed are you, Simon Son of Jonah! For flesh and blood has not revealed this to you, but my Father in heaven" (Mt 16:17). It is not simply a finite human understanding. It shares in something more.

Peter's confession and Christ's confirmation argues the identity of Jesus in His essential divinity and establishes His self-differentiation from the Father. It is of a piece with all that the New Testament has to say about the relationship of the Son to the Father in which the Spirit is comprehended as well. The identity of Jesus with God, and His self-differentiation from the Father as the Son, provides the necessary foundation for the understanding of God as Trinity.[9]

Through this understanding Simon becomes Peter. And upon this understanding (and no other), Jesus says *"I will build my church"* against which the gates of Hades will not prevail (Mt 16:18). But how well do we stand upon this rock of understanding? Again, Peter provides the paradigm.

For no sooner has he confessed Christ and been named Peter the rock when he is rebuked as Satan for denying Jesus' teaching about the necessity of what will unfold in His going up to Jerusalem; namely, the passion, death, and resurrection of Jesus Christ (Mt 16:21-23). Blessed by Jesus for an understanding revealed by God through him, he is then cursed by Jesus for His mind "not on divine things, but on human things" (Mt 16:23).

Peter does not fully understand the confession he has made. It is not that the confession itself is not true; rather, His understanding of it is not altogether adequate to its truth. He fails to understand the fuller meaning of what he has rightly and divinely confessed. There is the constant need to think the fullness of understanding contained *within* the confession of faith. As with Peter, so with us, both individually and corporately. Upon such a necessity stands the whole question of the renewal of the church, indeed, the whole being of the church.

Peter has first to learn that the sufferings of the Messiah belong to the glories of Christ. "He went not up to joy but first He suffered pain, and entered not into glory before He was crucified."[10] And so must we. Our worldly ambitions—to use God or ignore Him—and our temptations to despair—to abuse God or refuse Him—have to be crucified in us. The way of the Cross is required of us in our identity with Jesus. "If any want to become my followers, let them deny themselves and take up their cross and follow me" (Mt 16:24).

What follows is the Transfiguration in which the Cross is present by way of anticipation. It belongs to the glory and, ultimately, to the understanding of the glory. The story of the Transfiguration ends with Jesus' command to the disciples: "Tell no one about the vision until after the Son of Man has been raised from the dead" (Mt 17:5). The Cross belongs to the church's proclamation in the light of the Resurrection. Mark's comment that "they kept the matter to themselves, questioning what this rising from the dead could mean" (Mk 9:10) highlights, again, that what is seen and heard is not, at first, understood.

It awaits the accomplishment of what is here only anticipated. Only in the light of the Resurrection can the confession of "Messiah, the Son of the living God" who must "undergo great suffering...be killed, and on the third day, be raised" (Mt 16:16, 21) be understood more fully. The Gospels themselves are necessarily written from the standpoint of having come to understand what was, at first, not fully understood at all, though it was before their very eyes.

The mystery revealed is, nonetheless, the mystery to be understood, not in the sense of containing God in a box in our minds, but rather by our being contained by God's knowing love for us in His own eternal self-relation. The point in this moment of the Transfiguration is that the shape of the glory proclaimed is cruciform.[11] Through it we enter into the glory of the Trinity.

Luke, perhaps, puts the point more sharply. There are in the Transfiguration two essential moments: first, a presentation of the pageant of revelation leading, secondly, into the primary revelation itself. Jesus is seen transfigured in glory with Moses and Elijah, the Law and the Prophets respectively, who also "appeared in glory and were speaking of his departure, which he was about to accomplish in Jerusalem" (Lk 9:31). Thus, the Cross belongs to the content of the discourse of revelation. As in John's gospel, the Cross is inseparable from the glory of the Trinity. "Father, the hour has come; glorify your Son so that the Son may glorify you" (Jn 17:1; 16:14). So, too, on the Mount of Transfiguration, we enter into the revelation of God proclaimed and find ourselves in the company of the Trinity revealed. Behold, a voice.

The Father speaks out of the bright overshadowing cloud of the Holy Spirit to give birth to our understanding of the essential identity of the Son who was conceived by the overshadowing of the Holy Spirit and born of the Virgin Mary. Thus, to behold the voice of the Father is to enter into the understanding that the Trinity reveals. And it means to be transformed by what we behold; in short, to be transformed by the renewing of our minds and not to be conformed to this world.[12]

Peter has, secondly, to learn that our abiding with God lies in our understanding of Him. Not only is the church to confess the faith of Christ crucified, the church is also to be the place of our abiding with God. In the presence of the pageant of revelation, signified in the discourse between Moses and Elijah and Jesus, Peter's first reaction is to build three tents (Mt 17:4). He looks back to the Old Testament scenes of the giving of the Law and the form of God's occasional presence with His people above and within the tent of meeting.[13] But this scene would be something more.

While there is rightly a yearning to be in a place of abiding in what is revealed, it will not be in tents, tabernacles, or temples made of human hands but in the hearts and minds of the faithful who stand, individually and corporately, upon the rock of understanding in the revelation of God as Trinity. Such is the church. Peter's understanding will become transformed and deepened with the mind of Christ—"when [he has] turned back," Christ's prayers having overcome Satan's desires (Lk 22:31-32). With Paul it will become an exhortation for us all—"let the same mind be in you that was in Christ Jesus " (Php 2:5). Our incorporation into Christ as members of His body means our abiding in Him and He in us through His twofold identity as the Son of the living God and as the suffering servant; "God, of God" and God, "made man," the Trinity and the Incarnation.

The last and the greatest of the images of the co-inherence of God and man in John's gospel is Christ's statement: "I am the vine, you are the branches.…As the Father has loved me, so have I loved you; abide in my love" (Jn 13:5, 9). "Abide in me as I abide in you" (Jn 15:4). The Son of the living God is the Father's Son and Word who literally "lived among us" (Jn 1:14) in the soul and body of our humanity and only so could He "undergo great suffering…be killed, and on the third day be raised" (Mt 16:21). To paraphrase Athanasius, He borrowed a body so that He might borrow a death;[14] our body, our death. But only so we could "become participants of the divine nature" (2Pe 1:4).

"We have seen his glory, the glory as of a Father's only Son, full of grace and truth" (Jn 1:14) and "from his fullness we have all received, grace upon grace" (Jn 1:16). There is a double grace: the grace of our beholding and the grace of our being with Him whom we behold. The church is the spiritual place of our abiding with Christ. But what is that abiding? Our abiding is the understanding of His essential Trinitarian identity: "This is my Son, the Beloved; with him I am well pleased; listen to him" (Mt 17:5).

Dogma and Doctrine.

The doctrine of the Trinity is the great and central mystery of the Christian faith. It is not one doctrine in an unending succession of doctrines, one among many, as it were. Nor is it a doctrine for a particular time only to be set aside by the interests of another time, an old curiosity discarded in the dustbin of history, as it were. To the contrary, the doctrine of the Trinity is the primary and distinctive doctrine that clarifies every other doctrine and that remains for all time. No Trinity, no Christianity.

The doctrine of the Trinity emerges out of a necessity intrinsic to the Christian faith itself. The necessity is to be able to say what the faith is which is to be believed. That necessity centers on the identity of the God who is to be believed. The doctrine of the Trinity belongs to the intensification and clarification of the identity of God revealed in and through Jesus Christ.

The doctrine of the Trinity is, properly speaking, a revealed doctrine. That is to say, the identity of God as the Father, the Son, and the Holy Ghost is something which is primarily and essentially presented in the scriptural witness to Jesus Christ. It is something revealed through what is said and done by Jesus Christ and it is something proclaimed as that which is to be believed. As such it has a prior signification as a dogma.

The dogma of the Trinity is the principal dogma of the three great dogmas of the Christian faith: the dogma of the Incarnation, the dogma of redemption, and the dogma of the Trinity. However much these may be variously understood—and, indeed, the history of the church is very much about the quality of various understandings—they, nonetheless, constitute the essential core of what is proclaimed.

The word *dogma* in its simplest meaning is "opinion," an idea which is simply posited. Yet, it also means a public decree or ordinance, an opinion which is proclaimed with the intent of being publicly received or accepted. It is, thus, distinguished from mere private opinion and suggests, instead, something which belongs to the order of objective truth.

The word, moreover, is closely associated with doca meaning "glory." Δοχα and *dogma* both derive from the verb δοκεω. Consequently, a word like *orthodoxy* comes to mean not only "right opinion" but also "right worship" or "right glory." *Dogma*, then, refers to the rightly proclaimed opinion (truth) about God who is rightly to be worshipped and glorified. The church which exists for the praises of His glory stands upon the foundation of the dogma of God's glory—δοχα θεου—the revealed splendor of the fullness of God's being and truth.[15]

The dogma of the Incarnation, the dogma of the redemption, and the dogma of the Trinity are proclaimed to be believed from the witness of Scripture in the life of the church. They do not stand in isolation from one another as mere propositions arbitrarily set down. Neither are these dogmas simply dogmatisms which would stand against the possibilities of intellectual inquiry and/or understanding. They represent a dogmatic knowing as distinct from the dogmatic unknowing of, for instance, radical skepticism.

More importantly, perhaps, they are posited precisely as that which is to be known and entered through the understanding. Thus, they do not stand opposed to thought but rather as that upon which thought thinks. Doctrine, properly speaking, concerns the understanding or the thinking upon the *dogmata*—the things which are proclaimed to be believed.

Yet dogma already belongs to an activity of the understanding intrinsic to the Christian faith itself. For what are set down as the *dogmata* are themselves the expression of an implicit understanding. The three great dogmas, for instance, express the scriptural sense that the God who is to be rightly worshipped and glorified is the Father, the Son, and the Holy Ghost; that the Jesus who is glorified and crucified is both God and Man; and that the Jesus who died and rose again for us and for our salvation is the Savior of the world and the Redeemer of all mankind.

As dogmas, these are simply what are set down and proclaimed to be believed. As doctrines—specifically, essential doctrines—they are something more. They are the way of understanding what is essentially to be believed; the way of understanding the nature, the necessity and the inter-relation of the fundamentals of the faith. Ultimately, the great dogmas are proclaimed within a pattern of understanding. The creeds are that pattern of understanding.

By the creeds, we mean the three classical creeds of Christian orthodoxy—the Apostles' Creed, the Niceno-Constantinopolitan Creed, and the Athanasian Creed. Historically, these three have mostly had their play in the western church, but they also have an important ecumenical force (the *Filioque* controversy notwithstanding), particularly in their doctrinal unity, a point appreciated and articulated, for instance, by seventeenth-century Reformed divinity.[16] As the Irish Archbishop John Bramhall (*Athanasius Hihernicus,* as he was fittingly called) points out, the three creeds are really one creed, namely the Apostles' Creed.

> The Nicene, Constantinopolitan, Ephesian, Chalcedonian and Athanasian Creeds, are but explications of the Creed of the Apostles, and are still called the Apostles' Creed.[17]

He means this in Irenaeus' sense, that the Rule of Faith or Symbol, which ultimately emerges as the Apostles' Creed formally, is "this faith which the church has received from the apostles and their disciples,"[18] a pattern of teaching, moreover, handed on by the apostles who handed on the Scriptures. As Martin Chemnitz, the sixteenth century Lutheran theologian puts it: "the articles of faith which are set forth [in the Apostles' Creed] are not human inventions, but divine teachings delivered in the Word of God."[19]

The necessary interrelation of creed and Scripture is well expressed by Bramhall. "We have," he says, "a certain rule of faith, the Apostles' Creed dilated in the Scriptures, or the Scriptures contracted into the Apostles' Creed."[20] The two belong together as one rule of faith. Bramhall further explains:

> The Scriptures and the [Apostles'] Creed are not two different rules of faith, but one and the same rule, dilated in the Scripture, contracted in the Creed; the end of the Creed being to contain all fundamental points of faith, or a summary of all things necessary to salvation, to be believed "*necessitate medii*": but in what particular writings all these fundamental points are contained, is no particular fundamental article itself nor contained in the Creed, nor could be contained in it; since it is apparent out of Scripture itself, that the Creed was made and deposited with the church as a rule of faith, before the canon of the New Testament was perfected.[21]

The three classical creeds, moreover, belong to the essential ecclesiological identity of the churches that arise out of the magisterial protestant reformation as well as the counter-reformation Roman Catholic church. They belong to the underlying continuum of essential catholicism as the fundamental expression of the *consensus fidelium*—the consensus of the faithful. In other words, they provide the basis for a doctrinal ecumenicity precisely because they embody the consensual catholicism of both classical Protestantism and Catholicism. Equally, they provide an essential point of connection with the churches of Eastern Orthodoxy.

The creeds are more than formal statements of the faith. They are the formative principles which give shape to what they state. Far from being merely a list of dogmatic propositions, they present a pattern of understanding and provide a framework of interpretation. As well the creeds embody the substantial content of the faith, which is entered into and participated in sacramentally through baptism and the Holy Eucharist. In the one, we are named in God's own naming of himself, and in the other, we participate in the Son's thanksgiving to the Father. Again, there is a participation in what is proclaimed.

The creeds are the distillation of what the Scriptures essentially teach. They primarily arise out of the Scriptures, but, equally, they return us to them in an order of understanding. They provide the basic interpretative framework through which the essential things of revelation can be identified and understood and within which an host of secondary matters can also emerge and be measured. The creeds can be said to provide the necessary basis for speculative theological reasoning because they embody the essential form of systematic theology itself: the identity of the principle from which all things derive and to which they return.

There is a fundamental connection between the creeds and the Scriptures because the creeds embody the essential teachings of the Scriptures. The recovery of this sense of the unity between Scripture and doctrine is critical for the renewal of the church and for the renewal of theology. At issue in the divorce of Scripture and doctrine is a cluster of assumptions ranging from ambivalence and uncertainty about the essential philosophical content of revelation to repudiation and refusal of the possibility of the idea that the scriptural witness to the revelation of God is philosophical in content and philosophically coherent.

To be sure, the revelation of God in the witness of the Scriptures has an inherently positivistic form. What makes the creeds so critical is that they give a philosophical form to the philosophical content of revelation present in the inherent positivism of its scriptural witness. This is to say that the various images of God in the Scriptures are not simply relative to each other; that the images of God are not philosophically indifferent to the understanding of God; and that the *primary* images of God are not to be forsaken in the process of theological reflection or in the worship of the church.

The primary images of God are essential for understanding the host of biblical metaphors for the activity of God and the great variety of images which arise out of tradition and experience. The primary images are substantial both in themselves and as the understanding (lit., the "standing under") of these other images.[22] Apart from the primary images, they have no content and can have no meaning.

The creeds identify the primary images of revelation: God is Trinity is the fullest and the most comprehensive of these images. God as Trinity identifies the divine self-relation through the scriptural images of the Father, the Son, and the Holy Ghost which constitute the basis of His relation to everything else. The activity of God in creation, redemption and sanctification—the universal categories of God's relationship to all that is outside of himself, as it were—are attached to the distinctions of persons in the unity of the divine nature. And the creeds locate the primary form of our relationship with God in the church: our communion with God and one another in the communion of the Trinity.

The creeds are Trinitarian in form and content. They focus on the revealed identity of God in himself as the Father, the Son, and the Holy Ghost and locate the principal activities of God for us in terms of the divine relations. As such they embody the doctrinal understanding of the essential content of the revelation of God in the witness of the Scriptures. Insofar as they present a pattern of understanding they show that revelation is for thought and, moreover, that revelation is to be thought about *in this way.*

The Athanasian Creed, for example, the most didactic, the most rigorous and the most comprehensive of the three classical creeds (as well as being the most awkward for liturgical use, perhaps) concludes its dialectic of apophatic and cataphatic (negative and affirmative) ways of speaking about the Trinity with the words: "He therefore that would be saved, Let him thus think of the Trinity"[23]—that is to say, think of the Trinity in this way. The point is that the creeds intend to provide a pattern of understanding, a way of thinking divinity revealed.

The creeds, of course, are themselves the product of an understanding. It is here, perhaps, that we begin to engage the

contemporary situation in theology in its ambivalence or repudiation of the doctrinal and philosophical content of revelation.

It is clearly beyond the scope of this essay to deal competently
and comprehensively with the whole range of positions in contemporary Christian theology. It may be possible, however, to highlight
a few of the tendencies in contemporary theology which contribute
to the disparagement to one extent or the other of the classical *consensus fidelium*. Perhaps, too, it may be suggested that what is
properly wanted to be affirmed in some of these tendencies can be
seen to be best realized through the acknowledgment of the philosophical integrity of the classical formulations of the *consensus
fidelium*.

The *consensus fidelium* centers on the *sensus fidei*—the understanding of the faith objectively proclaimed in the Scriptures and
the creeds with which we subjectively and corporately identify. Thus,
the *consensus fidelium* is not something which is to be reinvented by
each and every generation, however much it is to be reappropriated
by each succeeding age.

At the very least, such a reappropriation requires a much more
thorough-going appreciation of the necessity of the consensual
catholicism of the classical tradition, without which we are left with
only the empty triumphs of our own modern chauvinism. For then
we are closed to the past, closed to the living thought present in it;
without which, too, we cannot think. "For though we but stammer
with the lips of men, yet chant we the high things of God," as one of
the Fathers so beautifully reminds us. The highest things are the
Trinitarian identity of God. Such high things are the content of our
praises. They belong to the understanding—our understanding as
entering into the divine understanding.

Our Refusals

There are two interrelated tendencies which color the contemporary appreciation and understanding of the *consensus fidelium*
and, in particular, the identity of God as Trinity. The one is a kind of
historical positivism which empties the history of doctrine of any

substantial content. The other is an existentialism which denies any philosophical integrity to the idea of God and the content of revelation. The creeds, for example, are viewed historically as the accidental results of certain temporal events, the products of the play of personalities, powers, and politics, all of which could have been otherwise; Arian, for instance, rather than Athanasian. The creeds become cultural artifacts, on the one hand, and embodiments of the will-to-power, on the other hand. There is no reason in history and no reason in the will, either of God or man. In their extreme form, these two tendencies comprise a denial of the *logos* of God and a refusal of eternity.

There is simply the parade of finite contingencies and the unending succession of temporal events. Being is time. But then history is emptied of meaning (a history of what?) and without a relation to the eternal, each and every temporal moment is equally insignificant.

On the one hand, the doctrine of the Trinity is subsequently viewed as an historical artifact and as something which is not intrinsic to the understanding and the identity of Christianity; hence, in the manner of Maurice Wiles, one imagines a Christianity without the Trinity and even without Christ.[24] On the other hand, the substantial integrity of the persons of the Trinity is denied and replaced with an existentialist understanding of personality.[25]

The Trinity is no longer definitively the Father, the Son, and the Holy Ghost. The names of spiritual relationship cease to have any significant revelatory content and any philosophical integrity. They have become relativized to an historical and sociological context (real or imagined), but only to provide justification for our context (real or imagined). The Trinity comes to mean simply that "God is being-in-relationship"[26]—any kind of relationship, however named.

The relations of the persons of the Trinity are rendered indeterminate so that the Trinity can be accommodated to each and every particular social and political agenda. In this view, God is really only for us;[27] God in himself is emptied of any intelligible content—so ineffably ineffable, so utterly unthinkable, as to be altogether insignificant.

What is less clearly seen is that this equally empties the forms of subjective experience of any substantial content as well, the very thing that is wanted to be affirmed. Without *God in himself* we are quickly bereft of God in *God for us*. "God" is reduced simply to a "for us," the product of the play of our own ambitions and aspirations.

An infinite content is, no doubt, wanted in the various contexts of contemporary finite experience. Unfortunately, it is wanted at the expense of the principle of its realization. Jesus Christ is, as Hans Urs Von Balthasar has put it, "the infinite content in the finite context" without whom all our particular experiences are empty and meaningless. "Apart from me," Jesus tells us, "you can do nothing" (Jn 15:5).

This existentialist tendency results in what may be called the "theology of indeterminate love"[28] in which the *logos* of the *theos* is effectively denied. Love is without reason. The understanding in the images of revelation is refused in the name of subjective experience. But the primacy given to experience in contemporary theology not only bankrupts theology, it also bankrupts experience itself, which discovers its own incompleteness even as it asserts its own self-sufficiency. Thus, the need to recover the understanding of God proclaimed in the *consensus fidelium* is not only *against* what is denied in this tendency but *for* what is wanted to be affirmed in it.

It is equally for the understanding of ourselves. The understanding of ourselves is bound up with the understanding of God and it places us in a relationship—the relationship of knowing love—with God and with one another. That place of understanding is the Church, the place of our living in the understanding and our acting out of it. To "take every thought captive to obey Christ" (2Co 10:5) is to discover the freedom of our understanding in thinking of God; indeed, to "think of the Trinity."[29] For the obedience of Christ is the Son's love for the Father in the bond of the Holy Spirit. Everything is to be understood in the knowing love of the Trinity.

The task of the church must be to proclaim this truth for the world and to be the place of our participation in the truth of the

Trinity. This means that the world's ambitions and aspirations are not only to be named to God, but, more significantly, they are to be placed under the name of God. The church speaks and can only speak in the name of the Father, and the Son, and the Holy Ghost. The intent is that whatever is proclaimed is measured by and subject to the substantial content of revelation itself.

What ultimately stands under the images of revelation is the understanding of God as Trinity. Everything that the church proclaims is intentionally placed under the knowing love of God. What the church proclaims, moreover, is in what the church participates, namely, a divine understanding articulated through our human understanding of the Trinitarian identity of God.

The fullness of the mystery of the Trinity is something that we enter into but cannot exhaust. To enter into it means acknowledging that the understanding in the images cannot be at the expense of the images themselves. Both historical positivism and existentialist theology tend to deny the philosophical integrity of the images of salvation.

Our Ambivalences

These tendencies also contribute to a climate of ambivalence about the categories through which the history and the doctrine of the Trinity can be thought. It is commonly said, for instance, that there is no doctrine of the Trinity in the New Testament. This is misleading and overstated. It begs the question "from where does the doctrine come?" and forecloses on the more primary question about the relation of doctrine and Scripture. That there is a development of Christian doctrine and, in particular, the doctrine of the Trinity, goes without saying, but "what kind of development?" and "from where?" are the principal concerns both for the historical account and for the understanding of doctrine.[30]

In saying that there is no doctrine of the Trinity in the New Testament, is it being argued that doctrine, specifically Trinitarian doctrine, is "the Hellenization of Christianity," as the great nineteenth-century liberal historian of dogma, Adolf von Harnack put it, or, for that matter, "the acute Hellenization," by which he described Gnosticism? Doctrine in either event stands in an external relation to the witness of the Scriptures. Its origins and development are presented as belonging to a thinking which has itself been historicized—"Hellenic" thinking. The weight is on the adjective at the expense of the integrity of the noun.

For in what sense it might mean to think without some relation to the philosophical achievements of the Greeks would be hard to say. But certainly for the development of doctrine the relation is of fundamental importance. It does not mean, however, a mere borrowing of terms and concepts which are then arbitrarily and externally imposed upon the poetic and prophetic voice of Scripture.

The more interesting and, perhaps, more important point is that the Scriptural witness in the life of the church impels a reflection upon what has been revealed and requires the development of terms and categories adequate to the thinking of what is revealed. These terms and categories are not simply borrowed from Greek philosophy. They are developed through the critical engagement of our thinking with what is presented for thought in revelation. Terms such as *homoousios* and *persona,* for example, are not categories taken directly from Plato and Aristotle. They are precisely the categories which are developed in order to think the relation of the Father, the Son, and the Holy Ghost.

The terms that are hammered out in the cauldron of controversy ultimately belong to the fundamental pattern of understanding embodied in the creeds and their conciliar explications. The terms belong to the understanding such that words in Greek come to be differently expressed in Latin. Basil, for instance, was able to see that the Latin phrase one *substantia* (substance) in three *personae* (persons) captured the understanding contained in the Greek expression one ουσια (essence) in three υποστασεις (hypostases). The point in question was the ambiguity of hypostasis which could be rendered as substance as well. Settling on the use of specific terms was part of the clarification of understanding and the achievement of the *consensus fidelium,* the working out of a common understanding in and through the diversity of languages.

That words are not univocal in their meaning does not mean that they are unimportant or indifferent. Quite the opposite. The achievement of the *consensus fidelium* is the setting of terms appropriate to each language which are precise enough to enable the essential understanding of the mystery revealed without reducing it to the arid formularies of a merely finite logic. At issue is how a finite logic can participate in an infinite understanding. That is the adventure of theology.

What is frequently forgotten is that these terms and categories such as *substance, person, nature, divinity, humanity,* and, for that matter, *Trinity,* which are embedded in the creeds and their conciliar explications, are more than formal and technical terms. They are part and parcel of the formative principles of the faith; part and parcel of a pattern of understanding intrinsic to the character of the Christian faith itself. When we forsake these terms and categories, we cut ourselves off from an entire language of theological discourse.

The history of doctrinal development is about something more than the parade of theological opinions, whether chronologically or randomly ordered. The theological enterprise may be seen historically and doctrinally to involve two different directions of thinking: the one working toward the articulation of the principle; the other moving from the articulation of the principle to its application and expression in the ordered life of the church. There is at once a deepening of the understanding of the faith proclaimed and the working out of the forms of our participation in the mystery of God.

Development is a loaded term. It should not be assumed that it is altogether and consistently progressive and linear. The pageant of history reminds us that there are ditches and dungeons, by-ways and dead-ends where "the right way is lost and gone,"[31] where what was once clear has become obscured, and where what was once known to be fundamental has become forgotten or refused. Consequently, there is the need for a resurrection of the understanding.

The word *persona*, perhaps, offers an illustration of what has been forgotten but needs to be remembered. Boethius, in the sixth century AD, provided for the Latin West the classic definition of the term *persona.* He recapitulated the history of its use from the Greek προσωπα to the Latin *persona,* and refined its meaning in relation to the more appropriate term (in Greek) υποστασισ. He defined *persona* as "an individual substance of a rational nature."[32] But the word and the refinement of its meaning is considered, first and foremost, with respect to the Trinity and, in particular, to the divine identity of the Son. It only subsequently comes to be applied to the understanding of our humanity—i.e., human personality.

To speak of the Trinity as "the three faces of Being" no doubt recalls the initial connection with προσωπα—masks through which the voice of an actor sounds *(sonus,* hence *personae)*—and connects with the contemporary emphasis on outward expression. But this is altogether at the expense of the classical definition of the term *persona* in the history of doctrinal development with its emphasis upon an inward and spiritual understanding of the reality of God. We move from that to an understanding of ourselves and not the other way around. What is lost is a deeper understanding of ourselves as spiritual creatures *imago Dei Trinitatis.* What is denied, too, is the philosophical impulse present in the analogical tendencies of Augustinian theology.

The doctrine of the Trinity belongs to an activity of the understanding: the understanding which composes and writes; the understanding which collects together and arranges in order what comes to be the books of the Bible; the understanding which establishes the canon of Scripture and develops the creeds. The doctrine of the Trinity constitutes the fullness of that understanding. It concerns the quality of the engagement of our thinking with the divine thinking.

It looks forward and backward. It looks back into the pageant of the history of salvation, gathering up the great host of scriptural images into this fullness of understanding. It looks forward into the unfolding pageant of the Spirit-guided church, gathering up the great host of the images of tradition and experience into this same fullness of understanding, "that nothing may be lost" (Jn 6:12).

Even our refusings of God's grace are made part of the gathering which is itself an activity of the understanding. There are our ignorances: we know not what we want nor what we do, yet "Father, forgive them; for they do not know what they are doing" (Lk 23:34), our unknowing gathered up into His all-knowing love. There are our discouragements: "Master, we have worked all the night long, but have caught nothing. Yet if you say so, I will let down the nets" (Lk 5:5), the net of His understanding into which we, too, are gathered. There are our denials: like Peter's threefold "I do not know him" (Lk 22:57), but "the Lord turned and looked at Peter. Then Peter remembered the word of the Lord…and he went out and wept bitterly" (Lk 22:61-62)—tears of repentance arising out of the look of Christ upon us whose gaze of compassionate judgment at once convicts but also anticipates His threefold restoration of Peter: "Do you love me?…Feed my sheep" (Jn 21:15-17).

Feed them what? Feed them with the bread of everlasting life in Word and Sacrament. "Give us this day our super-substantial bread"[33] the bread of understanding, the bread of doctrine, the bread of our abiding in the knowing love of the Trinity. Such things belong to the church as the place of our abiding in the fullness of understanding.

Exegesis

Jesus Christ clarifies the understanding even as He is himself the understanding as the Word and Son of the Father, and as the Lord and Savior of the world. One of the earliest credal utterances in the New Testament is the statement, "Jesus is Lord," a confession of faith which "no one can say except by the Holy Spirit" (1Co 12:3). It states an identity between Jesus and God. It is not something that "flesh and blood" could have revealed. It belongs to the spiritual understanding which arises out of the witness of the Gospels.

"No one has ever seen God. It is God the only Son, close to the Father's heart, who has made him known" (Jn 1:18). This is not simply a scriptural peg upon which to hang a whole hat of theological argument. Yet, it provides a window of understanding through which we may glimpse something of the mystery of God. What is suggested here is itself a principle of revelation. Not only is God made known, we may say, but God makes himself known. There is, indeed, an exegesis of God.

The word *exegesis* (εξηγησισ) is rich in meaning and significant in the range of its allusions. In its noun form, it means, first of all, *a statement or narrative, the telling of a story*, and secondly, it signifies *the explanation or the interpretation of the story*. Most anciently, as a verb (εξηγεομαι), it meant *"to lead, command or govern"* with the further sense of *leading or showing the way, even teaching or pointing out*. It also came to mean *to dictate or speak forth, to expound or set forth, to interpret*, moreover, and significantly, *to name in the sense of naming the gods*. More specifically, in relation to set forms of words, it means *to narrate, to relate in full* or *to give an exposition—a showing forth or a making known.*[34]

Most commonly, we speak of a scriptural exegesis, meaning an interpretative exposition of the argument of a passage or book of Scripture. Here, surprisingly and most tellingly, the application of the term goes beyond an exposition of words to the showing forth of God. Jesus, the Only Begotten of God who is in the bosom of the Father, *is* the exegete of God, the One who unveils God, as it were, definitively. Jesus narrates the story of God, but even more, He is the story. He is himself the exegesis, the one in whom God is made known. We might say that the story of Jesus is the *exegesis*, the interpretative exposition, of the story of God, and more importantly, of God himself: He "has made him known."

This is the only place in the New Testament where the word is used directly and emphatically about God himself as distinct from relating what has happened[35] or from telling about "God for us" in His signs and wonders done among His people.[36] And it is the only place where Jesus is the exegete.

Yet, the more profound point of His exegesis is that this is God revealing himself, for the identity of Jesus as God's own Word and Son has already been established. There is in this the sense of the fullness of revelation. Jesus' exegesis brings to light the identity of God as Trinity. It focuses on the naming of God. In Jesus there is an intensification and a clarification of the name of God into the names of spiritual relationship.

NAMING GOD.

Naming God belongs to the question of revelation. To put it starkly, if naming God means that we name God, then there is no revelation. But if naming God means that God makes himself known, that He names himself, then there is revelation. At the same time, though, if there is revelation, then it must be revelation to us. Somehow we are engaged with the revelation in order for there to be revelation.

The simple opposition between our naming God and God naming himself cannot hold. A clearer formulation is required. It is not so much that we name God as it is that God names himself through us. We enter into the understanding of God which He gives to us through our understanding. Only so can there be revelation. Revelation is mediation. Ultimately, and in the sense of its fullness, the revelation is in and through the mediator, Jesus Christ, who is both God and man in His twofold identity: His identity with the Father and His identity with us.

In the book of Genesis, Adam is given by God to name the other creatures. In so doing he enters, we might say, into God's own knowing of what He has called into being. Adam's naming of the other creatures is not an act that is simply independent of God's creation, for God not only knows what He has made but the act of creation is itself an intellectual act: "O God…who hast made all things by thy word."[37] Creation is a knowing act.

The creation, moreover, is known to be good. "God saw that it was good" (Ge 1:25), good in its parts and, indeed, very good as a whole, for "God saw everything that he had made, and indeed, it was very good" (Ge 1:31). There is a divine understanding of the creation which Adam's naming both presupposes and enters into. Indeed, God brings the creation to Adam who, having been made in "the image of God" (Gen 1:27) and enlivened by the breath of God breathed into him,[38] is able to enter into the understanding of what God has made and so name the other creatures according as they truly are.

Adam names the other creatures, we might suggest, through God's own understanding of what He has made. But while we read that

Adam named the other creatures, nowhere do we read that Adam named God. In the Scriptures, no one of Adam—that is to say, no human being—names God. God, on the other hand, reveals himself and gives us His name.

The critical arid definitive passage for the Old Testament on this question is the story of the burning bush.[39] The burning bush, which burns but is not consumed, gets Moses' attention, to be sure. More astoundingly, the bush does an equally unbush thing: The bush speaks. God, it seems, speaks out of the bush. But what is most astounding is what God says. God names himself in two kinds of ways: in relation to us, "I am the God of your father, the God of Abraham, the God of Isaac and the God of Jacob" (Ex 3:6); and in relation to himself, "I AM WHO I AM" (Ex 3:14).

These two sides form the creative tension that defines Israel's history and character. On the one hand, God identifies himself with a particular people, a particular tribe, a particular family over and against the gods of the nations and the tribes and the families round about. On the other hand, God shows himself to be the universal God, not one god among many gods, but the one God who is therefore the God of all people, indeed, the God of the whole universe. The tension for Israel is between "our god" and "the God," between the particularity of Israel as God's chosen people and the universality of the God of all creation.

Within this tension, there is no question about which understanding is primary. Israel is to be the people through whom God is made known to the whole world. The God of Abraham, Isaac and Jacob—God in a relationship within history—is subordinate to the God who names himself in a way that, at the very least, points to what is metahistorical and metaphysical: "I AM WHO I AM."

That Israel struggles to come to this fuller understanding does not negate the radical truth contained in what is here revealed. This is the great and sacred revelation of God's name entrusted to Israel, the *Tetragrammaton,* subsequently held in such reverence and awe that, around 300 BC, for instance, it came not to be spoken at all, save once a year by the high priest at Jerusalem in the Holy of Holies. Consequently, there are a number of circumlocutions—ways of speaking around this sacred name—which have become commonplace in religious discourse.

The sacred name is *Yahweh,* as it was probably pronounced; *Jehovah,* as it was traditionally (but mistakenly, however imaginatively) rendered in English. The Hebrew word *Elohim,* meaning God, or, more commonly, the Hebrew word for Lord, *Adonai,* were substituted in its place when reading Scripture, and subsequently, the rendering *Kyrios* in the Greek, *Dominus* in the Latin and the *Lord* in the Authorized Version (KJV) and the Revised Version as well.

The two namings are not simply left in juxtaposition in the story of the burning bush. There is a clear sense that the one serves as an historical modifier to the profounder reality of the other, the name by which "I am to be remembered" (Ex 3:15).

God also said to Moses, "Thus you shall say to the Israelites, 'The LORD ["Yahweh," meaning, I AM WHO I AM], the God of your ancestors, the God of Abraham, the God of Isaac, and the God of Jacob, has sent me to you': this is my name forever, and this my title for all generations.[40]

"The LORD is my name"—"the LORD" being the circumlocution for *Yahweh,* "I am who I am." Whether the circumlocution "LORD" or the name "Yahweh" is used in biblical translations, the primary sense of this naming of God cannot be that God needs a proper name by which to distinguish himself from other gods. The primary sense is the mystery of revelation. God makes himself known in the truth of His being.

When Jesus in John's gospel says, "I am the bread of life" (6:35); "I am the light of the world" (8:12; 9:5); "I am the gate" (10:9); "I am the good shepherd" (10:11); "I am the resurrection and the life" (11:25); "I am the way, and the truth and the life" (14:6) and, finally, "1 am the vine" (15:5), He is both making an identification of himself with the God who has revealed himself in the burning bush as "I AM WHO I AM" and He is intensifying the relationship of God with us through these metaphors of co-inherence or indwelling.

The abiding presence of God with us belongs to our being in the presence of the abiding love of God with God in God—the blessed

Trinity—God the Father, the Son, and the Holy Ghost. "God the only Son, who is close to the Father's heart, who has made him known" (Jn 1:18).

There is in this a sense of contrast and a sense of fulfillment. In the previous verse we read, "the law indeed was given through Moses; grace and truth came through Jesus Christ" (Jn 1:17). The contrast is between the Old Testament and the New Testament about what is made known and the mode of its being made known. The passage which follows, "No one has ever seen God" (Jn 1:18a), for instance, echoes the story of God's indirect revelation of himself to Moses in the cleft of the rock.[41] There is a constant tension between the hiddenness of God and His being made known, between the nearness of God and His remoteness from His people that is only fully resolved in the doctrine of the Trinity.

"No one has ever seen God" remains true for Moses and for all humanity according to our own powers of understanding. What follows is not revelation as additional information about God, however, but a new order of understanding. Jesus is not simply another Moses or another prophet. He is the only-begotten Son of God who is in the bosom of the Father; who has made him known."

What is invisible to the senses is made visible to the understanding. It is a divine understanding expressed through our human understanding; God making himself known to *us*. The Son's identity with the Father and His identity with us is at once the form and the content of the revelation. Thomas Aquinas puts it this way,

> The only begotten Son has made Him known…and this teaching surpasses all other teachings in dignity, authority and usefulness because it was handed on immediately by the only begotten Son.… But what did he make known except the one God? And even Moses did this: "Hear, O Israel, the Lord your God is one." What did this add to Moses? It added the mystery of the Trinity, and many other things that neither Moses nor any of the prophets made known.[42]

When we say "Jesus is Lord," we acknowledge the identification of Jesus with Yahweh, "I AM WHO I AM." The identification is something revealed through the incarnate life of Jesus Christ as presented in the Gospels. It deepens the understanding of the "proper name" Yahweh into the essential names of spiritual relationship: the Father, the Son, and the Holy Ghost. For when we say "Jesus is Lord" we are making a Trinitarian statement. The identification of Jesus with Yahweh—Jesus as Lord—means that the oneness of the Lord is not a solitary aloneness. God is Trinity, the Father, the Son, and the Holy Ghost.

Jesus, in whom this identification with Yahweh is revealed, ushers us into this more profound understanding. He names the relationships which are the names of God, the Father, the Son, and the Holy Ghost, to which all other images are subordinate and without which they cannot have any coherence or meaning. God's relationship with himself as Trinity is the basis for His relationship with all else.

METAPHORS AND NAMES.

This focus on naming God plays an important role in the renewal of the church. The variety of metaphors for the activity of God toward us are brought under the identity of God as the modifiers of the name of God revealed in the Old Testament and intensified and clarified into the Trinitarian names of spiritual relationship revealed by Jesus in the New Testament. Only as attached to the divine name/names do these metaphors have any meaning. They are the modifiers of the essential names of God and serve as illustrations for us of one aspect or another of the fullness of understanding contained in the identity of God, ultimately named as Trinity, God the Father, the Son, and the Holy Ghost.

The Song of Moses in Deuteronomy 32:1-18 illustrates the interplay between name and metaphor in the context of the Old Testament which is subsequently intensified and clarified by Jesus in the New Testament. Among the many Old Testament metaphors for God, the image of God as the Rock predominates. It is a metaphor for the stability and faithfulness of God which modifies "the name of the Lord" (Dt 32:3); that is to say, Yahweh, "I AM WHO I AM"

(Ex 3:14). "For I will proclaim the name of the LORD" (Dt 32:3). The Song goes on here to modify the name of the Lord, first, with the image of God as Rock and, then, with the image of God as the father "who created you, who made you and established you" (Dt 32:6).

Against the stability and faithfulness of God, the children of Israel have been inconstant and unfaithful, "a perverse and crooked generation" (Dt 32:5). They have forgotten the God who created them, the God who brought them into being. The image of God as Father here suggests the act of creation itself—the bringing into being of all that is.

The passage moves on to consider God's relation to what He has brought into being. There is the waywardness which places Israel "in a desert land, in the howling wilderness waste" (Dt 32.10). Israel has turned away from God. But God remains faithful toward Israel and turns towards Israel and finds her in the wilderness. There are the images of God's providential and loving care for what He has brought into being; the nurturing love for what has been made. "He shielded him; cared for him, guarded him as the apple of his eye" (Dt 32:10).

The act of begetting gives place to the activity of fatherly (and/or motherly) care for what has been brought into being,

> As an eagle stirs up its nest,
> and hovers over its young;
> as it spreads it wings, takes them up,
> and bears them aloft on its pinions....[43]

But Israel—*Jeshurun* (the upright one)—is not upright towards God's nurturing care, either. "Jeshurun grew fat and kicked" against God's word (Dt 32:15). There is Israel's rebellion against God who made Israel, on the one hand, and against God's care for Israel, on the other hand. This rebellion is put cognitively; in other words, in terms of our understanding:

> You were unmindful of the Rock
> that bore you,

> you forgot the God who
> gave you birth.[44]

There is our unmindfulness, our forgetfulness. It is, of course, a willing unknowing, a willful forgetting; there is in it a refusal to understand what is given to be understood. And regardless of whether or not the word should be rendered as "begot" or "bore" (either is possible) the passage as a whole suggests a critical distinction in the understanding of God's activity between the coming into being of an order of creation and what takes place within that order. In this case, the immediate sense of the image of God as Father of Israel and God's nurturing, motherly care of Israel belong to the activity of God within the order of creation and act as modifiers of the divine name which is altogether distinct from that order.

Yet there is contained in this the suggestion of the radical sense of creating—the coming to be of the order of creation—as distinct from the sense of creating within that order. The distinction comes to be expressed in terms of begetting, on the one hand, and giving birth, on the other hand, but as yet associated here with God's relation to Israel and only by extension to the whole of creation. And it has still to be extended to God in himself—the eternal begetting of the Son and Word of the Father.

There is a difference between creating and giving birth: the one an activity within the order, the other toward the understanding of the coming to be of that order. There is the intimacy of the image of giving birth and nurturing, and there is the sense of distance and difference in the act of creation. To collapse them together would be at the expense of the coming to be of what can only be subsequently nurtured. The intimacy of God's relation with Israel is an activity within the created order which has to be held in tension with the radical difference between God and what He has made, that is, its radical coming to be.

The revelation of Jesus Christ in the New Testament intends the resolution of this tension while maintaining the critical difference between the nearness and the remoteness of God, between transcendence and immanence. The doctrine of the Trinity is that resolution which holds these distinctions in unity without which neither transcendence nor immanence can have any coherence. The doctrine of the Trinity endeavors to explain how God can be perfectly and sovereignly in himself and wondrously and graciously *for us.*

What is in the Old Testament a metaphor for God's twofold activity in relation to us (like the father who creates, guides and protects, and like a mother who gives birth and nurtures) is intensified and clarified into the names of spiritual relationship to which all other metaphors and images are subordinate as modifiers. They qualify the understanding of God for us by being attached to the names of God.

What is wanted to be preserved is the sense of intimacy, on the one hand, and the sense of distance, on the other hand. The way this is done is through the principles of identity established by Jesus; namely, God the Father, the Son, and the Holy Spirit. This is not because the relationship of father and son is in any sense superior to the relationship of mother and daughter or any other kind of relationship *within* the created order but to indicate the prior relationship of God to the order, which He has made. What is wanted in the images or names are ways of expressing a primary metaphysical relationship that is then carried over into the life of faith and that gives spiritual meaning to all the ordered forms of human and divine relationship. They are gathered into the philosophical understanding of God revealed as Trinity, the God of knowing love. They serve as modifiers of the revealed names of God and amplify our understanding not only of *God for us* but also of *God himself.* They are not an addition but an explication.

"Before Abraham Was, I Am."

This can be seen in the New Testament in the connection between the "I am" sayings of Jesus and Jesus' exegesis of God as Trinity. The seven "I am" sayings of Jesus in John's gospel are all images about God's relationship with us in Jesus, which are explicitly gathered into and placed with the primary relation of Jesus and the Father. A brief consideration of each shows how this is so.

"I am the bread of life" (Jn 6:35) says Jesus, who goes on to make several references to the Father in which it is clear that our partaking of the bread of life is about our being sustained in the spiritual knowledge and love of God, both for us and in himself. "Just as the Living Father sent me, and I live because of the Father, so he who eats me will live because of me" (Jn 6:57); words, which He says are "spirit and life" (Jn 6:63).

"I am the light of the world" (Jn 8:12), Jesus says, and goes on, in the face of the animosity of the Pharisees, to speak of His relation to the Father and their ignorance. "I testify on my own behalf and the Father who sent me bears witness to me....If you knew me, you would know my Father also" (Jn 8:19), a witness that we are given to know and to will; in short, to "believe that I am he" (Jn 8:24). But "they did not understand that he was speaking to them about the Father" (Jn 8:27), nor did they understand that "before Abraham was, I am (Jn 8:58).

"I am the gate....I am the good shepherd" (Jn 10:7, 11, 14), says Jesus, and proceeds to connect the meaning of His shepherding with His relationship to the Father and the freedom of His sacrifice with the Father's love. "I know my own and my own know me, just as the Father knows me and I know the Father. And I lay down my life for the sheep...for this reason the Father loves me, because I lay down my life in order to take it up again....I have received this command from my Father" (Jn 10:14, 15, 17-18). We are known and loved in the knowing love of the Trinity.

"I am the resurrection and the life" (Jn 11:25), Jesus says, and goes on to place the illustration of this teaching—the raising of Lazarus—in the context of His prayer to the Father made known to us that we may believe that He is the resurrection and the life. "And Jesus looked upward and said 'Father, I thank you for having heard me...that they may believe that you sent me'" (Jn 11:41). Something of the glory of the Trinity is made visible to the understanding through the intimacy of His prayer which is opened to our view.

"Did I not tell you that if you believed you would see the glory of God?" (Jn 11:40). But, then, we, like Lazarus, are often pretty far gone.

"I am the way, and the truth and the life" (Jn 14:6), Jesus tells Thomas at the Last Supper and proceeds to show that this means His exegesis of the Father and our coming to the Father through the Son. "No one comes to the Father except through me. If you know me you will known my Father also....Whoever has seen me has seen the Father" (Jn 14:6-7,9).

Finally, Jesus says, "I am the true vine" (Jn 15:5). He goes on to develop the meaning of this image in terms of our abiding in the knowing love of God, "Abide in me as I abide in you" (Jn 15:4). "My Father is glorified by this , that you bear much fruit and so become my disciples. As the Father has loved me, so have I loved you; abide in my love...just as I have kept my Father's commandments and abide in his love" (Jn 15.8-10).

Immediately after this last image, Jesus proceeds to instruct the disciples most explicitly about the Holy Spirit. "Because I am going to the Father" (Jn 16:10, 17, 28) is the recurring refrain of Eastertide from John 16 in which Jesus teaches us about the person of the Holy Spirit: sent by the Father, sent by the Son, the Spirit of Truth, the Spirit of their mutual and abiding love.

In other words, these images of God in relation to us—"God for us"—are drawn into the intimacy of the primary relationship of the Father, the Son, and the Holy Ghost—God in himself—through which they have their content and meaning. Our abiding in God is through the mutually indwelling love of the Trinity. These metaphors of co-inherence are the modifiers of the sacred names of spiritual relationship clarified and revealed by Jesus in the witness of the Scriptures. They are, in a way, the metaphors for the church as the temple of God, the dwelling-place of the Trinity. This is suggested wonderfully by Thomas Cranmer:

> He that keepeth the words of Christ, is promised the love and favor of God and that he shall be the dwelling-place or temple of the Blessed Trinity.[45]

Conclusion

The renewal of the church turns upon this sense of understanding that we participate in what we are given to proclaim. The glory of the Triune God has been made known to us through the Incarnation of Jesus Christ. The doctrine of the "Double Trinity" may be seen as the crucial and typically Western way of acknowledging the sovereign freedom and truth of God in himself and the truth and freedom of our abiding in the Trinity through God's being *for us*.

The church finds her essential being identified in the creed: "the holy catholic church; The communion of saints; The forgiveness of sins; The resurrection of the body, And the life everlasting." Under the Spirit's guidance, these principles of faith belong to our fundamental fellowship with God the Father, the Son, and the Holy Spirit. They are the categories of our participation in the Trinitarian life of God. They give shape to the mission and life of the church as the place of our abiding in the fullness of understanding and as the basis for the church's engagement of the world in proclamation.

The recovery of the creeds as formative for the praying, teaching, and worshipping life of the church may be the way that this sense of the fullness of understanding God as Trinity can be renewed in us and in the churches. The renewal of the church must be a renewal in the high things of God which have been opened to our view to proclaim and enjoy.

For there are essentially two things which Jesus wants us to know: His divine identity and His identity with us. The fullness of understanding which He opens to view and into which He would have us enter is the Trinity both *in se* and *pro nobis*. And for the church, this is at once her delight and her mission. As always, it is what the poets sing.

> Thou hast but two rare cabinets fill of treasure,
> The Trinitie, and Incarnation:
> Thou hast unlockt them both,
> And made them jewels to betroth

The work of thy creation
Unto thy self everlasting pleasure.[46]

NOTES

1. Kim Ondaatje, *Small Churches of Canada* (Toronto, Ont.. Lester & Orpen Dennys, 1982), 52-53.

2. *"Rectus itaque Confessionis ordo poxebat, ut Trinitatis subjugeretur Ecclesia, tanquam habitatori domus sua, et Deo templum suum, et conditori civitas sua."*—Augustine, *Enchiridion*, XV.56, Oeuvres de Saint Augustine, IX, (Paris, Descle'e, de Brouwer et cie, 1947), 202.

3. *Book of Common Prayer, Canada*, 1959, 83.

4. *"Templum ergo Dei, hoc est totius summae Trinitatis, sancta est Ecclesia, scilicet universa in coelo et in terra."*—Augustine, *Enchiridion*, XV.36, 204.

5. Ambrose, *The Mysteries*, trans. Roy J. Deferrari, *The Fathers of the Church*, Vol. 44.

6. Matthew 16:13—17:9

7. This has, perhaps, its most dramatic literary representation in Dante's Divine Comedy. *Purgatorio,* Canto xxix, where Dante the Pilgrim is told, *"Guarda e escolta"*—*"Look and listen"*—to a sacramental presentation of the pageant of revelation.

8. The Common Prayer tradition gives particular expression to the interplay between these two classical principles of our life in Christ.

9. "The NT statements do not clarify the interrelations of the three but they clearly emphasize the fact that they are interre-

lated."—Wolfhart Pannenburg, *Systematic Theology*, Vol. 1, trans. Geoffrey W. Bromiley, 1991, (Grand Rapids, Michigan, Eerdmans Pub. Co., 1988), 269.

10. *Book of Common Prayer, America*, 1928, 138.

11. This has, perhaps, its most dramatic artistic representation in Fra Angelico's (1387-1435) depiction of the Transfiguration in the Dominican Convent of San Marco, Florence, Italy.

12. Romans 12:2

13. Exodus 33.:7-11

14. "He took to himself a body which could die" and, "Death does not appear by itself but in the body; therefore he put on a body, that coming across death in the body he might efface it."— Athanasius, *On the Incarnation* (London, Mowbray & Co., Ltd., 1949, reprint 1970), 153,247. Also, "He who was so full of life that when He wished to die He had to 'borrow death from others.'"— C.S. Lewis, intro., 9.

15. See Liddell & Scott, *Greek-English Lexicon*, ΔΟΚΕΩ, ΔΟΓΜΑ, and ΔΟΞΑ and Arndt & Gingerich, *A Greek-English Lexicon of the New Testament and Other Early Christian Literature*, δογμα and δοξα.

16. See David Curry, *The Recovery of Reformed Catholicism,* The Machray Review, Number 3, May 1993 (Prayer Book Society of Canada, 1994), pp. 11-12.

17. John Bramhall, *The Works* (Oxford: John Henry Parker, L.A.C.T., 1847) "Schism Guarded and Beaten Back," Vol. II, p. 478.

18. Εκκλησια...παρα τε των αποστολων και εκεινων μαθντων παραλαθσυσα...πιστιν. —Irenaeus, *Adv. Haer.*, Bk. I, chap. x, *Sources Chretiennes* (Paris: Les Editions du Cerf, 1979), p. 155.

19. Martin Chemnitz, *Examination of the Council of Trent*, trans. Fred Kramer (St. Louis, Missouri: Concordia Publishing House, 1971), Part I, p. 215.

20. Bramhall, "Schism Guarded...," *Works*, II, p. 630.

21. Bramhall, "Schism Guarded...," *Works*, II, p. 597.

22. David Curry, "'Something Understood': Doctrine in Devotion," *The Lord is Nigh: The Theology and Practice of Prayer*, ed. Michael Treschow (Kelowna, B.C.: Sparrow's Editing, 1997).

23. The Athanasian Creed, *Book of Common Prayer, Canadian*, p. 697.

24. In particular, the essays, "Reflections on the Origin of the Doctrine of the Trinity," "Does Christology Rest on a Mistake?" and "The Criteria of Christian Theology" in Maurice Wiles, *Working Papers in Doctrine* (London: SCM Press, 1976). While these points may or may not be what he advocates, he allows for a number of provocative and speculative possibilities for the contemporary expression of the Christian faith which arise from (a) a strong sense of the distance between ourselves and older traditional views, and (b) a strong sense of the distinction between the Jesus of history and the Christ of faith, leaning on the former at the expense of the latter: "Any full Christian theology must be brought into some sort of relation to Jesus...yet because of the fluidity of reference of the term Christ...Christ-centeredness itself may be a highly elusive concept," p.186. As Pannenburg explains, for Wiles the "historico-critical exegesis no longer justifies the thesis that the threefold form of deity is a datum of revelation in the form of an express statement with the authority of revelation."—*Systematic Theology*, Vol I, p. 271. The only real authority is "history."

25. Catherine Mowry LaCugna, *God For Us: The Trinity and Christian Life* (San Francisco: HarperCollins, 1991). Cf. Michael

Carreker's "Made in the Image of God: The Trinitarian Principle of Christian Personality," *Redeeming the Time: The Church and the Challenge of Secularity*, ed. Rev'd David Garrett (Charlottetown, P.E.I.: St. Peter Publication, 1994).

26. Ibid.

27. Ibid.

28. See David Curry, "Feminism and Homosexuality: Love without Reason?" *The Anglican Church and Same Sex Couples*, ed. Peter Armstrong, John Pearce (Halifax: Dal Printing, 1995), and Michael Carreker's "Made in the Image of God: The Trinitarian Principle of Christian Personality."

29. The Athanasian Creed, BCP, p. 697.

30. See William G. Rusch, "Introduction," *The Trinitarian Controversy: Sources of Early Christian Thought*, trans. and ed. William G. Rusch (Philadelphia: Fortress Press, 1980).

31. *"Che la diritta via era smarrrita."*—Dante, The Divine Comedy, *Inferno*, Canto I.

32. *"Naturae rationabilis individua substantia."*—Boethius, "Contra Eutyches," *The Theological Tractates*, trans. Stewart, Rand, & Tester (Cambridge, Mass.: Harvard University Press, 1973), III, p. 85.

33. Τον αρτον ημων τον επιουσιον δος ημιν σημερον.—Cyril of Jerusalem, Lecture V, "The Eucharistic Rite," *Lectures on the Christian Sacraments*, ed. F.L. Cross, (Crestwood, N.Y.: St. Vladimir's Seminary Press, 1977), p. 33.

34. See Liddell & Scott, *Greek-English Lexicon*, Εξηγησισ.

35. Luke 24:35

36. Acts 15:12; 21:19

37. Wisdom 9:1

38. Genesis 2:7

39. Exodus 3

40. Exodus 3:15

41. Exodus 33:18-23

42. Thomas Aquinas, *Commentary on the Gospel of St. John*, trans. J.A. Weisheipl with F.R. Larcher. (Albany, N.Y.: Magi Books, 1980), Lecture 11, p. 106.

43. Deuteronomy 32:11

44. Deuteronomy 32:18

45. *The First Book of Homilies, 1562* (Great Britain: Focus Ministries Trust, 1986), p. 2.

46. George Herbert, "Ungratefulnesse," *The Temple: The Classics of Western Spirituality* (Ramsey, N.J.: Paulist Press, 1981), p. 200.

The Trinity As Our Guide: The Centrality of the Trinity in Social Ethics

Donald Faris

A Collect for Trinity

Almighty and everlasting God, who has revealed Yourself as Father, Son and Holy Spirit, and ever live and reign in the perfect unity of love: Grant that we may always hold firmly and joyfully to this faith, and living in the praise of Your divine majesty, may finally be one in You: Who art three persons in one God. World without end.

The Trinity or Three Unitarianisms?

APPROXIMATELY fifty years ago, H. Richard Niebuhr observed that among "the newer tendencies in theology" was a rediscovered interest in the doctrine of the Trinity. His very perceptive article on this subject was entitled, "The Doctrine of the Trinity and the Unity of the Church."[1] He noted that liberalism had generally dismissed the doctrine of the Trinity as being primarily of historical or antiquarian interest. Niebuhr, however, appreciated the need to reappropriate the Christian faith for the current century and put this in terms of "men's enduring crisis." He wrote,

> The existential problem of God and of man's relation to Him led inevitably to the question about the deity of the Creator of nature, that is of His goodness, to the question about the deity of Jesus Christ, that is of His power, and to the question about the deity of the Spirit, that is whether among all the spirits there is a Holy Spirit.[2]

Niebuhr recognized that these problems were not solved independently of one another in the historic Christian faith. They were dealt with together in the unifying doctrine of the Trinity. This makes the doctrine of the Trinity an important subject in ecumenical theology as opposed to the "partial faiths and partial formulations of parts of the church and of individuals in the church."[3] It is then that Niebuhr turns to discuss "The three Unitarianisms in Christianity." While he recognizes the theoretical possibility of the Trinity falling apart into Tritheism (three gods), he says that it is nearer the truth to suggest that historically Christianity has been an association of three loosely held together unitarian religions. He speaks of a Unitarianism focused on the Creator; a Unitarianism focused on Jesus Christ; and a Unitarianism focused on the Spirit. He traces each of these Unitarianisms throughout the centuries and through several denominational traditions.

The Unitarianism of the Creator can be traced back to the Monarchianism and Arianism of the early centuries, through Socinianism and Deism right up to the Unitarianism of the twentieth century.

The Unitarianism of Jesus Christ can be traced back to Marcion in the second century. He rejected the worship of the Jehovah of the Old Testament as being "unworthy" and taught that in Jesus Christ a "better God had been discovered," one who is "nothing but good." This tendency can be seen in many twentieth century Christians who virtually ignore the Old Testament foundations of the New Testament.

The third Unitarianism is that of the Spirit. Separated from the Father and the Son, we can only hope that this is the Holy Spirit and not one of many spirits of the world. This tradition goes back to Montanus in the early centuries. Through Joachim de Fiore and his "Age of the Spirit" to modern day Quakers, Pentecostals and Charismatics.

American ethicist Richard J. Mouw describes the different Unitarianisms in terms of their worship. He says,

> Christians play favorites with the members of the Trinity. Some Christian groups find it most natural to pray to God the Father; their hymns and other expressions of spirituality seem to dwell mainly on

the first person of the Trinity, an emphasis that is also carried over into their theological reflection. Other groups find it very appropriate to employ "dear Jesus" prayers and songs and to center their theological discussions on the second person of the Trinity. And there are also Holy Spirit oriented Christians; because of the recent charismatic renewal, their numbers have been increasing, as more and more Christians have been invoking the power and presence of the third person of the Trinity.[4]

Mouw argues that the three different Unitarianisms not only produce different worship styles but also different "moral styles." He suggests that we ask ourselves this question. "When you think about *obeying God* which member of the Trinity do you view yourself as relating to primarily?"[5]

One ethical style is strongly centered on God the Creator. For example, some forms of Calvinism recite the Ten Commandments at every worship service and experience worship as regathering at the foot of Mount Sinai. Another ethical style is focused on Jesus Christ. You can see this in the emphasis on the imitation of Christ or the idea of "following Jesus" or "being like Jesus." Rather than regathering at the foot of Mount Sinai, this ethical style gathers people for worship at the Mount of Beatitudes. The third style of ethical Unitarianism is that which focuses on the third person of the Trinity, the Holy Spirit. This style would claim to go beyond either the Old or New Testament's moral guidance to seek moral guidance from an "inner experience" of the Holy Spirit.

In their liberal forms, the Unitarianism of the Creator can collapse into the worship of nature, and a moral style centered on following the laws of nature. A liberal Unitarianism of Jesus Christ can collapse into seeing Jesus as a "good man" or a model social activist. And a liberal Unitarianism of the Holy Spirit can be reduced to a worship which is open to the spirits of the age and a "feel good" ethic.

While Niebuhr seems to express the hope that these three Unitarianisms would all mutually correct one another, this does not appear to happen in real life. Unitarianism has historically been a resting place in the journey from faith to agnosticism. If we wish to recover the deep riches of the Christian faith and Christian ethics, then the church must recover a living understanding of the Trinity. We must return to our first love, the God who *is* love, the Blessed Trinity.

Return to the Trinity

We begin our Christian journey by being baptized in the name of the Father, Son, and Holy Spirit. We are strengthened on that journey by Holy Communion services where we participate in the communion of the Father, Son, and Holy Spirit and with one another. Christian Scriptures witness to the Father, Son, and Holy Spirit. Christian preaching proclaims the Father, Son, and Holy Spirit. And Christian prayer is both to and through the Father, Son, and Holy Spirit.

A Christian's entire life is a communion of life, a communion of our personal life with the life of the Father, through the Son, in the Holy Spirit. We believe that every human being is called into nothing less than this intimate personal union with the Father, Son and Holy Spirit. The eternal Father has freely given himself to us through the incarnation of His eternal Son, and in the eternal Holy Spirit. Just as Christ is a member of the divine family in virtue of being the eternal Son of the Father, so human persons are destined to be sons and daughters by adoption. Our communion with Christ and with one another in him, brings us into the eternal divine Trinitarian family. However, as Roman Catholic theologian J. A. Di Noia writes,

> …If we are destined to enjoy this ultimate communion we must change. We must become fit for it. Interpersonal communion with God is only "natural" to uncreated persons; for created persons, who are also sinners, such communion is possible only through justification and grace. Through the redeeming grace of Christ and, specifically, through the transformation that this grace makes possible, we are rendered "fit" participants in the communion of the Father, Son and Holy Spirit. Our transformation will be a confor-

mation: the more we become like Christ, the more surely we discover our true selves, the unique persons created by the triune God to share in the divine life and to enjoy the personal life of the Trinity. As Catholics pray in one of the Sunday prefaces, "Father...You sent Him as one like ourselves, though free from sin, that you might see and love in us what you see and love in Him."[6]

It is the blessed Trinity who is the God of Christians. When Christians use the word "God," this is the God we mean. The word "god" is a generic term which has been used to refer to many ideas, concepts, metaphors, images, and idols. Some people believe in many "gods." Some people believe there is only one "god" who by definition is "unknowable," raising the question of how they *know* this "god" is unknowable. Some people believe that "god" doesn't care about the creation. Yet others argue that "god" *is* the creation or that the creation is "part of god."

This pluralistic situation in regard to "god" or "gods" is not a new situation. The people of Israel lived at a time when most people believed that there were many gods. If you were to transport yourself back in time to early Israel to ask a non-Israelite whether they believed in god, they might well reply, "Of course I do. We have many household gods, but we give special honor to Baal and Asherah. Which gods do you honor?" If you were to ask a prophet of Israel if he or she believed in these gods, he or she might reply "Of course not. These gods are no gods. They are idols, The one living God has revealed himself to us. He has even named himself. We know Him as Yahweh, Adonai, the Lord."

If this pluralistic situation existed in the period of time covered by the Old Testament, it had not greatly changed by the time of the New Testament. Jesus and Paul lived in a society where some people worshiped the one living God of Israel, while others worshiped many gods. Both the Greeks and the Romans believed in many gods. While their personal devotion might be centered on a few gods, they increasingly made room for the divinity of their political leaders. Both Jews and Christians refused to worship these "many gods and many lords" (1Co 8:5). While the Jews continued to worship only Yahweh, "Adonai," the Lord, Christians had experienced a diversity within the unity of God. This diversity within unity had been revealed by Jesus Christ himself who spoke of the Father, the Spirit and himself in terms that could only be applied by any monotheistic Jew to God alone. The very earliest New Testament strata of pre-Pauline hymns, creeds and liturgies, all reveal that Jesus was worshiped, something that every Jew knew was reserved only for God himself! And baptism was in the newly revealed *name* of the triune God, "Father, Son and Holy Spirit." The earliest Christian experience was that after his crucifixion, the resurrected Jesus Christ was both "Savior" and "Lord" and both of these titles belonged to God alone. Yet, Jesus as "Savior" and "Lord" brought those who worshiped Him, to His eternal "Abba," Father. And the early Christians' experience was that this did not happen apart from the work of the Holy Spirit. It was not ivory tower speculation, but street-corner, life-changing experience that taught Christians that the one God had revealed himself as Father, Son and Holy Spirit. So, it was from the very first generation of Christians to this very day, that Christians reply to the question, "which God do you believe in" by answering with God's self-revealed name in which they were baptized. We believe in the Father, Son, and Holy Spirit. He is the God in whom we move and live and have our being. He is the God in whose Trinitarian life we share communion even now, and into whose image we are being transformed and conformed.

How do we know of this one God, Father, Son, and Holy Spirit? We know of Him because He has chosen to reveal himself to us. We have not chosen Him as one possibility among many. He has chosen to reveal himself to us. And He has done this by sending us His Word and Holy Spirit. The one Lord created all things visible and invisible by speaking His Word and calling all things into being even as His Spirit brooded over creation. He anointed His prophets, priests, and kings by His Holy Spirit and sent them His Word to guide them. Finally, when His people dwelt in great darkness due to their rebellion, He sent not a servant, but His only

Son, the Word, to dwell among them. John's gospel puts it this way (Jn 1:1-4, 14, 18):

> In the beginning was the Word, and the Word was with God, and the Word was God. He was in the beginning with God. All things came into being through him all things were made, and without him not one thing came into being. In him was life, and the life was the light of all people...

> And the Word became flesh and lived among us, and we have seen his glory, the glory as of the Father's only Son, full of grace and truth....No one has ever seen God. It is God the only Son, who is close to the Father's heart, who has made him known.

It is through His only Son that we know the Father, and it is in the Holy Spirit that we affirm that Jesus is Lord and cry "Abba," Father. The one revelation of God in Jesus Christ reveals God to be simultaneously, eternally and antecedently in himself the one Lord who is Father, Son, and Holy Spirit. But this revelation of God has itself a threefold form. While theologians have struggled for centuries to find some "vestige" of the Trinity within creation, Karl Barth argues that it is found only in the revelation itself. In the threefold form of the Word as Revelation, Holy Scripture, and Proclamation, we see the threefold form of God. In the revelation of Jesus Christ, the living Word, we encounter the Son, the Father, and the Holy Spirit. In the witness to this revelation in the Holy Scriptures, we are again irresistibly confronted by the living Word of God as Father, Son and Holy Spirit. And in the proclamation of the church through its preaching, liturgy and pastoral conversation, we again experience the living Word as the Father we praise, through the Son we adore, in the Holy Spirit in which we rejoice. We know God, only because He has freely chosen to give himself to be known by us, out of His self-giving love.

And here we must affirm that it is of supreme pastoral and ethical significance that what God is toward us, He is eternally in himself. God is personal, freely chosen, self-giving love.

GOD IS PERSONAL.

The three persons of the Trinity, Father, Son, and Holy Spirit are not three separate individuals. They are persons in communion. They are persons in relationship. The Father is Father of the Son. The Son is Son of the Father. The Spirit is the Spirit of God or the Spirit of Christ. God *is* persons in relationship and can only be known through personal relationships and as personal love.

GOD IS FREE.

There are no philosophical or theological principles or presuppositions that are superior to God. God did not "have to" create. God did not "have to" love His creation. He is what He is, and will be what He will be. He is an eternal communion of freely given love within himself and He has chosen freely to reveal this to His creation.

GOD IS SELF-GIVING LOVE.

Through all of the New Testament we see that God is *agape*-love. We see this self-revelation of love in Jesus' teaching that we should love God and love our neighbor equally. This double commandment is collapsed into one in the new commandment of John 15:9-12,

> As the Father has loved me, so I have loved you; abide in my love. If you keep my commandments, you will abide in my love, just as I have kept my Father's commandments and abide in his love. I have said these things to you so that my joy may be in you, and that your joy may be complete. This is my commandment, that you love one another as I have loved you.

This freely chosen self-giving love is seen in the suffering and cross that Jesus took upon himself. There we see not only the suffering love of Jesus, the Son of the Father, but also the suffering love that lies within the very heart of the Father and in which we participate through the personal inner working of the Holy Spirit.

The Trinity is not some intellectual abstraction in whom Christians may believe if they choose. Because God has communicated (revealed) himself to us in the three-fold way as Father, Son, and Holy Spirit, the Blessed Trinity lies at the very heart of the Christian message of salvation. Church of Scotland theologian, T.F. Torrance, makes this clear,

> ...Unless our salvation derives from the one ultimate being of God who is Father, Son and Holy Spirit eternally in himself, it is finally empty of divine validity and saving power. So far as belief in the Lord Jesus Christ as Saviour is concerned, it is clear that unless there is an unbroken continuity of divine presence and activity between Christ and God, then in the last analysis, Jesus Christ, with all He stands for, is irrelevant for the ultimate destiny of men and women. Unless Jesus Christ is God himself, God the Son incarnate, then the God proclaimed to us in the Gospel is not a God who loves us to the uttermost, but a God whose love falls short of identifying himself with us in Jesus Christ to the extent of actually becoming one with us in and through Him. Only God can forgive sins, so that unless Christ is God, His word of forgiveness is empty of any divine substance. Unless Christ is of one and the same being as God, as well as of one and the same being as ourselves, the atoning sacrifice of Christ on the cross for us and our salvation is in fact without divine validity or saving power.[7]

Trinitarian Ethics

If our salvation is grounded in the reality of the Blessed Trinity, so too are Christian ethics. Christian ethics are evangelical ethics, that is to say, they are ethics grounded on the good news of what God has done to accomplish our salvation. If they do not arise from the good news, the gospel of Jesus Christ, then they are simply arbitrary and arise merely from our own subjectivity. Anglican ethicist, Oliver O'Donovan, is helpful at this point. He writes,

> Every way of life not lived by the Spirit of God is lived by "the flesh," by man taking responsibility for himself whether in libertarian or

legalistic ways, without the good news that God has taken responsibility for him. Consequently, we cannot admit the suggestion that Christian ethics should pick its way between the two poles of law and licence in search of middle ground. Such an approach could end up by being only what it was from the start, an oscillation between two sub-Christian forms of life. A consistent Christianity must take a different path altogether, the path of an integrally evangelical ethics which rejoices the heart and gives light to the eyes because it springs from God's gift to mankind in Jesus Christ.[8]

Legalism and license are both ultimately the same in that they are both ways of living apart from God. If we can please God simply by following some rules (legalism), who needs the Cross and resurrection of Jesus Christ, or the guidance and power of the Holy Spirit? Or it we can simply ignore the guidance of God through His Word and Spirit, and do whatever we wish (license), then who needs God at all? Trinitarian ethics produce lives lived by the power of the Spirit, through the communion with the Son, to the praise of the Father. Just as God is antecedently in himself personal, freely chosen, self-giving love, so the Christian life is living in personal communion with this freely-given, self-giving love.

CHRISTIAN ETHICS ARE CHURCH ETHICS.

The profound communion, which exists eternally in God himself, is extended to humanity in the Incarnation. The depth of this communion is seen in the relationship of the divinity and the humanity of Jesus Christ. He reveals, at the same time, the self-giving love of God, and the real humanity that God intends for us. We have in Jesus Christ the revelation of the eternal communion which exists in God himself: the revelation of the communion which exists between God himself and our humanity; and the foundation and content of the new relationship which we are to share in the communion of the church.

The depth of this communion has been expressed in the Greek term, *perichoresis*, and the Latin term, *circumincession*. These terms suggest an embracing movement, a "proceeding around," or "walking about on all sides" and refers to the interpenetration of the persons of the Trinity. The Father, Son, and Holy Spirit all interpenetrate one another in their mutual communion. This same *perichoresis* or mutual interpenetration exists in the Incarnation of the Son in our humanity. Hence, the church is interpenetrated by God as the "body of Christ," the "bride of Christ," and the "temple of the Holy Spirit." God, the Father, Son and Holy Spirit dwell in each and every Christian. Christians should be a sign and reminder of the Holy Trinity to one another. The Holy Communion service should remind us that we live in communion with one another, but also through our communion with the humanity of Jesus (His body, His blood) with the Blessed Trinity.

The Christian church is a community shaped by the Word of God. Certainly this means to be shaped by proclamation through faithful preaching and liturgy. Certainly it means we are to be shaped by Scripture.[9] But even more than that, it means to be shaped by the living Word of God, who is at one and the same time the one God, Father, Son, and Holy Spirit.

CHRISTIAN ETHICS ARE BIBLICAL ETHICS.

Unless God had freely chosen to reveal himself, we would not be able to know Him. It is only God himself who knows himself completely (1Co 2:11). We do not comprehend God, we apprehend Him. And we apprehend Him through His self-revelation, or self-communication to us. This self-communication is through the three-fold form of the living Word in Jesus Christ, the written Word of Scripture, and the spoken and lived Word of Proclamation. We know God's intentions for human life through His commands. God's Torah, His commands, His law, are intended as loving Fatherly guidance. It is our stubborn sinfulness and rebellion that turn this loving guidance into a burden. From beginning to end, in every part of Scripture, God reveals himself to us. The Trinitarian form of His eternal self-giving love is made explicit in the New Testament. This is clear from the baptismal formula Matthew 28:19, "in the name of the Father, and of the Son and of the Holy Spirit"; and in the benediction from 2 Corinthians 13:13, "The grace of the Lord Jesus Christ, the love of God and the communion of the Holy Spirit, be with you all"; and in the discussion of the church in I Corinthians 12:4-6, "There are a variety of gifts, but the same Spirit; and there are a variety of services, but the same Lord; and there are varieties of activities, but it is the same God who activates all of them in everyone."

There are, of course, many other texts in Scripture which only make sense in a Trinitarian context, but the biblical witness to the Trinity is not just a matter of a number of proof texts, rather it is a matter of being open to what Scottish theologian, Alasdair Heron, calls "The whole sweep of the biblical message."[10] The Trinity and Incarnation are the deep underlying currents that hold together the Old and New Testaments. They are a lens that provides a focus on the entire biblical witness. The doctrine of the Trinity, "…Far from being a piece of dusty patristic or scholastic metaphysics or an 'unbiblical accretion,' can come alive as setting the horizon and providing the grammar of Christian Theology. This can happen when the doctrine is not simply seen *as a doctrine* dubiously related to this or that New Testament passage or collection of passages, but as pointing to the identity of the God of Scripture…."[11]

Christians through the centuries have experienced the fact that the living Word, Jesus Christ, speaks to us through the written Word of Scripture, through the inner testimony of the Holy Spirit to bring us to the Father. The doctrine of the Trinity tells us that it is the living God who speaks to us through Scripture. "Indeed the Word of God is living and active, sharper than any two-edged sword, piercing until it divides soul from spirit, joints from marrow; it is able to judge the thoughts and intentions of the heart." (Heb 4:12).

CHRISTIAN ETHICS ARE SOCIAL ETHICS.

The persons of the Trinity live in perfect relationship to one another. The Trinity is a social Trinity, not an isolated individual. Therefore, the personal relationships and personal love in the Trinity are social relationships and social love. They constitute the perfect communion which is both the source and goal of all that exists. Human beings are created in the image of God, male and female (Ge 1:27). We are created social beings. The modern isolated "individual" is an intellectual fiction. The relationship of Christ to his church is likened to that most basic social relationship, the unity and diversity of marriage (Eph 5:32). The profound impact that a Trinitarian social ethic would have in our society's understanding of marriage has been pointed out by Scottish theologian, James Torrance, "We have too one-sidedly interpreted 'the individual' as someone with rights, duties (Thomas Jefferson), the thinking self (Descartes), endowed with reason (Boethius), a self-legislating ego (Kant), motivated by a work ethic, with needs, physical, emotional, sexual, cultural. Two such individuals can contract together in marriage but soon find that their marriage is on the rocks, each claiming their individual rights to realize their own potential or seeing the other as there simply to meet one's own needs. The relationship disintegrates because there is no real covenant love, no mutual self-giving and receiving, no "perichoretic unity."[12] Human sexual, economic, and political relationships are intended to reflect the relationships of free, self-giving and receiving love which exists between the Father, Son, and Holy Spirit.

CHRISTIAN ETHICS ARE ETHICS OF FREEDOM.

Just as Christian ethics are social ethics because they are based on the social nature of the Trinity, so they are freedom ethics because they are based on the freedom of God. God alone is truly free and unrestrained by the necessary limitations of creatureliness. But in the love which the persons of the Trinity bestow upon each other, there is perfect freedom, a freedom in which we participate by accepting the free gift of grace in Jesus Christ. That free gift frees us from the self-centered bondage of individualism. In that self-centeredness, we think we are free because we are free to sin. Indeed, we are not only free to sin, we are *inclined* to sin. As Martin Luther pointed out, we are not simply a donkey choosing between two straw piles, we are a donkey with a rider. And that rider is either Satan or the Lord. Truly, it is for freedom that Christ has set us free (Gal 5:1), but it is a freedom to be obedient to the One who loves us and gave himself to set us free. The American Presbyterian theologian Alexander McKelway writes,

> Freedom in obedience is radical freedom, because the obedience required is not to law, but to grace. Faith owes obedience, not to some abstract absolute, but to the God who acts, lives, and loves in freedom. Thus the command that we must obey establishes our freedom because it demands that we accept this grace as our own, that we understand ourselves as women and men who have been justified, whose sins have been borne and borne away by Christ, and who thus may live in freedom.[13]

This freedom from the bondage of sin, this revolutionary freedom in obedience, lies behind Paul's reply to the licencious false prophets of Corinth and their modern disciples. Paul writes (1Co 6:9-11, 19-20):

> Do you not know that wrongdoers will not inherit the kingdom of God? Do not be deceived! Fornicators, idolaters, adulterers, male prostitutes, sodomites, thieves, the greedy, drunkards, revilers, robbers—none of these will inherit the kingdom of God. And this is what some of you used to be. But you were washed, you were sanctified, you were justified in the name of the Lord Jesus Christ and in the Spirit of our God...Do you not know that your body is a temple of the Holy Spirit within you, which you have from God and that you are not your own? For you were bought with a price; therefore, glorify God in your body.

Christian ethics are ethics of radical freedom in obedience to God's loving guidance given us in the form of clear commands. But, it is more than that. It is an ethic grounded in our sharing the very life of the eternal Trinity through the communion of the Holy Spirit.

CHRISTIAN ETHICS ARE BASED ON COMMUNION WITH GOD.

Unitarian ethics are based on the notion of a distant, remote God. Christian ethics are ethics grounded in our participating in the eternal communion that exists between the Father, Son and Holy Spirit. We are caught up through the incarnation of the Son, and in the fellowship of the Holy Spirit to share in the eternal life which comes from and returns to the Father. While in the rationalistic tradition of the West, we may tend to separate faith and ethics, in the Eastern Christian tradition faith, worship and life are held together in "godliness" (*theosebeia, eusebeia*). T.F. Torrance summarizes it this way, "Faith is itself an act of godliness in humble worship of God and adoring obedience to Him, and godliness is a right relationship to God through faith which gives a distinctive slant to the mind and molds life and thought in accordance with "the word and truth of the Gospel."[14] "Godliness" is used in the Pastoral Epistles in the same manner as "The Way" is used in the Acts of the Apostles. (Compare Ac 9:2; 19:9; 22:4; 24:14 and 1Ti 2:2; 3:16; 4:7; 6:5; 2Ti 3:5; Tit 1:1; 2Pe 1:3, 6; 3:11.) The key passage is 1 Timothy 3:15-16 where we see that the "mystery of godliness" is revealed in the incarnation of Jesus Christ. Paul writes,

> ...If I am delayed, you may know how one ought to behave in the household of God, which is the church of the living God, the pillar and bulwark of the truth. Without any doubt the mystery of our religion [godliness] is great:

> He was revealed in flesh,
>   vindicated in Spirit,
>   seen by angels,
>   proclaimed among Gentiles,
>   believed in throughout the world,
>   taken up in glory (1Ti 3:15-16).

CHRISTIAN ETHICS ARE ETHICS OF GRATITUDE, PRAISE, AND JOY.

Because Christian ethics are a response to God's gracious gift of himself, they are ethics driven by gratitude, thanksgiving, praise, and, joy. Even if they involve us in a participation in the suffering of Christ, we are to '...look to Jesus, the pioneer and perfecter of our faith, who for the sake of the joy set before him endured the cross, disregarding its shame..." (Heb 12:2). We are to "Consider it nothing but joy," my brothers, whenever we face trials (Jas 1:2). Life in the Christian community is to be characterized by grateful thanksgiving.

> [L]et the peace of Christ rule in your hearts, to which indeed you were called in the one body. And be thankful. Let the word of Christ dwell in you richly; teach and admonish one another in all wisdom; and as with gratitude in your hearts sing psalms, hymns and spiritual songs to God. And whatever you do, in word or deed, do everything in the name of the Lord Jesus, giving thanks to God the Father through him (Col 3:15-17).

Our entire lives should be a song of praise. And if we are truly living from our new center in Christ, then it is God who is the singer, and our lives which are the song.

An Example of Trinitarian Ethics

If we are searching for an example of Trinitarian ethics, one of the best modern examples will be the *Church Dogmatics* of Karl Barth. Barth taught that the doctrine of God includes both the foundation and content of theological ethics. Each volume of *Church Dogmatics* concludes with an ethical section as the command of God as Creator, Reconciler, and Redeemer.[15] For a more accessible North American example of Trinitarian ethics, it is worth outlining the thought of American Episcopal ethicist, Philip Turner. He has written a very important book grounding social ethics in Trinitarian theology.[16] He bases his definition of social ethics on the work of the French sociologist, Marcel Mauss. Mauss noted that in all societies, gifts are given, received and returned. He argued that society may be understood as a complex system of exchanges that express, establish and maintain the two basic elements of social order: alliance and hierarchy. Moral obligations arise from these exchanges and social obligations are literally a form of indebtedness.

The French anthropologist Levi-Strauss carried these arguments a step further. He proposed that society may be understood as a system of communication in which exchanges take place on three significant levels: the exchange of sexual partners, the exchange of goods and services, and the exchange of language or meaning.

Taking this model of the nature of social life, Philip Turner declares that "Social ethics asks what sorts of obligations our sexual, monetary, political and linguistic exchanges ought to recognize or engender, and what purpose these engagements ought or ought not to serve."[17] While Mauss and Durkheim believed that human nature is the product of sociological laws, Turner is willing to argue that society is as much a product of human nature as human nature is a product of society. He states that, "In both an individual and communal sense, to be is to give, receive and return; not to be is to refuse such engagements."[18]

At this point, we can see how the Christian doctrine of the Trinity informs the Christian understanding of social ethics. Through the life, death, and resurrection of Jesus Christ, we believe that we not only know how God is related to the world (the economical Trinity) but also who He is in himself (the immanent Trinity). We believe God is in himself eternal self-giving love. The Father eternally freely gives or bestows to the Son all that He is. The Son receives this gift of love and returns it to the Father. As Turner states it, "All that is given is returned. God thus lives and is love. His inner life eternally is one of giving, receiving and returning, and all this takes place in and through the Spirit. Between Father, Son and Spirit there is coinherence, a total presence, a giving, receiving and returning."[19]

Because all human beings are created in the image of God, the perfect community of love in God's inner relationships are the foundation of all social ethics. Presence, reciprocity, giving, receiving and returning define the deep law or structure of both divine and human life. In this understanding, the eternal exchanges of freely given self-giving love become both the model and the motive for all human exchanges, be they of sex, money, power, or language. But this raises a second important issue. It is the question of how the distorted, disoriented social exchanges of our sinful, broken world can be transformed.

Once again, it is the revelation of God's free self-giving love that not only reveals our sin but also provides its remedy. In Christ, divine love is freely bestowed on us as a gift, pure and simple. In terms of social exchange, Turner explains it this way,

> God does not seek to change our motives and intentions by entering the game of social exchange and playing it so successfully by earthly rules that He conquers us all. God's way of changing the social game we play is to continue to bestow himself in truth, as He is, and in so doing absorb into himself the negative return, or rejection, of that gift. The absorption of this negative return into the life of Christ and so into the life of God, Christians believe, is love's deepest expression, with the power to draw from us the poison of self-interest and so transform our motives and intentions.[20]

This Great Exchange has been expressed in many ways through the centuries. The apostle Paul spoke of how our Lord, though He was rich, yet for our sake became poor, that through His poverty we might become rich (2Co 8:9). The fourth-century Cappadocian theologian, Gregory Nazianzen, put it this way:

> He hungered, but He fed thousands...
> He was wearied, but He is the Rest of them that are weary...
> He was heavy with sleep, but He walked lightly over the sea...
> He prays, but He hears prayer.
> He weeps, but He causes tears to cease...
> He is sold, and very cheap, for it is only thirty pieces of silver:
> but He redeems the world...
> As a sheep He is led to the slaughter, but He is the Shepherd
>   of Israel, and now of the whole world also.
> As a Lamb He is silent, yet He is the Word.
> He is wounded, but He healeth every disease.
> He dies, but He gives life.[21]

God gives us his eternal life and love, and receives in return, in exchange, our sorrow, sin, and death. It is this great costly love which motivates Christians to transform our sexual, economic, political, and linguistic exchanges, first within the church and then within the larger society.

Philip Turner's discussion of the issues of sex, money, and power are all highly critical of the way the mainstream North American "denominations" have sold out to the superficial, individualistic, selfish influences of the surrounding culture. Take for example his devastating critique of the so-called "personalist" sexual ethics popularized by James Nelson in his book, *Embodiment*.[22] Turner points out that Nelson is working with the classic Greek error of dualism in his person/body dualism, that he does not take the body seriously by arguing that male/female distinctions are "merely" biological and that he diminishes the deep significance of sexual engagements by using the "personalist metaphor" of conversations. Here we can see the clear danger of thinking that because a writer is using the words "person," "relational," or even communion," they are somehow a Trinitarian or even a Christian thinker. Turner unmasks the superficiality of the so-called "personalist" ethics most powerfully in a chapter on "Real Sex,"[23] where he brings to bear the content of Genesis 1-3 and Ephesians 5:21-33 to reveal the depth of a real biblical understanding of sex.

He also expresses a deep concern about the debasement of language which has occurred in our society, and in our churches. There is a great deal of talk about "responsibility, care, love, trust and openness." But, as Turner points out, "Each of these virtues begins to sound in the mouths of many of their users highly qualified, and certainly as something less than the love, responsibility, care, trust, and openness manifest in Christ's giving up of himself for the church. Many contemporary presentations of fidelity and permanence will also seem disturbingly hedged about with qualifiers. We will wonder if, with such a qualified love, the man and the woman love their partner as themselves, and we will certainly wonder if the love they show is like the love Christ shows for the church."[24]

Turner's Trinitarian ethics offer a truly prophetic and liberating perspective on the exchanges of sex, money, power, and language that take place in our society. The various Unitarianisms that pervade the mainline denominations have debased our understanding of all these issues. It has never been more important for "the church to be the church" and not a social or religious appendage of a society in rapid moral decline. One does not have to be a prophet, or the son of a prophet, to predict that in the next century the liberal "denominations" will have almost entirely disappeared, to be replaced by a World Christianity comprised of three great Trinitarian Traditions: Roman Catholic, Eastern Orthodox, and a Reformation-based Evangelical Protestantism.

A Collect for Trinity

Almighty and eternal God, You have revealed yourself as Father, Son and Holy Spirit. Enable us to live by the Spirit, that, walking with Christ and rejoicing in Your fatherly love, we may become partakers of the mystery of Your divine being: through Jesus Christ our Lord, who lives and reigns with the Father in the unity of the Holy Spirit, three persons in one indivisible God, for ever and ever.

NOTES

1. *Theology Today* 3, (October 1946): pp.371-384.

2. Ibid, p. 372

3. Ibid.

4. Richard J. Mouw. *The God who Commands* (University of Notre Dame Press, 1990), p.150.

5. Ibid. p.151.

6. J.A. Di Noia. "Jesus and the World Religions," *First Things* (June/July 1995), pp.24-28, citation from p. 26.

7. T.F. Torrance. *The Mediation of Christ* (Helmers and Howard, 1992), p.124.

8. Oliver O'Donovan, *Resurrection and Moral Order* (Eerdmans, 1986), p.12.

9. See Richard B. Hays, *Echoes of Scripture in the Letters of Paul* (Yale University Press, 1989), p.191 and Wayne A. Meeks, "A Hermeneutics of Social Embodiment," (HTR 79,1986), pp.184-185.

10. Alasdair Heron, "The Biblical Basis for the Doctrine of the Trinity," pp.33-43 in the book he edited for the British Council of Churches, entitled *The Forgotten Trinity*, (BCC/CCBI. 1991).

11. Ibid, p. 43.

12. Ibid, Professor James B. Torrance, "The Doctrine of the Trinity in our Contemporary Situation," pp.3-17, citation from page 16.

13. Alexander J. McKelway, *The Freedom of God and Human Liberation* (Trinity Press, 1990), p.100.

14. T.F. Torrance, *The Trinitarian Faith* (T & T Clark, 1988), p.28.

15. See Eberhard Jungel, "Gospel and Law: The Relationship of Dogmatics to Ethics," pp.105-126, in *Karl Barth, a Theological Legacy* (Westminster Press, 1966).

16. Philip Turner, *Sex, Money and Power: An Essay in Christian Social Ethics* (Cowley, 1985).

17. Ibid, p.16.

18. Ibid, p.17

19. Ibid, p.19.

20. Ibid, p. 22

21. Gregory Nazianzen, orat., XXXIX.20, NPF 2V11, p.309.

22.　James Nelson, *Embodiment* (Pilgrim Press, 1978).

23.　Ibid, Turner, pp.45-70.

24.　Ibid, p.69.